Financial Management of Travel and Tourism

Financial Management of Travel and Tourism

B.S. Badan
Harish Bhatt

Commonwealth

Financial Management of Travel and Tourism

Edition : 2024

ISBN 81-311-0066-9

Published by :

COMMONWEALTH PUBLISHERS
4831/24, Prahlad Street,
Ansari Road, Darya Ganj,
New Delhi - 110002
Ph. : 23275511, 23257835
e-mail : commonwealthbooks@gmail.com

Printed at :
Roshan Offset Printers
Delhi

PREFACE

Tourism can be defined as the act of travel for the purpose of recreation, and the provision of services for this act. It is a service industry, comprising a number of tangible and intangible components. The tangible elements include transportation systems—air, rail, road, water and now, space; hospitality services, accommodation, foods and beverages, tours, souvenirs; and related services such as banking, insurance and safety and security. The intangible elements include: rest and relaxation, culture, escape, adventure, new and different experiences.

Travel and tourism is a major industry in the world and is at the top of the league of invisible earners of foreign currency. Many sovereignties, along with their respective countries and states, depend heavily upon travel expenditures by foreigners as a source of taxation and income for the enterprises that sell services to these travellers. Consequently the development of tourism is often a strategy employed either by a non-governmental organization or a governmental agency to promote a particular region for the purpose of increasing commerce through exporting goods and services to non-locals.

During recent years the tourism industry has witnessed unprecedented growth. Increasing consumer demand for educational and participatory travel experiences has resulted in a variety of specialty niche markets such as ecotourism, cultural-heritage tourism, and agritourism. New paradigms link strategic tourism planning with sustainable development.

The leisure and tourism industry is one of the leading global economic activities, a multi-billion-dollar industry with

700 million international travellers per year around the world. Tourism is a motor for employment and income creation and, especially in poor countries, a vehicle for development. But today it is not sufficient to simply create employment without regard for the quality of jobs and the social and environmental effects of tourism in vulnerable areas. A growing number of organizations, including the tourism industry leadership, are increasingly conscious of the risks and are adopting a more responsible attitude.

The present publication provides an authoritative look at how to manage travel and tourism industry in a better way. It introduces the complexities of the tourism system so that they will be better positioned to eventually assume the managerial challenges and responsibilities in a diverse and challenging industry. The latest advancements in tourism theory and thinking, retaining the thoroughness of content, diversity of applications, regional and international issues, economic significance, tourism operators and the role of technology in the tourism industry etc. are also described elaborately. Numerous regional and global case studies and examples are included to provide an appropriately broad geographic context. This work will be highly informative and useful to students, researchers, policy makers, managers and working groups of travel and tourism industry.

B.S. Badan
Harish Bhatt

Contents

1

Attractions in Tourism

Introduction

The attraction—whether called the 'tourist' attraction or the 'visitor' attraction—has a central place in the tourism system. It includes a large number of very diverse phenomena, including architecture, nature, museums, public sculpture, theme parks, retail parks and events in fact, the sector is so diverse that it is hard find a definition that covers them all. Nevertheless, the importance of the visitor attraction (as it will be called here) is obvious: it helps 'make' a destination, sometimes it *is* the destination. It *attracts* tourists in some way, it gives the tourist a *motivation* for travelling and, therefore, it becomes a reason for paying a visit to a place. Everybody who is involved in tourism at any level will appreciate how crucial this makes the attraction in tourism generally. By definition, that which attracts a tourist also makes tourism possible, opening up opportunities in transport, catering, accommodation, guiding, publishing, souvenir production, and so on.

The purpose of this chapter is to look at the attraction in its own right, in order to understand what it is and how it works. It will also look at the particular issues which the tourism industry and tourism managers (and others working in the sector) have to deal with in relation to attractions at both the micro and macro levels.

The Historical Background

Have there always been attractions, and have they always motivated tourism? If, for the moment, we forget about any distinction between 'tourism' and 'travel', there were probably always visitor attractions of one sort or another. That is, it is likely that people have always travelled in order to see or experience something 'for its own sake', in addition to the other reasons they might have for going somewhere. Of course, we cannot know for certain why people travelled to Stonehenge, for example. Undoubtedly they went for religious reasons, to perform rituals or some other social or religious duty. However, it is also very likely that they went to a place like Stonehenge because it was—and is—such an exceptional monument, such a unique piece of religious architecture, so exciting in its own right. Thus, we cannot know, though we can guess or even assume, that visits to Stonehenge also led to some kind of activity in the travel, catering and accommodation sectors. The people who lived at the time when Stonehenge was in use were not radically different from us and it is, therefore, reasonable to imagine that what amazes and preoccupies us today could also have some kind of parallel then.

Moving forward in history to Ancient Egypt, Greece and Rome, there were certainly religious and civil monuments and institutions which people travelled to see for touristic reasons. During the time of the Roman Empires, Greece had already come to be seen as an artistic and cultural ideal which the Romans travelled to see and whose artistic works they reproduced for their own homes. By the Middle Ages, religious tourism became widespread, leading to the creation of pilgrimage 'trails' across Europe which Christian pilgrims would follow, collecting souvenir tokens at the great religious attractions so that they could eventually prove back home that they had been there. The great cathedrals and monasteries and sites of religious miracles and revelations became religious attractions, as they have remained to this day.

Modern tourism has its roots in developments going back several centuries. In Europe, its roots lie in the Grand

Tour of the 17th and 18th centuries, when young noblemen toured Europe as part of their general education, to visit the sites that had come to represent the origins of their contemporary civilisation. Co-incidentally, there were also many of the sites which the ancient Romans had visited—for example. Athens—plus newer attractions dating from Roman times, such as Rome and Pompeii and great cities which represented a more modern cultural tradition, such as Paris and Venice.

Of course, the Grand Tour was only for the few and, to a great extent, the wealthy. The 19th century, however, saw the development of a more widespread kind of tourism, resembling more closely what we see today. With industrialisation came the creation of a working class with—eventually—leisure time and a certain amount of surplus spending power: this was the foundation of a new mass market. The steam engine was the technological advance that made mass tourism possible: trains and ships could now transport people from place to place, quickly and reliably, according to fixed timetables. The way was open for Thomas Cook to bring that market and that technology together in the UK, to create a modern tourism which was less exclusive and which enabled the many to take shorter, cheaper holidays, following a predetermined route to destinations with a series of attractions appropriate to the kind of tourist that went there. Soon this new concept was spread across Europe, inviting new tourists to visit known attractions across the Continent and benefit from new transport and accommodation.

The Destination and the Attraction

The 'destination' is, effectively the 'unit' which the tourism industry puts together and which it then presents and markets to the tourist/visitor as a complex product. The destination needs to have a range of facilities for the tourist, such as accommodation and catering, for a range of customer types. It must also have the appropriate infrastructure to allow tourist to travel there (by road, rail, air) and move around within it (public transport, roads) and communicate (telephone, postal services, etc.).

More than anything else, however, it must offer a reason or a motive for tourists to go there—it must be able to attract tourists. It can do so in a number of ways. Ski resorts, for example, offer a well-defined range of winter sports-related leisure activities, based on the landscape. Some towns and cities are well-established and; over the centuries, have built up a longstanding reputation as tourist destinations, offering a particular kind of attraction, such as the cultural destinations of Florence, Paris or Dresden. In the UK, York in this category, though perhaps at a slightly more modest level. Some landscapes can have a similarly longstanding reputation, as is the case with England's Lake District, famous for its scenic qualities and its association with the Romantic poets. Importantly, age is not in itself a qualification for success. For example, Blackpool and Agia Napa are seaside resorts, differentiated not by age but by appealing to different kinds of tourists with different expectations.

Each of these types of destinations has something which will motivate tourists to go there. However, there also has to be enough of that 'something' for the tourist to do so - the destination needs 'critical mass' before tourists can be expected not only to visit but also to stay. In the UK, a tourist might decide to stay for a length of time in London and, perhaps for shorter periods, in a range of other cities. Official statistics can show which cities are most attractive in these terms (Table 1.1).

Clearly, there is a connection between size and attractiveness, although size is not a sufficient reason for visiting in itself: all of the cities on the list have a variety of attractions to tempt the tourist. Of the cities listed in Table 1.1, London clearly has critical mass. Edingburgh is not only architecturally and historically attractive, but also has an annual Festival to attract visitors. Oxford, Cambridge and Bath are all traditional centres for visitors with their historical and cultural connections, whilst Glasgow, conversely, has only recently been established as a tourist centre.

Table 1.1 : Top towns visited by overseas residents, 2000.

Rank	*City/town*	*Visits*
1.	London	13,150,000
2.	Edinburgh	910,000
3.	Manchester	560,000
4.	Birmingham	520,000
5.	Glasgow	430,000
6.	Oxford	410,000
7.	Cambridge	370,000
8.	Bristol	360,000
9.	Bath	300,000
10.	Cardiff	240,000
11.	Nottingham	190,000
12.	Newcastle-on-Tyne	180,000
13.	Stratford-on-Avon	170,000
	Coventry	170,000
	Reading	170,000
14.	Bournemouth	150,000
15.	Leeds	140,000

Interestingly, although Stratford-on-Avon, because of its Shakespeare connection, is a standard stop on the tourist itinerary, it did not receive as many visitors in 2000 as did Newcastle-on-Tyne, which is now building up an image, along with Gateshead, as a tourist centre. This is principally because the latter two cities have decided to collaborate instead of competing—by sharing resources, they have a greater chance of achieving sufficient 'weight' as a destination. The two cities have also embarked on a programme of creating new facilities and attractions which, it is hoped, will help transform the reputation of the North East from being an area of heavy industry and coal-mining into being a cultural destination, potentially the European Cultural Capital in 2008. Included in this programme are the Millennium Bridge (opened in 2001), the Baltic Centre for Contemporary Art and the Gateshead Music Centre, as well as a sculpture trail along the River Tyne.

Defining the Visitor Attraction

Visitor attractions can be many things. They may be things which tourists travel purposely to see, such as a trip to India specifically to see the Taj Mahal, or which they visit when they are on their travels anyway ('when in the US, don't miss the Grand Canyon!'). They can be man-made (Sydney Opera House) or natural (the Lake District), it can be there anyway (St. Peter's Church in Rome) or it may have been constructed specifically as an attraction (Disneyland). It may be part of a destination (the Manneken Pis in Brussels) or it may the destination itself (inland resorts, such as Center Parcs).

From a tourism management perspective, the definition should embrace the concepts of both 'tourism' and 'management', thus permitting the inclusion of some things which are not *intended* to be visitor attractions, but which tourists visit anyway and in such numbers that the tourist flow has to be managed (as is the case with many religious buildings, such as Westminster Cathedral or the Blue Mosque). Conversely, it also makes us think carefully before we include the Sidney Opera House or Nelson's Column in London: they may help attract tourists to the destination, but they may not be managed specifically for that purpose, nor are they necessarily major reasons for visiting. However, a magnificent view of the Scottish Highlands can be included, as it can be deliberately managed by offering tourists a simple lay-by with a interpretation board explaining the landscape.

Several definitions of the visitor attraction exist. The Scottish Tourist Board (STB), for example, defines it as :

> *A permanently established excursion destination, a primary purpose of which is to allow public access for entertainment, interest or education, rather than being principally a retail outlet or a venue for sporting, theatrical,*

> *or film performances. It must be open to the public without prior booking, for published periods each year, and should be capable of attracting tourists and day visitors as well as local residents.*

More simply, Middleton (1988), defines the visitor attraction as:

> *A designated permanent resource which is controlled and managed for the enjoyment, amusement, entertainment and education of the visiting public.*

Swarbrooke (1995) defines the attraction in the context of the destination:

> *Attractions are generally single units, individual sites or very small, easily delimited geographical areas based on a single key feature. Destinations are larger areas that include a number of individual attractions together with the support services required by tourists.*

Hanna (1997) formulates it in this way:

> *The attraction must be a permanently established excursion destination, a primary purpose of which is to allow public access for entertainment, interest or education; rather than being primarily a retail outlet of a venue for sporting, theatrical, or film performance.*

From these four definitions, it is evident that the visitor attraction must, in particular:

- be *permanent,* in the sense of being permanently established or regularly repeated, as in the case of a festival or sports event;
- not simply *frame* the actual attraction, as a theatre would;
- be *enjoyable* and function as part of the (tourist) visitor's *leisure time* but also possibly be *educational;*
- *attract visitors* (not only tourists but as members of the public), and be designed and managed to provide a *service* to *satisfy their needs;* and
- it may *charge.*

Therefore, this chapter will concentrate on the kind of facility that has been specifically designed and created to function as an attraction. In other words, many things attract visitors, but only some are primarily or entirely designed and managed for that specific purpose. These include:

- Museums (or special exhibitions in museums).
- Arts centres and arts museums/galleries.
- Nature centres, national parks and other managed landscapes.
- Historical buildings, open-air museums and managed townscapes.
- Theme parks and amusement parks.
- Visitor centres.
- Zoos and aquaria.
- Historical and archaeological reconstructions and research centres.

Amenities

All of these would normally have a number of standard features which would be part of the service to be provided (and therefore part of the experience to be managed). These features—or amenities—include :

- On-site amenities
  - — Parking
  - — Visitor Centres
  - — Signs and labels, audio-visual presentations and guides and guidebooks
  - — Shops, catering and lavatories
  - — Litterbins, seating, lifts and on-site transport
- Off-site amenities
  - — Signposts
  - — Hotels

Classifying the Visitor Attraction

Having defined the visitor attraction, it is also important to find a means of classifying it in order to help isolate aspects that distinguish one type of attraction from another. Therefore, this section considers the criteria that can be used to distinguish different types of attraction and to provide an overview of this richly varied sector.

Attraction types

The degree of variety is clear from classifying which attractions by type. Such types include :

- Natural history attractions
- Science based attractions
- Attractions concerned with primary production
- Craft centres and craft workshops
- Attractions concerned with manufacturing industry
- Transport attractions
- Socio-cultural attractions
- Attractions associated with historic persons
- Performing arts attractions
- Pleasure gardens
- Theme parks
- Galleries
- Festivals and pageants
- Field sports
- Stately and ancestral homes
- Religious attractions
- Military attractions
- Genocide monuments
- Towns and townscape
- Villages and hamlets
- Countrysides and treasured landscapes
- Seaside resorts
- Regions

With the exception of 'Genocide Monuments', most, if not all, these types may be represented in most areas. The drawback, however, is the very variety: there may be so many types that the classification becomes confusing. Equality, it could be argued that there are many more types. For example, is a 'theme' park the same as an 'amusement' park? Is a 'region' not too large to qualify as a single attraction? In any case, classification of this kind require constant updating to ensure that they include new types of attractions, such as the increasingly important themed retail parks.

Private public

Other kinds of classification use broader criteria in order to help distinguish between the different types. One distinction is between privately-owned and publicly-owned attractions.

Privately-owned attractions

Normally, the primary concern of these attractions is to earn a profit for their owners/shareholders. This means that they have to focus carefully on what their customers want, so that they can attract them, not only once but for repeat visits. To do so, they need to focus on developments in their own sector in order to maintain or improve their competitive position. They also need to monitor their customers' levels of satisfaction through regular surveys.

For example theme parks, such as Alton Towers or Disneyland, are designed to attract and entertain large numbers of paying customers and are, therefore, closely focused on the needs and wants of their core visitors, as well as on their own need to survive and prosper. Attention is also paid to the activities of any competitors in their own industry or to other activities that compete for their customers' attention and money. They will also consider the (relative) importance of customers drawn locally, day-trippers and tourists coming from further a field and will work out to what extent they have to serve, say, overseas tourists as well as domestic ones. Marketing, as well as good business management generally, becomes a crucial factor in their success.

Publicly-owned attractions

These can be owned by local or national government and, therefore, can usually rely on an element of financial support from their owners. This sector includes attractions run by charitable trusts, such as the National Trusts for England and Scotland. Public-sector attractions include such facilities as museums and other public buildings, whose primary purpose is not usually to service tourists but which may nevertheless do so. Thus, they are usually service institutions, created to meet the needs of the local population, although this is not always the case. For example, the Burrell Collection in Glasgow was created by a rich collector, who donated it to Glasgow without attempting to discover whether there was a real local *need* for such a collection.

Publicly-owned attractions are usually created to meet non-tourist needs. Thus, museums normally exist to educate the local population in an aspect of their own heritage to collect, preserve and exhibit artefacts and to make them accessible to the public. In the case of the national museums in the UK, the purpose is the same at the national, and possibly even international, level. Charitable trusts, such as those owning and managing the National Trusts' properties or other attractions, such as the Centre for Life in Newcastle, do not have to make a profit. However, they do have to earn their own revenue—the National Trust, for example, depends entirely upon members subscriptions, entry fees at its sites, donations, retail activities and special appeals for its income. Similarly, publicly-owned museums (most are either publicly-owned or are run as charities) are nowadays expected to raise their own revenue through retailing other commercial activities, such as corporate hospitality. In the case of charitable trusts, all revenue is earned (or donated), meaning that they are increasingly 'commercial' in their attitude to management and to the visitor: their management is inevitably coloured by the need to attract and please visitors. This is also increasingly the case for attractions owned by local and national government, which is why it is possible to deal with them all under the same heading of 'attractions management'. But, significantly, such attractions may also be subsidised, allowing them to focus on the local audience rather than tourists.

The distinction between privately and publicly owned attractions may only seem one of degree: they may all seem to be run along commercial lines, using modern management methods. However, the actual difference should not be underestimated. In practical management terms, it is often the case that an attraction within the publicly-owned sector will not only *distinguish* itself from the privately owned sector, but will also *distance* itself from it on qualitative grounds, arguing that the two types of organisations are fundamentally different. One exists to make profit (by serving the customer explicitly), whereas the other aims to add to the quality of life of members of the community (by helping the visitors discover their identity and heritage or discover their position as citizens). Thus, in their day-to-day work, these privately and publicly-owned institutions will priorities differently when balancing the needs of their specialist staff (perhaps researchers and scientists employed in a museum) against the needs of operations managers (looking after the running of the building as a visitor attraction) and the visitors (who may be students, schoolchildren, tourists, families etc.).

Natural, man-made or special events

It is possible to distinguish between attractions that are:

- natural,
- man-made,
- man-made and purpose-built to attract tourists,
- special events.

Natural attractions

These include landscape features, which, for one reason or another, attract the attention of visitors. The Foot and Mouth crisis in the UK in 2001 confirmed the fact that the farming industry helps to maintain the landscape for tourism purposes as well as for agriculture. Without the constant attention from farmers, the cultural landscape would lose qualities that currently attract tourists. However, landscape may be more explicitly designed and managed as a tourist attraction through, for example, the provision of managed paths for walkers, huts for climbers and visitor centres which can both act as information offices and interpretation centres. The National Parks are prime examples of this kind of landscape management.

Man-made attractions

Man-made attractions are features in landscapes or townscapes (or entire townscapes) that have been created by human beings for purposes other than tourism. These include religious buildings, castles, examples of special architecture (which may be special because it is typical of an historical period or of a particular architect's work), or areas in towns and cities of particular aesthetic or historical value. Also included in this category are ruined buildings, which are often preserved for historical or other reasons and presented as tourist attractions.

The National Trust is a good example of an organisation devoted to the preservation and interpretation of buildings (and landscape features) that are significant parts of England's national heritage, from ancient times to (almost) the present day. The Trust presents buildings in a manner that makes them accessible in intellectual terms to the visitor (that is, which allows the visitor to understand what their significance is). At the same time, it is increasingly adopting modern teaching and learning methods to make the visit not only educational but also entertaining.

Man-made, purpose-built attractions

Attractions built with the specific purpose of attracting tourists include theme parks and amusement parks, holiday centres, such as the Center Parcs or Disneyland, and recent attractions, such as Newcastle's Centre for Life and Edinburgh's Dynamic Earth. These latter attractions combine the theme park with the educational facility, but they are not there specifically to serve the local community: they appeal to a national (and possibly an international) audience. Thus, they fulfil a dual attraction and the public service role exemplifying the trend towards mixing both entertainment and education in new contemporary attractions. Theme parks, conversely, aim specifically to earn a profit by providing an experience and facilities that will attract visitors.

Special events

Festivals and sports events, such as the Olympics, are examples of special events that play a large part in contemporary tourism. Festivals—in particular arts festivals—are numerous in the UK. Major examples are the Festivals in Edinburgh, Chichester and Glyndebourne, which attract audiences and performers from all over the world. Because they are recurrent, they can become part of a region's or a city's tourism strategy. Some festivals, such as the Munich Beer Festival, are not only visited but also copied in other countries and others occur in a similar form, such as the

Newcastle Hoppings, a great, annual meeting of travelling show-people.

Managing the special event as an attraction largely involves the same skills as other kinds of attraction management but also involves specific aspects, such as programming, arranging venues, co-ordinating sales and merchandising. Customer research is a difficult aspect of the special event, in particular where the free event is concerned. If, for example, a festival takes place in the streets of a town, it is difficult to estimate the number of people attending and why they have come. However, as is the case with other attractions, the special event will also provide opportunities for a range of local and other entrepreneurs and suppliers in the tourist business, including catering and accommodation.

The nature of the visitor attraction product

All attractions serve visitors directly by providing the kind of experience that is appropriate to the tourist (and to others), which includes a *core experience* (heritage, architecture, mountain-climbing, fun and excitement, learning, art) set among a variety of other facilities which service the visitors and provide employment and other opportunities for local people.

As with the tourism product as a whole, the attraction is a service and, therefore, displays the characteristics of intangibility, inseparability, heterogeneity and perishability. This means, amongst other things, that people are central to the attractions industry: employees must be appropriately trained to deal with visitors. It also means that the attractions industry—like tourism generally—belongs to a sector, the service industries which is becoming increasingly important in contemporary industrialised societies. Citizens are increasingly used to acting as customers for services and the demand for quality service and professional management grows ever stronger. This affects all parts of the industry, including the not-for-profit element.

The Market for Attractions

Given the sensitivity of tourism in general to a variety of external factors, it is difficult to measure and accurately predict the market for attractions. Nevertheless, in recent years, the 'travel facilities and attractions' market has enjoyed some growth, though spread unevenly across the market. Figure 1.1 summarises recent developments:

- The market for travel facilities and attractions in the United Kingdom grew by 12.4 per cent over the 1995-1998 review period, reaching an overall value of £2,608.3 million in 1998.
- All sectors benefited from the increasing popularity of the United Kingdom as a tourist destination, attracting foreign tourists with large disposable incomes, resulting in escalating consumer expenditure throughout the United Kingdom travel and tourism industry.
- The travel facilities and attractions market also benefited substantially from the rising number of United Kingdom residents holidaying in the United Kingdom rather than travelling abroad. Similarly, the market benefited from the increasing incidence of United Kingdom residents enjoying weekend breaks and visiting tourist attractions.
- The strength of the United Kingdom travel facilities and attractions market is expected to continue into the near future. Over the 1998-2003 forecast period, growth of 30.9 per cent is expected, underpinned by the focus on millennium celebrations and increased commercialisation of all attractions, with the overall market reaching value sales of £3,413.6 million in 2003.

Figure 1.1 : The market for travel facilities and attractions.

This would suggest that:

- the facilities and attractions market is a market in growth and therefore worth investing in;
- the UK attracts increasing numbers of relatively wealthy tourists;
- more British tourists holiday at home and more British tourists go on weekend breaks; and
- more growth is expected.

The events of 2001, in particular the Foot and Mouth crisis and the terrorist attacks in the USA, cast some doubt on these projections. Nevertheless, it is reasonable to expect that the market will return to where it recently—that is, the estimated market growth may not happen by 2003 but it will happen eventually.

Supply-side aspects

In 1999, the English Tourism Council (ETC) published a report which reveals a great deal about the 'shape' of the visitor attractions market from the supply side. It is summarised in Figure 1.2.

- There are at least 6,215 attractions in the UK; 74 per cent of these are in England.
- The attractions sector is split as follows (**top 10 categories**):

Museums and Galleries	1,756	28%
Historic Properties	1,521	24%
Visitor Centres	489	08%
Gardens	378	06%
Workplaces	382	06%
Wildlife Sites	315	05%
Country Parks	290	05%
Farms	247	04%
Steam Railways	106	02%
Leisure Parks	85	01%
Other	646	10%

- Although only 4 per cent of attractions are in London, they account for 13 per cent (52,860,000) of visits.

Figure 1.2 : The supply of attractions in the UK.

Heritage in the UK visitors attractions market

The dominant position of 'Museums and Galleries' and 'Historic Properties' in the UK market should be noted. Many of these attractions are non-profit-making, being funded by national or local government, and often they do not charge admission or do not charge much (as in the case of many museums) or they are run by trusts (as in the case of the National Trust). There is a tendency, at the moment, for these sectors to become increasingly dependent on earned revenue (as opposed to funding from the public purse), although the present government has made national museums free of charge. This benefits all visitors, from local, socially excluded schoolchildren to wealthy foreign tourists. In all, some 41 per cent of all attractions in the UK did not charge for admission in 1999, suggesting that they could be an important service to the visitor, adding to the leisure experience without costing the visitor anything.

In 1999, visitor attractions earned an estimated £1.4 billion gross revenue, of which 49 per cent came from entrance fees or donations (donations are preferred by some attractions such as some cathedrals and museums), whilst 41 per cent was earned through sales of merchandise in shops and 10 per cent came from catering (ETC 2000a). These revenue figures do not, of course, include income from public-sector bodies in the shape of grants. As long as public funds go into the attractions sector, competition will always seem unfair. Local museums do not usually have to fend for themselves financially, unlike, say, a local theme park. On the other hand, the local museum usually serves quite different purposes from the theme park: where the former aims of educate, the latter seeks to entertain. The two are not, however, mutually exclusive.

The London/South-East factor

Of the 404 million visits in 1999, by domestic and international visitors, the vas majority (81 per cent) was to attractions in England and a large proportion of those were in London and the Southeast. There is nothing surprising in this. Some of the most famous heritage attractions and museums are in or near the capital, and the largest theme parks are constructed where they will have the largest catchment area—that is in the South and the Southeast of England, which also has the largest population density. The large attractions are visited both by international, national and local visitors and will locate where they can reach those audiences.

It is clear that the domestic and foreign markets present different challenges to the tourism marketer (Table 1.2). Domestic tourists are more focused on the 'other England' than are foreign tourists, whose interest is clearly in the London and the South East. To the latter, the United Kingdom appears, at first sight, to be divided into the London area and the not-London area.

Table 1.2 : Leading UK destinations for domestic and foreign tourists (all purposes), 1999.

Region	*Domestic tourists (% trips)*	*Overseas tourists (% trips)*
Heart of England	13	7
London	12	45
West Country	12	6
East of England	11	6
Southern	9	8
South East	9	9
Other England	20	9
Scotland	7	7
Wales	7	3
Northern Ireland	1	—
Total	100	100

The ability to attract visitors: size matters

The market is not only concentrated in terms of where the attractions are, but also in terms of their ability to attract an audience: attractions with over 200,000 visits make up 7 per cent of all attractions, but account for 58 per cent of visits. Thus, the market is heavily concentrated on a relatively small number of attractions with a very large number of visitors. This does not mean, however, that smaller attractions cannot exist or survive in the market. As ETC (2000a) report points out, '57% of attractions receive fewer than 20,000 visits per year; three quarters (76%) receive less than 50,000 visits'.

Evidently, because they are all 'attractions', all the sites included in the ETC (2000a) report clearly belong to the same sector. However, that is not to say that they are also in the same *market* seen from the customers' view. Not only geography but size determines that, for example, Metroland in Gateshead does not at any level compete with Alton Towers. That is important for both: they are not competing for the same customers, one does not threaten the existence of the other.

Attractions over-supply

Attractions of different sizes are designed and operated at very different levels: it is also a sector with a great turnover For example, it is known that at least 859 attractions closed throughout England between 1978 and 1999 whilst, between 1990 and 1999, over 1,200 new attractions opened to the public (South West Tourist Board 2001). These figures could be taken to mean that the market for visitor attractions is buoyant. However, the reality seems to be different: there is an *oversupply* of tourist attractions in the UK. It appears that 'demand for attractions is slowing' and that the 'average number of visits per attraction is declining, yet supply is increasing.' (ETC 2000a).

The National Lottery

One possible reason for this oversupply in the UK is the role played by the National Lottery, in particular in the construction of the Millennium projects, such as the Millennium Dome in London. In many ways, these projects are exciting opportunities for the areas where they are built. They potentially enhance the lives of local people as well of visitors generally. They are also, generally speaking, exciting as buildings: they add to the quality of the built environment and contribute to a general upgrading not only of the UK as a tourist destination but as a place to live. However, the Millennium projects—like some other Lottery-funded projects, not least new arts venues - have been criticised on several grounds :

- Being publicly-funded and owned, they are seen as competition for the commercial, for-profit sector. There is nothing new in the public sector owning attractions in the UK, and they are not in a majority, with 69 per cent (4,139) of attractions being privately owned (including charitable trusts); of the remainder, 1,406 are owned by local authorities and 453 by the Government. However, the arrival of new publicly-funded attractions in an already crowded market is seen by some commercial operators as excessive and unfair competition.

- There is a suspicion that some of the Lottery-funded projects are based on over-optimistic business plans with exaggerated expectations of visitor numbers (indeed, some projects, such as the National Centre for Popular Music in Sheffield, have since closed). Although potentially drawing increased numbers of visitors to a region, new attractions also threaten existing ones, particularly if the overall market remains static in terms of revenue and/or visitor numbers.

Table 1.3 : Summarises the status of major lottery-funded projects in the UK *Lottery-funded attractions.*

Name	*Place*	*Status*	*Problem*
Centre for Life	Newcastle	Highly popular	Well-visited
Dynamic Earth	Edinburgh	Highly popular	Well-visited
Earth Centre	Doncaster	Staff numbers reduced	Low visitor numbers
Eden Project	Cornwall	Highly popular	Well-visited
Nat. Centre for Popular Music	Sheffield	Temporarily closed	Low visitor numbers
National Glass Centre	Sunderland	Staff laid off	Low visitor numbers
National Space Centre	Leicester	(recently opened)	Difficult location
Tate Modern	London	Highly popular	Well-visited

The attractions sector, therefore, seems to be skewed in ways that seem important:

- Museums, galleries and historic houses make up the largest number of attractions.
- London and the South East attract the largest number of tourists, with London being the be preferred destination for international tourists.

- there is oversupply in the sector.
- Competition is coming from new directions.
- Currently, in the year 2001, the tourism sector generally is facing major crises, nationally and internationally, which can limit the number of overseas tourists but which may also strengthen domestic tourism.

These factors might influence the attractions owner (and various organisations with an interest in the success of attractions) to consider:

- Whether this means that attractions outside the museums/heritage sector will be less successful.
- Whether the dominance of London in the tourist market is inevitable.
- Whether it will be necessary to respond to oversupply by reducing the number of attractions or by attracting more visitors.
- Whether the sector will be able to meet the new competition and the changing market conditions.
- How the sector can best respond to national and international crises.

The answers to these issues relate partly to changes which individual attractions have to make, partly to changes at governmental level or at the level of lobbying groups and professional organisations. Ultimately, they all have to do with the strategy of visitor attraction management and with the business environment within which that strategy is worked out.

Feasibility Studies and Attractions Design

Management is about controlling resources and delegating work and, in the case of the attraction, those tasks start before the attraction opens its doors for the first time. The modern attraction is a sophisticated 'machine', designed, equipped and manned to give visitors an enjoyable and memorable experience. This section looks at some of the processes that this involves. By outlining the process of creating a new attraction, it throws light on aspects of attractions planning that are applicable in a range of situations, from the development of a small theme park to a major heritage site or, indeed, the continuing development of an existing attraction.

Planning and preparation

The planning and preparation of a new attraction must be carried out with great care so as to ensure that the original concept is not only practicable and marketable, but also that:

- it will be able to attract investors.
- once opened, that it will be manageable.
- over the years, that it will have potential for further development; so that
- it can continue to attract visitors.

The process can be illustrated as in Figure 1.3.

Stage 1
Idea

↓

Stage 2
Project Description &
Project Organisation

↓

Stage 3
Feasibility Study

↓

Stage 4
Attraction Development

↓

Stage 5
Customer Experience & Profit

Figure 1.3 : The attraction, from idea of realisation.

Stage one

At the initial, idea generation stage, the new idea for an attraction is measure against whether, at this stage, there is likely to be sufficient back-up, resources and perceived need for it. Subsequently, the concept development can start, addressing questions such as:

- What is it you want to achieve and why?
- Does the idea seem simple, unique, innovative?
- Does it, at this early point, appear viable, given the competitive environment and the resources that would be needed?

Stage two

The project development stage is a more 'real' phase. A team of people must be identified to create a real project out of the idea and the concept, who can provide expertise at all levels of the development of the project, who can timetable and organise the actual venture, and the legal and financial expertise. At this point, detailed costings of building and running the project will also be undertaken to help with financial projections. In short, the project organisation will involve the establishment of a team to turn the project from plan to reality, with changing membership so that it can deal with different tasks as the project develops.

Stage three

The first task in the feasibility study is to establish whether a market exist for the new attraction, firstly through secondary research (using existing, published sources), then through the commissioning of primary research that aims to establish who the visitors would be, where they would come from geographically, what their socio-demographic profile is, and so on. A second phase would establish where the best location is (assuming that this is not a natural or heritage attraction tied to an existing location), in particular with respect to proximity to major cities, how much land is needed, and whether the right infrastructure and labour force exist. An environmental audit would also be considered, given not only the interest in sustainable tourism but also national and international rules and regulations concerning environmental protection.

Stage four

The feasibility study allows the project developer to complete the project description and project organisation, moving forward to the actual attraction development stage, planning the construction of the attraction in detail, with financial costings. At this stage, the project developer is aiming to create a workable plan for how the original idea of the project can materialise as a real attraction with real experiences and facilities for the visitors, created within given financial and physical constraints. Here, not only is the nature of the individual 'ride' or stage on the visitor's tour through the attraction considered: attention is also paid to the actual building materials, queue management and the provision of catering for visitors with different purchasing power. At this stage, the project developer also takes into account budgeting and the raising of finance. The latter will depend on the quality of other planning work done so far, given that investors would need reassurance that the project would, indeed, be feasible.

Stage five

This stage involves the realisation of the project and, therefore, requires concentration on:

(a) The customer experience, which is all-important for the continued success of the project.

(b) Making a surplus on the activities of the attraction, if in the private/charitable sector, or at least balancing the books, if in the public sector.

The first issue requires constant research into customer satisfaction levels through, for example, questionnaire completion or focus groups. The second requires an equal level of vigilance in keeping an eye on whether all parts of the attraction are achieving the anticipated results, and on plans for future investment requirements. Both can be seen as an attempt to maintain the momentum that has been built up during the entire planning process, as described above.

In really, the development of an attraction is a much more is a lengthy process than described here, involving repeats of many of the stages as new ideas are brought forward and as new constraints are encountered. Similarly, large numbers of specialists of different kinds may be involved in the project planning and development, as new issues of the practical implementation and funding arise. The attraction that finally opens may well be the result of a series of compromise, yet it may still be a success as long as the process is managed and guided firmly throughout the process and any changes are made with due regard for the original vision of the project. Once the attraction is open to the public, it will be subject to evaluation not only by technical and other specialists but also by its customers who will be the ultimate arbiters of what works and what does not. Their views will be important, as the attraction develops and perhaps expands throughout its lifetime, to take account of changing fashions in the leisure market.

Management Issues

The visitor attraction, as defined in this chapter, requires management. This implies that it is usually staffed with several people with different duties relating to the maintenance of the building and serving the visiting members of the public.

Managing a visitor attraction is like managing any other organisation. There is a core product or a core product range. It has to be marketed to customers and it is important, therefore, to try and find out what those customers need and want. At the same time, income and expenditure have to be planned, monitored, controlled and reported, whilst there will be staff to manage, sometimes with very different kinds of expertise and duties. Finally, the attraction has to be operated on a day-to-day basis, as well as developed on a longer-term basis. In this respect, the visitor attraction is like any other organisation and it is necessary to pay attention to the kinds of management issues that normally arise, particularly:

- Operations management.
- Marketing.
- Finance.
- Human Resource Management.

Operations Management

Operations management is concerned with the day-to-day running of the attraction. Given that visitor attractions are services, people are central to the process, both as visitors and as attraction staff and management. Even where the attraction is in itself important—as in the case of major heritage attractions such as Stonehenge—the attraction does not fully come into its own until it has an audience, a visitor, who has decided to devote resources, such as time and money, to experiencing the attraction.

Operations management is there to ensure that the attraction functions properly; that any machinery is functional and safe; that catering outlets and shops are stocked and open, that staff are present and correct; that all facilities are presentable; and, that the site in general is tidy. In other words, although others have planned, designed and built the attraction, operations management is there to ensure that it operates as it should. Operations management is on the frontline between attraction and visitor. Issues such as queue management, problem solving and safety concern are in its remit. This is, therefore, the area within attractions management that will be particularly interested in quality management, possibly in accordance with accepted quality standards, such as those represented by ISO 9000.

Marketing

Marketing is the management discipline that brings visitor attractions' unique strengths together with the 'target visitor', by creating a story around the attraction that will appeal to that visitor. Successful marketing depends on a thorough understanding of the 'core experience'. In general terms, that is what the visitor is primarily looking for—'a good day out, exploring our heritage', perhaps, or a day with my friends on the scariest rides available in theme parks'—

and which the visitor attraction than seeks to turn into a 'real' experience. That real experience is a composite product. It comprises many subcomponents, including the moment the visitor becomes aware of the visitor attraction through, for example, advertising; the process of buying the entrance ticket; going on the rides; and, using the ancillary services which the visitor attraction has to offer, such as catering, that ideally makes the visit even more enjoyable and merchandise from the shop provides opportunities for shopping both for gifts and souvenirs.

Visitor research is the fundamental route to marketing success in the visitor attraction. Regular questionnaire exercises monitor the satisfaction level of existing visitors, whilst specially commissioned research investigates the expectations and motivations of non-visitors, both those who are currently visitors at other attractions and those who are not yet visitors but might be converted. Arms with knowledge about visitors, the attraction can attempt to aim its promotion as directly as possible at potential visitors, by selecting to advertise or otherwise publish in appropriate media, promoting through other appropriate channels (e.g., flyers at tourist information offices and hotels) and perhaps even promoting through directly mail to the target audience.

Finance

Finance is usually concerned with two aspects:

- Day-to-day finance, in the sense of looking after the cash flow that results from revenue earning at the entrance and at other outlets and franchises with the attraction.
- The raising of finance for new projects: capital expenditure.

The finance department will monitor income and expenditure in order to ensure that the attraction is solvent and that it achieves the appropriate financial result. The main income for the attraction may come from admissions, which means that the attraction must pay careful attention to pricing and the relationship between the price and value which the visitor feels that the attractions visit represents. The modern services customer looks for value for money and it becomes one of the central tasks of attractions management to find out how that can be provided at each individual attraction.

Instead of the admissions price, the attraction may rely on the 'average spend' of the visitor during the visit. This can enable the attraction to lower its admission price (thereby removing a financial barrier to visiting) in the expectation that the visitor will spend additionally at outlets within the attraction. Shopping is a staple part of the attraction visit in the UK and visitors expect to find appropriate merchandise, at a range of prices, as part of the service. The budget is the main instrument for financial control, enabling the financial officer to check forecasts against actual performance and suggest ways of dealing with temporary problems.

Human resource management

Human resource management is concerned with how staff are best recruited, trained and employed at the attraction. Staff salaries is likely to be the largest item on the attractions overall costs and the temptation—indeed, the need—may well be for managers to seek to reduce staff costs by making staff more efficient and productive. This may happen through the employment of temporary staff or through multi-skilling of existing staff, to ensure that they are able to function at more than one point in the attraction experience. Given that the attractions market is seasonal with the majority of visitors arriving during peak holiday times a flexible workforce is a must for many attractions which need to close down, wholly or in part, during the low season. This makes staff motivation a constant issue in the visitor attraction; it is not easy to maintain morale in a workforce which is not prepared to offer permanent employment to its staff. Since staff are crucial in delivering a high-quality visitor attractions experience, that becomes a major issue for the attractions manager who must maintain staff morale and staff numbers at a sufficient level to keep the visitor satisfied.

Quality Management

Now-a-days, the concept of quality prevails in the business in general, and in the tourism sector in particular. As previously, quality management is an essential task in tour operations, and the same is true for attractions management.

Quality in attractions related to at least two different areas. Firstly, since the attractions product is an 'experience, the staff delivering that service need to be skilled both in the particular jobs they carry out, such as manning rides, guiding tourists, or guarding sensitive areas, and in human relations, so that they know how to interact with visitors in an appropriate manner. Secondly, the attraction normally uses a range of 'hardware'. This may include machinery that is part of the experience which needs to be safe for the public to use and at an appropriate level of quality. The attraction also relies on a variety of produce bought in for sale to the public, such as food, drink, guidebook, and merchandise. All of this has to be of the right quality and therefore the attractions manager is responsible for ensuring that suppliers meet the attraction's quality demands.

Getting quality levels right

Quality levels have to be appropriate for the attraction, but determining quality is difficult. Quality is relative; there is no scientifically-based scale to indicate when the right level has been achieved. However, there are other ways of measuring it. For one thing, quality levels must reflect the image of the attraction: the attractions manager must know what the attraction ought to be able to deliver to the customer. That particular decision must be made with reference to what kind of person the attraction wishes to attract and what that customer is entitled to expect; meeting customer expectations is an important part of deciding quality levels. Customer expectations will be coloured both by what the attraction itself offers and by what other attractions and other service organisations have to offer: the competition is always a factor in creating customer quality perception.

The attraction can turn this to its advantage by benchmarking itself against other similar organisations in the industry, so that it can decide at what point it reaches appropriate quality levels. It may also adopt quality assurance standards through schemes such as the International Standards for Quality Management Systems: ISO 9000. It may also adopt the Total Quality Management (TQM) approach which aims for the implementation of a culture of quality throughout the organisation.

Although these ideas have long been current in general management, the attractions industry remains slow in their adoption. However, the demand from the public for good quality - or even excellence—will not go away and the industry will have to consider how to approach it. The Scottish attractions industry has introduced a quality scheme to help visitors know what service levels to expect at the visitor attraction. The English attractions industry has, however, refused to introduce a similar scheme, and now finds itself the subject of an 'attack' from the Consumer Association (Winter 2000), which has published its own Guide to Tourist Attractions, judging each on:

- **Quality of attraction** (welcome, what there is to see and do, interpretation, guides, range of appeal).
- **Standard of facilities** (restaurant, shops, toilets, parking, maintenance).
- **Value for money.**

World Heritage

The World Heritage Committee (WHC), a part of UNESCO, is an attempt to create not only a network of globally important heritage sites but also a global set of standards for heritage attractions. In order to quality for inclusion in the network, sites must conform to criteria specified by the WHC. Currently, the WHC includes 690 cultural and natural sites across the world, preserved so that future generations can inherit the treasures of the past. Among the UK sites are Stonehenge, Hadrian's Wall and the Old and New Towns of Edinburgh.

The WHC is not only concerned with heritage in an abstract sense; it also has views on how that heritage can be preserved and made available to visitors in a more specific sense. Thus, the WHC stipulates that any site included on the official list must have 'agreed plans, (e.g., regional, conservation plan, tourism development plan)' (WHC 2001) and that it must address issues of among other things, management, finance and visitor facilities.

Hadrian's Wall

Hadrian's Wall was placed on the list of World Heritage sites in 1987. It is a requirement from the UK government (in line with the WHC requirements listed above) that this long site, stretching across 12 local authorities, should have a management plan. This plan aims 'to balance and accommodate the different and sometimes potentially conflicting) interests of those whose purpose of to management and conserve the Site and those who use it' (Underwood 2001). Part of the purpose of the management plan is to balance the economic need to attract tourists with the need to ensure that the site is not eroded by too many visitors. This, the plan states, will happen through 'targeted tourism marketing campaigns... that bring added value from tourism to the area'. Similar plans exist for other sites in other countries, helping not only to identify internationally significant heritage sites but also to ensure that they are preserved and managed, so that they can serve the several purposes they have to serve as part of local and global history and culture, as national status symbols and as tourist visitor attractions.

Visitor Attraction Organisations

By creating a trade association, businesses can achieve several important things. They are able to speak with one voice, putting their industry's case to government, when they negotiate national regulations and legislation. They are also able to establish and maintain agreed quality levels within the industry. It is sometimes argued that as a tourist destination, the UK lags behind other countries where customer care is concerned. A national organisation could help improve this situation.

Trade associations

Since the visitors attractions sector is so varied, setting up a truly representative network in the UK has proved to be different. However, several associations have been formed:

- The Association of Leading Visitor Attractions (ALVA) has some thirty members (out of the approximately 6000 that make up the sector) who between them attract over 85 million visits annually, including Tyne and Wear Museums, Blackpool Leisure Beach, Stonehenge and Longleat. ALVA is involved in a benchmarking project for the sector (Locum Destination, 2000).
- The Historic Houses Association (HHA) is a trade association for stately homes, lobbying about taxation issues and co-ordinating its members' tourism and commercial activities, such as weddings and film location work. Among its members are Alnwick Castle and Burghley Castle.
- The British Association of Leisure Parks, Piers and Attractions (BALPPA) represents the interests of 256 of the UK's commercial leisure parks, piers, zoos and static attractions.
- The International Association of Amusement Parks and Attractions (IAAPA) with more than 5,000 members in 91 countries, aims to promote professionalism in the amusement industry and to represent the industry before government.
- The Association of Scottish Visitor Attractions (ASVA) is concerned with providing the Scottish visitor attractions sector with services that help the development of its members by supplying information about trends in the industry and arranges staff development courses and workshops in topics of interest to members. It also supports product development by providing consultancy and 'mystery visits' to allow managers to understand where there might be room for improvement.

National (state) organisations

There are also national organisations concerned with the standard of visitors attractions. The Scottish Tourist Board (STB) runs several standard), *Commended* (a good overall standard) and *Approved* (an acceptable good overall) quality assurance schemes, one of which grades visitor attractions according to the standard of services they provide, classifying them as *Highly Commanded* (a very good overall standard (Perthshire Tourist Board 2001). The English Tourism Council (ETC), responding to a general decline in the English visitor attractions sector, has developed an attractions strategy, which aims to 'improve the sustainability of attractions, encourage them to embrace change and be more customer orientated and to inform relevant organisations of the operational context, characteristics and needs of attractions' (ETC 2001). This not only indicates where some of the industry's structural problems lie, it also implies that a centralised strategy for the entire industry may help solve its problems.

In this context, the Regional Tourist Boards must not be forgotten. They are responsible for creating the regional matrix of destinations and attractions will provide not only a regional strategy to guide members of the industry but also a forum for local attractions.

Conclusion

The centrality of the visitor attraction, as part of the tourism system, is clear—along with the other elements in the system, it helps make the destination what it is. The exciting thing about visitor attractions, from the manager's point if view, is the great variety that exists in the sector; the challenge of managing them and making them successful is endless. In addition, the visitor attraction has the potential to make a difference, not only to the economy of the destination (and, sometimes, the wealth of its owner). It can also make a difference to the visitors who may not only be entertained by it but who may also learn from it and take new knowledge back into their lives from it. Its attraction can, to coin a phrase, be endless to all those who come into contact with it.

Appendix

Visitor Attraction Cases

The two cases below offer insights into to quite different visitor attractions. Read both separately and together, they throw light on some of the current issues in this type of attraction, in particular in the areas of interpretation and customer service.

Case One

The Space Centre at Leicester

'When I visited the National Space Centre at Leicester in June 2001, I arrived by train, I had expected to find signs at the station telling me how to get there but none were present. I took a taxi and expected that the taxi driver would be able to find the National Space Centre but discovered that at first he was not sure where it was. It was a very new attraction, but as a tourist-student I was a little disappointed. However, as the taxi driver got nearer to the attraction, road signs—both general road signs and the characteristic brown attraction signs--began to announce where we had to go to find it.

Once we were at the National Space Centre, the unusual architecture of the new building was in itself enough to tell me that we were there. I had, in fact, spotted the unusal building from the train and guessed that it had to be one of the new Millennium buildings. Progressive architecture has become a distinctive part of the contemporary attraction in the UK, often made possible by funding from the National Lottery. A large car and coach park was the first facility I encountered, although the taxi could drive close to the main entrance and did not have to enter the car park as such.

There were signs telling me where to find the main entrance although the modern architecture made it difficult for me to recognise the front door as such. As a visitor, I expect to be guided all the way to the attraction nowadays, without having to ask directions, just as I expect to be able to find products in the supermarket without having to ask staff.

There were speaking spaces for the disabled near to the entrance and disabled access was available everywhere. That, of course, is becoming a legal requirement but it is also satisfying in itself to see that provision is made for disabled visitors so that they do not feel disadvantaged when they enter and use the building. Of course, I am talking about physical access for the physically disabled: there are many other kinds of disability which do not require special access but which may require other facilities such as signs in Braille or large letters for visually impaired visitors, or induction loops for the hard of hearing.

Once you enter, a large Soyuz spacecraft, hanging from the ceiling, clearly signals to the visitor what kind of attraction we are in: one dealing with science and technology. Of course, that is what you expect when you visit a National Space Centre, but it is also the responsibility of attraction designers to make it obvious from the start what we are dealing with. In this case, although this is not a museum as such, the Space Centre does in fact own and exhibit important artefacts, including the Soyuz spacecraft. We are not just visiting a virtual reality experience, we will see authentic objects, we are facing reality, although as the exhibition then shows us, we are also in the world of conjecture, speculation and, most importantly, calculation. After all, this is about space, and much of it is still unknown.

That means that the Centre has to be well organised: otherwise, how can it take us through material that seems quite abstract at times? The exhibition itself has been theomatically organised: we can explore a series of themes, each interesting in its own right, and together they form an overall picture of contemporary space exploration, carried out in space and from Earth. There are many interactives, including computer interactives and various 'toys' allowing us to learn about things like gravity. It soon becomes clear that you come to this attraction to learn things and I suspect that one of the major target audiences is schools.

A special information area tells us about space exploration here and now, with a large screen for the projection of images from, for example the Internet. There is a completely up-to-date cinema with the capacity for film screening with audience feedback. There is a hall for special exhibitions, a lecture room, a restaurant and a cafeteria, toilets (of course) and a gift shop with space-related gifts for any purse. The catering is not very space orientated—I wondered if they would be selling space food in tubes and that kind of thing. The merchandise plays, very obviously, to people's interest in science fiction, but it also includes some fairly sophisticated items like rockets. In addition, you can buy a guidebook and, if you want to and have the computer access, a homepage on the net.

The Space Centre has a large tower, the spectacular and very obvious architectural feature, covered in inflated plastic material and heated by heaters designed to look like solar panels. Inside the tower are two full-size rockets as well as more exhibitions on each of the floors off the tower space, including full-scale models of satellites. Of course, there is a lift for those who do not want (or are not able) to walk upstairs. You expect that kind of facility, but this lift is special: it is rattly and shaky. The reason is that it is exactly the same kind of rattly lift that takes NASA astronauts up to the cockpit of the space shuttle. Now, that is mixing customer facility with exhibition design in the most elegant and pleasing way.

This is how a really well-designed attraction works: it is a single experience, it offers a quality exhibition and a quality environment with good quality facilities. This should help ensure that the visitor has an enjoyable time, stays as long as possible (but not for too long: you also need to move people through the attraction) and has opportunities to spend, so that the attraction can earn the revenue it needs to.

The National Space Centre has been developed to attract a number of different audiences. It targets the educational market very clearly with excellent educational facilities including the schools space resource building at the entrance to the centre. This is not surprising: Leicester University, which has been instrumental in developing the Space Centre, is in itself a national centre for space research, as it has been for decades. That is also why it seems aimed at schoolchildren. But it is also aimed at tourists, who may not want to spend their entire holiday at Leicester itself but who may day-trip from London. It certainly has the facilities to satisfy that market, although only time will tell whether it can actually attract them.

They may be able to get to the Space Centre on the new City Tour Coach, which takes the visitor to main sights and attractions in Leicester. The centre is meant to be part of a wider launch of Leicester as a tourist destination and there are clear hopes that tourism will form part of the economic regeneration of the City. Many cities are trying this approach at the moment and it is one of the exciting aspects of visitor attractions that they are in such a central position in the tourist economy now and that so much money is being invested in them. Again, only time will show whether there is an audience, of schoolchildren, families, tourists and others to fill this attraction, and the many others which have appeared in Britain in the last ten years'.

Case Two

The Anatomical Museum, Innsbruck, Austria.

'I had a scary experience on my holiday one year ago. My parents took me to something called the 'Anatomical Museum' in a city in Austria called Innsbruck. The whole family had 'passe' which we could use for two days, and the 'Anatomical Museum' was one of the things we could see. So we went.

The Anatomical Museum is in a building called the 'Anatomical Institute'. It is part of the University. At first we could not find it. It was not at the address on the map that we got with the passes. We had to walk past the University Hospital through several streets before we got to a big house in a quiet street. There were no signs in the street but there was one on the house: That was the Anatomical Institute. First we went into the basement. There was nothing there. We went upstairs to a corridor with cases with glass fronts. It was spooky: the cases were full of skulls with maltese crosses painted on them in black, and green oak leaves. The ceiling was high and the corridor was very dark and quiet. On one door was a large sign saying 'Strictly no unauthorised admittance.' We could not find the museum anywhere, so my dad knocked on some doors and eventually a man came out. He looked surprised, but then he said he would open up for us. They were closed, we said, but dad had a brochure which he got with the pass and it said that they were open on Tuesday and today was Tuesday. The man had a key and opened the door. He walked into a dark room and switched the ceiling strip lights on, one by one. Then he waved us in and left us.

We were in a brightly lit room surrounded by display cases. But the first thing you really noticed was the smell: a kind of musty, chemical smell. To the left and right were display cases full of specimens. I have always been interested in the skeleton and muscles and there was skeleton and muscles everywhere, in bottles and in boxes, in rows on shelves and so on. Even an entire person, in a glass case. At the back of the room was this huge skeleton which belonged to a man who had been very tall when he died five hundred years ago. Behind him was a collection of skeletons of animals: dogs, seals, horses, everything.

We were all very quiet in there. My sister went out first. Mum did not seem to know where to look. Daddy was taking picture. I was thinking about tomorrow when we were going riding at a riding school.

We did not stay long. Afterwards we went to a place called a 'Konditorei', where you get coffee and cakes. We talked about the museum. My sister though it was scary. She hated the lights. My mum was not sure it was a good place for children. The smell was a bit much, too. I thought it was OK but not that interesting. Some of the books they have in the library showed the human anatomy better. The skins were cool, though. My dad said he was not sure what all the exhibits were. There was so much in that one room and some of the labels were hand-written. All in all, we thought it was quite interesting, though, and we had never seen anything like that before. Anywhere.'

2

Tourism and the Environment

Introduction

'The environment is the foundation of the tourist industry.' (Mathieson and Wall 1982: 97).

From the intrepid trailblazer back-packing through Laos and Cambodia to the sun-loving package tourist basking on the beaches of the Costa del Sol, tourists decisions to visit particular destinations are strongly influenced by their perception of their differing environments. Moreover, how they get there, where they stay, and whatever they do whilst staying there will all have a discernible impact on the physical environment. In short, tourism is what we refer to as an **environmentally dependent industry.** The physical environment is a fundamental part of the tourism product and, as tourists, we seek out different and distinctive environments. However, in doing so, we may threaten the very nature and physical well being of these environments; our actions may even end up destroying the very thing that attracted us in the first place.

International tourism has increased rapidly since the 1950s to become one of the world's largest industries. There are over 600 million international arrivals per year and a choice of over 200 foreign destinations. As a result, very few countries in the world do not attract any foreign tourists at all. However, since the heyday of mass international tourism in the 1960s, concern about the environmental consequences of tourism development has grown. During this period, people have become more aware of environmental issues generally as the environmental impacts of rapid economic growth have become increasingly experienced both locally and globally.

Importantly, however, although the deleterious impact of human activity on the physical environment is by no means a new phenomenon, what is new is the scale and severity of this impact. Indeed, there are now very few places on earth which have not been subject to some form of human interference and economic exploitation. At the same time, global news media networks have heightened our awareness of environmental issues and it is perhaps not surprising, therefore, that people are becoming more aware of the impacts that tourism in particular can have upon the physical environment.

Tourism is a form of exploration and, throughout history, explorers have always gone in search of new lands, partly out of curiosity but also out of a desire or necessity to discover new resources for exploitation. The success of the capitalist enterprises which make up the tourism industry is, therefore, partly dependent upon their ability to 'discover' and market new destinations for our consumption. However, although tourism is sometimes described as a 'smokeless industry', as an activity it has several important and unique characteristics (Fig. 2.1) which mean that, in many cases, it is far from being environmentally benign. From deforestation in the Nepalese Himalayas to the threatened extinction of loggerhead turtles on the Greek island of Zakynthos, there are now many well documented examples from all over the world of where tourism is a contributor to some form of environmental damage.

- Unlike the consumption of most manufactured goods, in the case of tourism the customer (tourist) must go to the point of production to consume the product. A defining characteristic of tourism is, therefore, travel and, in the modern age, most travel necessitates the consumption of fossil fuels. Moreover, there is a social cache associated with distant travel whereas the constraints of modern life dictate that such journeys should be completed as quickly as possible. These dual demands for travel over greater distances and speeds further increase the consumption of fossil fuels. Tourism essentially encourages millions of people to travel much greater distance, consuming more fossil fuels, than they would otherwise normally do in their daily lives.
- Tourism tends to be a relatively short-term, transitory experience characterised by a rather escapist philosophy. For most people, tourist activity is restricted to, at most, a 2-week holiday each year. Tourism encourages consumerist behaviour, as there is a tendency for most people to consume proportionately more of certain products and services whilst on holiday than they would normally do at home (e.g. food and drink, clothing, souvenirs, fuel, water, suntan lotion, tobacco). Consequently, tourism is a wasteful industry and encourages the consumption of both renewable and non-renewable resources.
- Our cultural fascination for and attraction to relatively pristine natural environments (e.g. lakes, mountains, forests, coasts, and islands) necessitates that tourism development often takes place in relatively fragile and previously undisturbed ecosystems.
- Tourism is a complex and multi-faceted industry and so are its associated impacts. Several different industries (e.g., transport, construction, hospitality, services, and entertainment) contribute to the making of the tourism product and each has distinctly different environmental impacts in terms of their nature, location, scale and severity. The enviornmental impacts of every tourist trip are not, therefore, just limited to one particular location (e.g., the destination area) but can be geographically widespread.

Figure 2.1 : Some potentially environmentally threatening characteristics of tourism.

Before discussing the environmental impacts of tourism in some detail, it is worth noting that the study of them is by no means a straightforward task, for a number of reasons:

- It is often difficult to differentiate between environmental changes attributable directly to tourism and those caused by other human activities.
- The environmental impacts of tourism may not always be immediately obvious as it may be sometime before perceptible changes to land, air, water, flora or fauna become apparent.
- It is necessary to consider the indirect as well as direct effects of tourism development on the environment. Direct effects may be relatively obvious and are usually experienced in and around the tourist destination areas themselves. However, environmental impacts can also occur elsewhere in areas that are either on transit routes to the destination or are linked to them in some way through the supply of goods, labour or services to the tourist industry. For example, tourism development has been a catalyst for rural to urban migration in some developing areas, leading to the abandonment of low-paid agricultural employment in favour of more lucrative work in the tourism industry. The consequent reduced labour input in agricultural areas is likely to precipitate some form of enviornmental change as agricultural infrastructure is no longer fully maintained.
- Frequently, there is a lack of sufficiently detailed information about what environmental conditions were like in the destination area before tourism development took place (e.g., an inventory of local flora and fauna or measures of seawater quality) and so it is difficult to derive a precise baseline from which comparisons can be made.

It is sometimes easy to place the blame for environmental damage, such as coastal pollution, on the tourism industry, in particular when other factors may have already been contributing to the problem long before any significant tourism development took place. It is also worth considering, as emphasised in the next section, that not all of the environmental changes induced by tourism development are necessarily negative.

Different Types of Relationship between Tourism and the Environment

According to Mathieson and Wall (1982), there are three possible relationships between tourism and the physical environment.

(i) Neutrality

This is, perhaps, the rarest and almost certainly the most short-lived condition. Neutrality exists when there is little or no interaction between tourists and the physical environment. Thus, this relationship is only experienced, if at all, in the very early stages of tourism development when there are only small numbers of tourists and no additional facilities provided. However, it is difficult to envisage how even a small number of visitors would not create extra demands for local resources and, thus, disturb the human-environment equilibrium in some way. After only a short time, as the destination becomes more popular this relationship is likely to be destroyed by the additional environmental pressures created by tourism development. It would be naive to assume through, that, prior to the arrival of tourism, all societies coexist in a state of neutrality with the physical environment and that only tourism disturbs this equilibrium.

(ii) Opposition or conflict

The most widely commented upon relationship between tourism and the environment, this is where the interests of tourism and the environment are in opposition to each other so that, as tourism develops, natural resources are degraded and eventually destroyed. Many argue that this condition is particularly caused when rapid growth in visitor numbers coincides with unplanned, uncontrolled, profit-led forms of tourism development.

(iii) Harmony or symbiosis

Symbiosis occurs where there are positive benefits provided by tourism development to the physical environment and vice versa. In this context, tourism is seen as a lesser evil than other forms of development as the revenues from tourism may be ploughed back in to the preservation or protection of fragile ecosystems that may otherwise have been developed or destroyed. As an environmentally dependent industry, it is obviously in tourism's long term interests to protect the environment for the enjoyment of future generations. However, as discussed later in this chapter, this goal may be practically very different to achieve in a climate of increasing tourism demand.

Factors influencing the nature and scale of environmental impacts

Before looking at some examples of the negative environmental impacts of tourism, it is first necessary to consider some of the factors that are likely to determine the nature and scale of the environmental impacts. Some of these factors relate to the environment itself, whereas others relate more to the socio-political context in which tourism takes place and the type of tourists attracted to the destination.

According to Burns and Holding, the factors affecting the environment impacts of tourism include:

- **The scale of tourism development and rate of growth:** Sometimes, tourism development occurs so rapidly that there is not time to develop sufficient infrastructure and sanitation services to cope with the increased demand.
- **The fragility and sensitivity of the environment:** Some ecosystems are more sensitive to environmental changes than others (e.g., coral reefs and wetlands) or take longer to recover from any environmental damage (e.g., mountain environments).
- **The sensitivity of the development in terms of its integration with the local environment and culture:** For example, the design of tourist related buildings are not always in keeping with local architectural styles, leading to a form of aesthetic pollution. Also, the building materials used may have been imported from elsewhere, creating further environmental costs in transportation.

- **The political context of development:** In some destination areas there is neither the political infrastructure nor the will necessary to ensure proper development planning and control and, as a result, resorts may be developed in a very piece-meal, 'laissez-faire' fashion.
- **The range of development incentives and the importance attached to tourism by national regional government:** Development incentives offered by local, national or international government bodies (e.g., EC) might influence both where tourism development occurs and the type of development initiated. Some national governments in the developing world, for example, have offered incentives to encourage inward investment (e.g., by foreign transnational tour operators) in their tourism infrastructure. Their need for foreign exchange earning and capital investment in tourist infrastructure, such as airports and resort complexes, has sometimes taken precedence over a concern for the impacts of such development on the local environment.
- **The cultural attitudes of local people to the environment:** Cultural attitudes to the environment vary from place to place. Some cultures regard certain environments as sacred—for example Ayers Rock (Uluru) is a sacred site for Australian Aborigines—and so are likely to strongly resist certain forms of tourism development in such areas (e.g., airstrips, hotel complexes). In Western Christian societies, the Romantic Movement of the eighteenth century fundamentally changed cultural attitudes towards wild landscapes, such as forests, mountains and moorlands, inspiring the creation of protected areas such as the US National Parks.
- **The type of tourists attracted to the destination and the characteristics of their behaviour:** Some tourists create more environmental damage than others simply because of both their actions and their attitudes towards the environment. The type of accommodation stayed in, the extent and mode of travel to and around the destination, the places visited, the activities engaged in, and what is actually consumed whilst on holiday will all have an influence on the degree of environmental stress created by each individual tourist. Clearly, a

cycling holiday around your own country, staying in locally owned bed and breakfast accommodation and eating local organic produce will cause less environmental damage than, for example, flying to Nepal for a trekking holiday involving overnight stays in tourist lodges which consume large quantities of local fuel wood to provide hot water and cooked meals.

- **The availability of information to educate the tourist:** The more information tourists have about the potential environmental consequences of different forms of behaviour, the less likely they are to engage in behaviour that they know to be harmful to the environment. Many tourists are simply not aware of the environmental implications of their actions (e.g., the damage done to coral reefs by trampling on them and breaking off pieces as souvenirs) and, therefore, by improving most tourists' basic environmental awareness, many problems could, in principle, be alleviated.
- **The volume of tourists using the destination:** In some areas, even a few tourists can create a perceptible environmental impact if there are insufficient local resources (e.g., food, water, shelter) and inadequate infrastructure to meet these additional demands. Nevertheless, we tend to assume that more tourists mean more damage. This is only really the case when the carrying capacity of an environment is exceeded, when additional numbers do create additional damage.
- **The physical robustness or fragility of the environment to different types of tourist activity:** Some ecosystems are more sensitive than others to the kind of environmental pressures initiated by the increased presence of tourists. The trampling of plant species in mountain environments, for example, is a particular problem because their relatively cold temperatures, short growing seasons and poor quality soils mean that regeneration of damaged vegetation is a lengthy process.

Tourism and Environment in Conflict

Academics have tended to approach the study of the environmental impacts of tourism in a number of different ways. For example, Mathieson and Wall simply divide the physical environment up into its constituent parts (e.g., vegetation, wildlife, air, water, and land) and report on the impacts of tourism on each of these separate elements. Although perhaps the most straightforward, this approach can, however, be a little misleading as it is possible that any one tourism development or activity could impact on all of these elements either simultaneously or sequentially. For instance, the clearance of vegetation for the construction of a ski piste may not only lead to the loss of wildlife habitat but can also expose the soil to increased rates of erosion and, consequentially, alter sediment loads in local rivers and streams because of increased run-off. Ultimately, it may also contribute to increased levels of carbon dioxide in the atmosphere because of deforestation as well as perhaps reducing the overall aesthetic appeal of the area. Therefore, just one form of tourism development impacts upon flora, fauna, land, air and water.

An alternative approach, then, is to study the environment as an integrated, holistic system and, therefore, structure the analysis around different aspects of tourism development. At the same time, it is also necessary to consider the environmental impacts of tourism at different stages in the tourism system. For example, there are impacts created in the generating areas, during transit, at the destination area itself and in other areas linked into the tourism system by the supply of tourist goods and services.

Perhaps the most comprehensive and integrated framework for studying the enviornmental impacts of tourism was developed by the OECD in the mid 1970s as part of their tourism and environment programme (Pearce 1989). The framework focuses upon a number of tourism-generated stressor activities (e.g., resort construction, generation of wastes and tourist activities), the nature of the stresses themselves and the primary (environmental) and secondary (human) responses to this environmental stress.

The OECD identify four environmental stresses related to tourism, which are considered below.

Permanent environmental restructuring

The first major source of environmental stress identified by the OECD is described as permanent environmental restructuring. This is caused by major construction activity, such as the building of new resorts and associated infrastructure (e.g., roads, airport terminals and runways, railways). Such development leads to a change in the physical fabric of an area.

The ribbon-style beach resort developments along the most of the Spanish Costas provide a striking example of this transformation. The famous British novelist Laurie Lee, looking back on his visit to the area in the 1930s, described it as 'a beautiful but exhausted shore, seemingly forgotten by the world. I remember the names San Pedro, Estepona, Marbella, and Fuengirola. They were salt-fish villages, thin-ribbed, sea-hating, cursing their place in the sun. At that time one could have bought the whole coast for a shilling. Not Emperors could buy it now.' Indeed, over a period of just 40 years, the Costa del Sol has been transformed from a relatively barren coastline dotted with poverty-stricken fishing villages into a virtually unbroken strip of high rise hotels, apartments, motorways, marinas and urbanisations stretching nearly 60 kilometres from Malaga in the east to Estapona in the west.

The planned coastal resorts of the Languedoc-Roussillon development on France's western Mediterranean coastline are another extreme example of this form of permanent environmental restructuring. Resorts in this area were planned on a grand scale, with ribbon-style coastal developments like those found in Spain and on the neighbouring French Riviera deliberately avoided. Despite this, the development did involve the wholesale drainage and 'reclamation' of large areas of wetland, including coastal marshes and saltwater lagoons leading to a loss of habitat for many wetland species of flora and fauna.

As well as wetlands, coral reefs are another coastal ecosystem that has come under threat because of the construction of coastal tourism resorts. Coral reefs are thought to be home to 25 per cent of all known marine species and constitute the second most biologically diverse ecosystem on earth. They are, however, very sensitive to environmental change and require specific water quality conditions to survive, hence their limited geographical distribution. For healthy growth, the coral requires fairly constant sea temperatures of between 25 and 29 degrees Celsius, a shallow platform less than 100 metres below sea-level and clear, highly oxygenated water that is free from sediment and pollution. Although coral reefs have become a tourist attraction in their own right, such as the Great Barrier Reef, tourism development and the activities of some tourists threaten them.

The construction phase of tourism development—digging of hotel foundations, clearance of vegetation, road construction, and so on—often leads to increased sediment loads in the coastal waters surrounding the developing. The consequent clouding-up of coastal waters can starve coral of essential sunlight and effectively, choke the reef to death. The dumping of inadequately treated sewage into coastal waters from resorts can also effect the vitality of coral reefs by increasing salinity and reducing dissolved oxygen levels. Additionally, of course, tourists themselves contribute directly to coral damage by both walking on reefs and plundering them for souvenirs. The extensive reef systems off Egypt's Red Sea coast attract thousands of divers to resorts such as Sharm el Sheik and Naama Bay but, according to Goudie and Viles (1997), 73 per cent of coral reefs off the coast of Egypt have been adversely affected by tourism.

Another obvious consequence of the permanent environmental restructuring that accompanies most tourism development is a change in land use patterns, usually with predominantly urban land use replacing predominantly rural. This transition is often quite rapid and not only leads to a change in wildlife habitats but also a change in the livelihoods of the local human population, with employment opportunities in the construction and hospitality sectors replacing those in traditional primary industries such are agriculture and fishing. In southern Andalucia (i.e. the Costa del Sol), where agriculture tended to be dominated by a relatively small number of large landowners (*latifundia*) and the majority of the generally poor local population either relied on migrant work elsewhere on seasonal employment as landless day-labourers (*braceros),* such a transition has been mostly welcomed and the environmental changes accepted (Barke *et. al.,* 1996).

Elsewhere, though, where tourism development has been externally imposed on an indigenous population without their support and has involved the enforced confiscation of their land and the diversion of water resources to the tourism industry (e.g., Goa, India), such changes have not been universally welcomed and local farmers and environmentalists have formed protest groups to resist these forms of development (Lea 1993).

The construction of coastal resorts is not the only form of tourism development to cause permanent environmental restructuring. Mountain areas are the second most popular location for tourism yet these areas are particularly sensitive to environmental change because their cold temperatures, short growing seasons and poor quality soils mean that regeneration of damaged vegetation is a lengthy process (Holden 2000). According to the World Tourism Organisation figures, winter sports are estimated to account for about 4 per cent of all international tourist arrivals and the construction of ski resorts to satisfy this demand can lead to considerable and irrevocable environmental change. In addition to the visual impacts associated with the construction of an urban environment within an often remote mountain setting, the creation of ski runs, depending on altitude, usually necessitates deforestation resulting in a loss of wildlife habitat. The removal of vegetation is also likely to increase surface run-off and may precipitate hydrological changes together with gulling and even landslides. There is also evidence of an increased incidence of avalanches and mudslides due to the removal of trees and other vegetation for ski resort development (Simmons 1988).

The generation of wastes and pollution

The second major source of environmental stress created by tourism development is the generation of new or increased waste materials and, consequently, the pollution of air, land and water resources. The pollution of air and water resources resulting from wastes generated by tourism is a problem on a global as well as a local scale.

The transportation of tourists is, not surprisingly, a major source of air and noise pollution. Air and car transport contributes significantly to both local and global atmospheric pollution. According to the United Nations Environment Programme (UNEP), it is estimated that approximately 2 million tons of aviation fuels are burned each year, producing 550 million tons of greenhouse gases and 3.5 million tons of chemicals responsible for acid rain (WTO 1997). It is also estimated that, in the US, aircraft contribute 10 per cent to CO^2 emissions and that globally airlines account for 2.3 per cent of CO^2 and NO^2 emissions (Burns 2000; Pearce 1989). Cars are, however, the main mode of tourist transpor-tation and by far the biggest contributor to atmospheric pollution. According to Cooper *et. al.*, (1998), within Europe alone—by far the biggest tourist generating area—the car accounts for 83 per cent of tourist passenger miles. Air pollution is no respecter of national boundaries and the knock-on effects of atmospheric pollution, such as acid rain, may well in turn contribute to the degradation of tourism resources, such as ancient monuments and conife-rous forests. In addition, the increased local air pollution levels experienced in both major transit and destination areas at peak times can have an adverse effect on the health of the local population. There are clearly considerable secondary human costs of increased air pollution in terms of paying for the amehoration of the local effects (e.g., repairing damaged stonework, treating asthma sufferers, installing air conditioning). Globally of course, the consumption of fossil fuels by tourist related transport is also a major contributor to the creation of greenhouse gases and possible future global warming.

However, these negative aspects of tourism must be put within some sort of perspective. It is worth pointing out that sustaining other aspects of our everyday western lifestyle, such as travelling to work, school, and the shops, the production of consumer goods and the supply of domestic gas and electricity, contributes far more to the consumption of fossil fuels and air pollution loads.

As well as contributing to air pollution, tourism development is also a major polluter of the world's water resources. Throughout its history, tourism development has been drawn to water resources of one kind or another. The seventeenth century onwards, the European aristocracy's belief in the curative properties of sea bathing and spa waters greatly influenced the pattern of tourism development (Towner 1998). the Romantic poets, painters and writers of the late eighteenth and early nineteenth centuries also helped fashion a taste for lonely lake shores, meandering rivers and dramatic coastal scenery amongst the social elite (Andrews 1989). Even in the contemporary period, tourism's umbilical link with water continued with the western fashion for sun, sea and sand holidays and the popularity of water sports.

Often, however, resorts have developed without the prior construction of adequate sewage facilities and so our seas, lakes and rivers have acted as cheap and convenient depositories for untreated effluent. While tourism is by no means the only contributor to marine and fresh water pollution, its role has been significant in many parts of the world. Coastal pollution through the inadequate disposal of human sewage not only threatens marine life, but can also have a negative effect on human health, possibly causing anything from a mild stomach upset to typhoid through either bathing in infected waters or eating contaminated seafood. In addition, the effects of water pollution can be off-putting for visitors because it is both unsightly and smells unpleasant. In recent years, many European, resorts have been encouraged to clean up their coastal waters under the European Blue Flag initiative and, as a result the quality of bathing water and the cleanliness of beaches in many resorts has improved significantly. Thus, at the launch of the campaign in 1987, only 244 beaches in Europe satisfied the Blue Flag's water quality standards; by 2001, however, they had granted the award to 2041 beaches in 21 countries (see Table 2.1). Nevertheless, despite these measures, in the Mediterranean basin only 30 per cent of over 700 towns and cities on the coastline treat their sewage before discharging it into the sea (Holden 2000). Moreover, such voluntary

Table 2.1 : Numbers of awarded Blue Flag beaches and marinas in 2001 in the different European countries.

Country	*Beaches*	*Marinas*
Belgium	7	4
Bulgaria	9	0
Croatia	16	14
Cyprus	34	0
Denmark	188	79
Estonia	2	3
Finland	6	30
France	403	85
Germany	33	204
Greece	351	8
Ireland	75	4
Italy	154	40
Latvia	3	0
Netherlands	18	30
Norway	1	6
Portugal	133	7
Slovenia	4	3
Spain	390	85
Sweden	60	74
Turkey	99	11
United Kingdom	55	26
Total	2041	713

Source: Foundation for Environmental Education, Blue Flag Campaign, 2001.

regulations are only applicable inside Europe and the costs of improving coastal sewage infrastructures may be prohibitive for many resorts in developing nations.

As well as contributing to the disposal of untreated sewage, tourism is also partly responsible for the water pollution caused by the fertilisers and herbicides that are used extensively in the maintenance of golf courses and hotel gardens.

Tourism is generally a rather profligate activity we consume more and we waste more when on holiday. Consequently, the industry produces large quantities of solid wastes. Improper disposal of solid wastes generates litter and resort areas can start to look and smell unpleasant with rubbish attracting vermin and possibly affecting human health. Disposal techniques include landfill and incineration, but these are not without their own environmental impacts potentially leading to the contamination of land, water and air. Not all of the solid waste produced by the tourism industry is biodegradable either and, in some locations, disposal opportunities are more limited than others. There have even been reports from the Masai Mara game park in Kenya of elephants being poisoned by eating zinc batteries that had been left on a tip outside one of the tourist lodges (Holden 2000).

One only has to think of the hundreds of different holiday brochures lining the walls of your local travel agent, and how these are replaced and discarded at least once every year, to realise that the tourism industry is an inherently wasteful one. Nevertheless, it is clearly not in the industry's best interests to foul-up resorts with untreated effluent pumped into the seas and piles of uncollected garbage left around the hotels. Somewhat ironically, although most tourists are very wasteful, they also like to visit clean, pristine environments and other people's dirt puts them off, as does the potential threat of communicable illnesses spoiling their holiday. The impact on human populations of the generation of wastes by the tourism industry is not just about the impact on human health, but also the escalating financial costs involved in pollution abatement measures and in cleaning-up already polluted environments in order to maintain their attractiveness.

Whose responsibility it should be for meeting the costs of cleaning up after the tourists is, however, a matter for speculation. In many resort areas, the local population bears the greatest burden of these costs through the local taxes they pay for public services, yet we might ask ourselves why the polluter (the tourist) doesn't pay more towards the costs of 'cleaning-up'.

Tourist activities

The third source of environmental stress and, perhaps, the one that is most widely documented is that which results directly from the recreational activities of tourists themselves. Mention has already been made about how the souvenir collecting antics of some tourists can threaten the vitality of coral reef ecosystems, but there are many other ways in which the activities of tourists can disturb, damage and even destroy sensitive flora and fauna.

Some forms of tourism, such as safari tourism, are explicitly designed to bring tourists into close contact with wild nature. In some of the more popular game parks, such as the Masai Mara in Kenya, the breeding and eating habits of some wild animals, including the rare black rhino, cheetahs and lions, have been disrupted by the intrusive activities of tourist buses. There are reported instances of up to 40 minibuses at a time around a single animal (Mathieson and Wall 1982; Shackley 1996). Through close contact with some animal populations, particularly fellow primates such as gorillas, tourists can also inadvertently spread human ailments, such as colds, flu, pneumonia and measles. For other species with no source of protection, these illnesses can often be fatal (Ryan 1989).

Other forms of tourism also impact directly upon wildlife. Ryan (1991) describes how, on the Greek island of Zakynthos, the breeding habits of loggerhead turtles were severely disrupted by tourism development until the Greek authorities took action to protect this endangered species. The turtles lay their eggs on what have now become popular tourist beaches. If the eggs manage to survive the beach activities of the tourists then it is when they hatch that the young turtles are in most danger. The lights and noise from the tourist resorts can disorientate the turtles and, instead of heading for the sea by the light of the moon, they can head straight for the headlights of motor vehicles or the bright lights and noise of the local taverna or disclose. Failing to reach the sea, many young turtles were dying on the roads or of dehydration. However, the introduction of building restrictions and strict controls on the use of the beaches at certain times have helped protect the turtle population (Williams 1998).

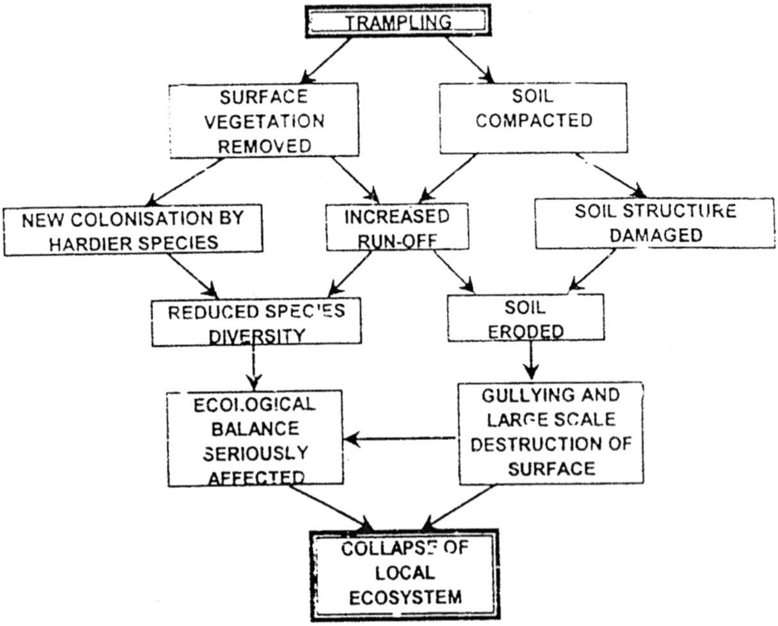

Figure 2.2: Effects of trampling at tourism sites.

Other seemingly innocuous activities, such as walking and trekking, also pose a considerable environmental threat in some areas. The trampling of vegetation and compaction of soils along popular recreational paths and trails has attracted a considerable amount of research (e.g., Liddle 1975). In mountain environments, where the vegetation recovery process tends to be very slow, trampling by walkers can reduce vegetation cover and species diversity with more resilient species becoming dominant around heavily used areas. The widening and erosion of heavily used footpaths in several of the National Park areas in England and Wales has resulted in costly rpairs and maintenance for the park authorities, with duckboards and gravel having to be used along parts of the Pennine Way to prevent further environmental damage.

The impacts of trekking in the Nepalese Himalayas have also attracted a considerable amount of academic attention (Holden 2000; Nepal 2000). The Nepalese Himalayas now attract well over 100,000 trackers a year (Nepal 2000) and, in the Sagarmatha National Park and Annapurna Conservation Area in particular, the relatively high numbers of visitors have created a number of environmental problems. The littering of tracks in remote mountain locations with garbage has become a particular problem—Nepal (2000) estimates that an average trekking group of 15 generates 15 kg of non-biodegradable, non-burnable garbage in just ten days. The other major issue, though, has been the accelerated deforestation of some hillsides in order to supply fuel wood to the numerous trekking lodges that offer tourists hot showers, cooked meals and a welcoming real fire. Deforestation has exposed some hillsides to soil erosion and gullying.

In other parts of the world, forest fires sometimes caused by the careless activities of tourists, such as not properly extinguishing campfires, barbecues or cigarette butts, have also damaged areas. Thus, some tourist activities are not only clearly a threat to the physical environment in some areas, but there is also a considerable financial cost involved in repairing damaged environments and in setting up appropriate controls on access and on certain activities. Resource management techniques that are commonly employed to protect the environment are introduce later in this chapter. However, the final area of tourist related environmental stress identified by the OECD is that associated with population dynamics, in particular population growth as a result of tourism development

Effect on population dynamics

The seasonal increases in population densities experienced by most resort areas create a number of environmental impacts. The most obvious of these is the physical congestion and over-crowding experienced at key tourist sites, such as beaches, ski-slopes, and historic town centres, during peak periods of demand (Pearce 1989). In some popular resorts, the population density during the peak season may be as much as twenty times higher than that experienced during the low season. In Torremolinos on the Costa del Sol, for example, the official population of 33,055 swells to over 200,000 in the summer months (SUR in English, September 6th-12th, 1996).

Congestion is not only unpleasant for the tourists. It can also inconvenience members of the local population not directly involved in tourism who are delayed by traffic jams and have to compete with tourists for access to local services such as shops, banks, and restaurants. Tourists and locals also compete for relatively scarce natural resources, such as and and water, with the behaviour of many tourists sometimes exacerbating the situation. Whilst on holiday, most western tourists on average consume a much greater quantity of water than they would normally do at home. For many package tourists, it has also become an essential part of the holiday experience to stay in relatively luxurious hotels. Operational standards in these establishments help perpetuate an expectation on the part of the tourist that sheets and towels will be laundered daily. Also, the daily activities of the average sun, sea and sand seeker encourage the excessive use of water in the form of regular showers and baths to remove the bodily accumulations of sand, salt water and sun tan lotion acquired from an average day on the beach. The hospitality industry, therefore, consumes copious amounts of water when compared to both other industries, such as agriculture, and to local residents. It has been calculated, for example, that 100 luxury hotel guests would consume as much water in 55 days as 100 urban families consume in two years and 100 rural farmers in three years (Salem 1994). In areas where water resources are scarce anyway due to climatic conditions, excessive water usage by tourists can be a particular problem. Not surprisingly, many Mediterranean sun, sea, and sand destinations fall into this category (Figure 2.3).

Another consequence of increased population densities as a result of tourism is the stress placed on inadequate local transport infrastructures, together with increased levels of local pollution levels due to the number of idling engines in slow moving traffic.

Tourism and the Environment in Harmony

So far, we have only examined the negative environmental impacts created by some forms of tourism development. However, tourism is by no means the main cause of enviornmental damage around the world. Other industries, such as mining, logging, petrol-chemicals and even agriculture, pose a much more significant threat to the physical environment. Moreover, in some circumstances, tourism development can actually be the driving force behind schemes to protect environmentally sensitive areas and prevent other potentially more damaging forms of development taking place. Without tourism, for example, it is unlikely that protected areas such as the national parks in both the US and UK would have ever been established. In many areas, tourism provides an economic rationale for the maintenance of a healthy and attractive physical environment. In general, when tourism impacts upon the health of the physical environment then it threatens to impact upon its own health and future well being as tourists are not normally attracted to degraded, congested, dirty and polluted environments. Therefore, it is in the long-term interests of the tourism industry, unlike some other industries, to sustain the quality of the environment for future generations of tourists.

Cost of water protest in Marbella
Sur in English, September 23rd-29th 1994
Andalucian government seeks urgent measures to alleviate prolonged drought.
Sur in English, September 23rd-29th 1994

Further drop in Costa reservoir water level *Sur in English,* October 28th-Nov. 3rd, 1994
Water cuts inevitable until it rains: Marbella has no water between midnight and six in the morning.
Sur in English, Dec. 9th-15th 1994.

The Costa del Sol is located on the southern coast of Spain and, as the local newspaper headlines above suggest, it is an area that regularly experiences long periods of drought. (e.g., 1994-95). Many of the rivers in this area are dry from one year to the next and are seasonally used as convenient transport routes by the local population. In the height of summer, one is more likely to see cars and motorbikes running up and down the river beds than water !

Irrigated agriculture (e.g., citrus fruit, vegetables and salad crops), supplying food to the local tourist industry as well as for export to the rest of Europe, competes with the tourism hospitality sector for water resources. In addition, the Costa del Sol also has one of the highest spatial concentrations of golf courses in Southern Europe with over 30 courses located along a 125 km stretch of coast (Priestly 1995). The use of extensive sprinkler systems to keep the hundreds of greens and fairways in lush, verdant condition for the thousands of golf tourists requires the use of considerable water resources. According to the US National Golf Foundations, maintaining the turf grass on one golf course requires between 500,000 and 800, 000 gallons of water per day.

In recent drought years, the situation has reached crisis point with water having to be rationed for a few hours a day for the local population in resorts like Torremolinos and Marbella whilst supplies to the hotels were unaffected. Considerable amounts of local taxpayers money has had to be invested in the construction of expensive sea water desalinisation plants in order to cope with the fresh water shortfall.

Figure 2.3 : Tourism and water resources on the Costa del Sol.

Mathieson and Wall (1982) identified four different ways in which tourism makes a positive contribution to the conservation of the physical environment:

(i) Rehabilitation and restoration

Tourism provides the economic rationale for the rehabilitation and restoration of historic sites, buildings and monuments. The funds generated by tourist admission fees are now often used to refurbish and restore historic houses, castles, and other heritage attractions.

(ii) Transformation

Tourism has been responsible for the transformation of old redundant sites into completely new tourist facilities and attractions. This has been particularly the case with industrial heritage attractions in the UK, where run-down dockside and canal areas have been transformed by urban development corporations into vibrant riverside areas with smart shops, restaurants, cafes and bars (e.g., the Quayside area in Newcastle upon Tyne, the Albert Dock in Liverpool, and Salford Quays near Manchester). Mothballed coal mines have also been transformed into heritage attractions with cafes, shops and interactive sight and sound museums, such as the Woodhora colliery near Ashington, Northumberland. These new attractions also have the effect of relieving congestion at other popular attractions.

(iii) Conservation

Tourism provides the incentive for the conservation of natural resources. As noted above, tourism and recreation have usually provided the main rationale for the establishment of protected areas such as national parks and nature reserves. Indeed, many would argue that there is little point in preserving unique and spectacular environments unless people are able to see them and that it is the demand created by tourists that gives the environment value and creates the need for protection. It is also recognised that, if it was not for the establishment of national parks in East Africa to protect one of the world's large wildlife populations, then some of the greatest wild species on earth such as lions, leopards giraffes, zebras and elephants could have been threatened with extinction through poaching and over hunting. It is tourism, though, in the form of safari tours, that has provided the main justification for wildlife preservation by creating a valuable source of foreign exchange, income and employment in developing countries such as Tanzania and Kenya.

(iv) Planning and administration

Finally, tourism has often been the impetus for the introduction of planning and administration controls in some areas in order to restore and maintain environmental quality and to ensure the provision of satisfying experiences for visitors. Such planning initiatives, although more often than not introduced in response to resource damage, have also produced other benefits for the local community in terms of the wider adoption of environmental planning and development control. In addition, some authors has argued that tourism itself has been instrumental in promoting environmental awareness and the broader appreciation of conservation issues.

Figure 2.4 below provides a summary of the positive and negative environmental consequences of tourism development. Having discussed these negative and positive impacts in some detail, we can conclude that the environmental costs associated with tourism development are by no means inevitable. In fact, in many areas tourism offers a much more environmentally friendly alternative to other forms of economic development and it is in the best long-term interests of tourism to preserve environmental quality. However, in order for the positive environmental benefits of tourism to be realised, development needs to be carefully planned and controlled, with the population both involved in development decisions and sharing fully in the sustained financial rewards that can accrue from sustainable tourism development.

Area of effect	Negative Impacts	Positive Impacts
Biodiversity	• Disruption of breeding/ feeding patterns • Killing of animals for leisure (hunting) or for souvenirs • Loss of habitats and change in species composition • Damage/destruction of vegetation	• Encouragement to preserve flora and fauna as attractions • Establishment of protected or conserved areas primarily to meet tourist demands
Erosion and Physical damage	• Soil erosion • Damage to sites through trampling • Overloading of key infrestructure (e.g., water, sewage, transport)	• Tourism revenue used to finance ground repair and site restoration • Improvement to infrastructure prompted by tourist demand
Pollution	• Water pollution through sewage disposal, fuel spillage, construction activity and rubbish discarded by tourists • Air pollution (e.g., vehicle emissions) • Noise pollution (e.g., construction work, traffic, bars and discos etc) • Disposal of solid waste materials (e.g., landfill) • Littering	• Cleaning programme to protect the attractiveness of environment to tourists (e.g., European Blue Flag initiative)
Resource Base	• Depletion of ground and surface water • Diversion of water supply to meet tourist needs (e.g., golf courses, pools, hot showers etc) • Depletion of local fuel sources (e.g., firewood) • Depletion of local building-material sources	• Development of new/improved sources of supply
Visual/structural change	• Land transfers to tourism (e.g., from agriculture) • Detrimental visual impact on natural and non-natural landscapes through tourism development. • Introduction of new architectural styles • Changes in (urban) functions • Physical expansion of built-up areas.	• New uses for marginal or unproductive lands (e.g., beaches, moors and mountains) • Landscape improvement (e.g., to clear urban dereliction). • Regeneration and/or modernisation of built environment • Reuse of disused buildings (e.g., conversion of derelict coat mines into heritage attractions)

Figure 2.4: Balance sheet of the environmental impacts of tourism.

The next section considers some of the management and planning techniques that are employed to control the environmental impacts of tourism. However, if tourism development occurs without detailed planning and is dominated by the interests of external agents, such as foreign tour operators, whose primary motivation is providing short-term profit for their share-holders and hedonistic pleasure for their customers, then this harmonious relationship between tourism and the environment is likely to be threatened as the human and physical resources of the destination area are rapidly exploited and degraded.

Resource Management Techniques for Controlling the Environmental Impacts of Tourism

The now well-documented environmental costs associated with some forms of tourism development have led to the increased application of planning and resource management strategies in many destinations in an attempt to avoid the same problems and to, instead, generate potential environmental benefits from tourism development.

These different planning and resource management strategies can be divided into five distinctive but complimentary approaches:

- Spatial planning strategies.
- Alternative development strategies.
- Education and marketing techniques.
- Access control measures.
- Site management techniques.

Spatial planning strategies

Essentially, these are measures designed to encourage tourism development in alternative locations and relieve pressure on sensitive or already degraded sites. A number of different spatial planning techniques have been used, including the strategy of concentrating tourist numbers at specially designed 'hardened' sites, sometimes referred to as 'honey-pot' sites. In several national park areas this is achieved by providing free car parking facilities in certain areas, perhaps accompanied by information and interpretation boards as well as other facilities such as picnic tables, public toilets and even cafes. Visitors may also be encouraged to stay near to the site by promoting well-marked trails. Access to other areas may be physically restricted or simply not encouraged through lack of parking, limited access roads or absence of marked trails.

In contrast, an alternative spatial planning strategy is to disperse rather than to concentrate visitors. The aim of this policy is to spread any potential benefits to a wider area and to dilute visitor numbers at the most popular sites to ensure that carrying capacities are not exceeded. Dispersal may be achieved by creating new attractions or alternative resorts elsewhere, or by directing visitor traffic to alternative areas by the use of sign posting and marketing. The consequences of such an approach, however, may be to attract a greater number of visitors to the area rather than to help disperse the existing numbers more evenly around the area. Thus, the unintended net outcome may be increased environmental pressures over a larger area. It is, therefore, believed that dispersal techniques are only effective in low-use places, such as in some of the larger, less accessible US wilderness areas, whereas concentrating visitors and their impacts is most effective in popular locations (Cole 2000).

Zoning is one of the most popular town and country planning strategies and involves identifying certain areas of land where some land uses are considered desirable (e.g., residential, industrial, commercial, recreational, agricultural) and are, therefore, encouraged whilst other less suitable land uses will be restricted through planning legislation and control. This approach is designed to minimise the potential for land use conflicts. For example, busy tourist developments do not always make the most suitable neighbours for quiet residential areas and a coal-fuelled power station is unlikely to be chosen as the ideal view from the window of a luxury hotel complex. In countries with strong planning legislation and procedures, zoning can be used effectively to improve the visitor experience and to minimise conflicts between host and guests. However, there is a danger that the over-zealous use of land use zoning can produce physically isolated modern resorts devoid of local character and interest.

Zoning may also be used on a micro scale in order to avoid user conflicts between different types of recreational activities. For example, zoning strategies are commonly used in the management of water resources—all over the world, popular beach and lakeside resorts tend to allocate separate areas of the water for jet skis, powerboats, windsurfs, sailing dinghies and bathers in order to avoid accidents and user conflicts.

Alternative development strategies

There are a number of alternative development strategies that can be implemented in order to manage the environmental impacts of tourism. Firstly, alternative types of tourism development such as 'soft' and 'green' tourism can be encouraged. Soft tourism attempts to restrict development to more environmentally tolerable levels and tourist activity is, therefore, restricted to existing developments. The only growth that is encouraged is that which complements other major economic activities, such as agriculture, rather than supplanting or threatening them. Activities such as farm tourism are, therefore, encouraged and small-scale accommodation provision, such as family-run bed and breakfasts or campsites, may be favoured rather than large scale hotel developments.

Green tourism has, unfortunately, become a rather meaningless term as it is often wrongly used to describe many different types of tourism activity, not all of which are neces-sarily designed to minimise environmental impacts and to foster environmentally friendly behaviour. Some tour operators, for example, have tended to jump on the green bandwagon, promoting an array of eco-tourism products as 'green' simply because they bring the participant into close (and therefore potentially very damaging) contact with wild nature. However, there is an attempt to encourage forms of tourism development that do potentially make a more positive contribution towards the environment. For example, holidays are available that combine more environmentally friendly forms of transportation, such as railways and cycling, with accommodation provision on organic farms. Less extreme, perhaps, were the efforts made by the UK Government's then Rural Development Commission (now part of the Countryside Agency) to encourage the English hospitality industry to adopt more environmentally friendly forms of consumption. The Commission produced as 'do-it-yourself guide to greening the tourism business' in which they encourage enterprises to look carefully at their purchasing policies, energy consumption and waste generation, suggesting action that they can take, such as recycling, reusing or reducing, in order to be more environmentally responsible (Rural Development Commission 1996).

A third type of alternative development strategy is to create new resources and attractions nearer to existing centres of population in order to increase capacity, reduce motor vehicle travel and reduce overcrowding at more environmentally sensitive sites. The creation of urban forests, city farms, and water parks, together with improved recreational provision along regenerated riversides and canal areas in and around many British cities, are a good example of this approach.

Education and marketing techniques

There are a number of measures, collectively described as education and marketing, that are designed to influence the attitudes and behaviour of both visitors and/or staff employed in the tourism industry.

One strategy that can be employed to reduce the environmental impacts of tourism is to educate industry staff more thoroughly in environmental conservation issues. This may involve appraising staff of the ways in which they can reduce energy consumption and produce less waste during their day-to-day working activities. In the US, a number of environmental educational schemes (e.g., 'Soft Paths' and 'Leave-No-Trace) have been developed by the National Park Service and other organisations in order to educate key workers, such as park rangers, and visitors in low-impact behaviour within wilderness areas (Cole 2000). In a similar way, some package tour operators are trying to improve the local environmental awareness of their resort representatives so that they can positively influence their customers' behaviour by, for example, warning visitors of the environ-mental threat posed by collecting souvenirs from coral reefs.

Visitor behaviour can also be influenced by the provision of multi-lingual information and interpretation boards located strategically around environmentally sensitive sites explaining the environmental threats posed by certain forms of behaviour. This approach has been adopted in an effort to protect the fragile dune systems along France's popular Vendeen coastline.

It is well known that marketing has a powerful influence on tourist patterns and this is particularly the case when tourists have limited access to other information about a destination area. Therefore, some local authorities may heavily promote less sensitive environments and less environmentally damaging activities whilst restricting the availability of information about those sites which they consider are under threat. In many cases, strategic marketing techniques are used as a complimentary measure to other educational techniques.

Access control measures

The fourth method of minimising the degradation of popular but sensitive tourist environments is to introduce any one of a number of access control measures. These tend to be the most controversial of the resource management techniques as they tend to be exclusionary, restricting resource access perhaps to only a limited number of individuals and sometimes coupled with both temporal and spatial restrictions.

Some destination areas protect their environmental assets by maintaining exclusivity by effectively pricing themselves out of the mass market. Only the very rich can afford to visit these areas and so visitor numbers are restricted and carrying capacities are never exceeded. The small Himalayan Kingdom of Bhutan, for example, has one of the most exclusive tourism development policies in the world. Since the 1980s, it has restricted its visitor numbers to fewer than 3,000 a year by only granting access visas to those who have purchased their exclusive package tours.

Alternatively, some heavily used areas may restrict visitor numbers by introducing quotas and permits. Spain's number one tourist attraction, the Alhambra Palace in Granada, sells time-allocated tickets to visitors each day on a first-come, first-served basis. Only a certain number of visitors are given access to certain parts of the palance complex at any one time and once the capacity has been reached, no more tickets are sold. In a similar way, in order to visit the Upper Mustang region in northern Nepal, tourists are obliged to obtain a permit and, although these only cost a fairly modest sum, only 1000 permits are issued each year to tourists belonging to an agency-handled tour group. In an attempt to reduce the pressures on local supplies of fuel wood and to prevent further deforestation, the Nepalese government also insists that trekking groups take with them their own supplies of kerosene (Nepal 2000).

Access to protected areas may also be controlled by only permitting entry at a limited number of entry points, whilst physically controlling vehicular access to the park area can also be used to restrict visitor numbers. Gating all access points to the park area and only permitting vehicular access to residents is one example of this form of access control. Alternatively, placing physical limitations on car parking availability within and around the park area can also be an effective measure for controlling numbers. Some of these schemes have been implemented in Britain's national park areas. In the Peak District, for example, the capacity of the main Dove Dale car park was reduced in an attempt to reduce the flow of walkers through the popular but sensitive limestone gorge (Ryan 1991).

Some more remote areas can control access by choosing to remain physically inaccessible to all but the most intrepid visitors. No developing transport infrastructure, such as road, rail, air and sea links, can be perhaps the most effective means of controlling visitor numbers.

Site management techniques

Finally, there is a range of local site management techniques that can be implemented to protect sensitive areas and to allow the regeneration of already damaged sites.

The creation of sign-posted walks, together with the provision of information points along the route, can be used to encourage visitors to use paths which have been designed to sustain high pedestrian flows and discourage them from using more fragile areas. In addition, a number of 'site-hardening' measures can be implemented to protect vegetation and reduce soil compaction and erosion around heavily used sites. Several different techniques have been used to prevent path erosion and widening due to excessive trampling. In the Peak District, paths have been re-laid using synthetic materials, such as nylon netting, as a permeable base but then overlain by natural local materials such as gravel produced from gritstoen and basalt (Ryan 1991). These paths produce a much more hard-wearing surface than the underlying peat, which was subject to severe erosion in heavily used areas. In a similar way, footpaths through the sand dunes along the French Vendeen coast have been replaced with boardwalks to protect the grasses and maintain dune stability.

Where possible, site-hardening techniques try to make use of local materials and maintain the natural appearance and aesthetic appeal of the area under threat.

Table 2.2 below, compiled by the WTO, provides a summary of some the resource management strategies discussed in this chapter.

Table 2.2 : Planning and management strategies for alleviating tourism impacts.

Policy/planning	• Development plans which include tourism and which set out zones or sites for tourist use, determine rights of access to areas, and consider what sort of activities are suitable for the area. • Develop and enforce regulations to control aspects of development and tourist activity. • Require environmental impact assessments and monitoring for tourist developments. • Use economic mechanisms such as subsidies to encourage more sustainable practices and 'user pays' to control use and provide income for conservation and rehabilitation of the environment.
Development/ Construction of Facilities	• Consider choice of sites and site design carefully to ensure minimal impact. • Use minimal impact construction techniques. • Use native species for landscaping and appropriate architectural styles.
Management of Resources	• Conduct environmental audits. • Develop and use recycling, waste minimisation and energy efficiency programs. • Use environmentally friendly products and technologies.
Management of Visitors	• Design systems which control visitor flows. • Use interpretation/education to encourage sustainable behaviour.
Adapting the Environment	• Harden sites for protection • Provide facilities which influence visitor activities.
Marketing and Promotion	• Consider tourism concepts and products better suited to the environment. • Provide accurate information in advertising to ensure that visitors have appropriate expectations.
Education	• Use effective interpretation services to encourage visitors to engage in more sustainable behaviours. • Provide environmental education for tourism personnel. • Develop codes of conduct for tourist, staff, operators and other tourism sectors.
Research and Monitoring	• Support research which seeks to improve understanding of the tourism-environment relationship. • Evaluate the effectiveness of any programs and activities conducted. • Monitor environmental quality.

Source: World Tourism Organisation (1997).

Conclusions

Although virtually any form of tourism activity will have some impact on the physical environment, these impacts are not necessary always negative. In fact, we have argued here that it is in the tourism industries long term interests to try and engender a symbiotic relationship with the physical environment as this is a key, but potentially fragile, resource for the future sustainability of the industry. Achieving this kind of relationship is not, however, always possible and development of any kind always leads to some form of environment change. It is necessary, therefore, to think in terms of the limits of acceptable change and to introduce planning and management measures, such as those discussed above, that are designed to reduce the environmental impacts of tourism to acceptable levels. For this to be possible, however, there needs to be the necessary political will and planning infrastructure which enables local populations, as well as representatives from the tourism industry, to be involved in the tourism planning and development process as stake holders.

3

Government and Tourism

Introduction : The Essence of Politics and Government

Politics can sometimes be a bit of a dirty word. Most 'ordinary' people seem to love to have it. 'They should keep politics out of sport'; 'they bring politics into everything these days' or 'politics and business don't mix' are typical, sincere laments. Such refrains, however, reveal a profound misunderstanding of the nature of politics and its all-pervasive, everyday significance. Times of war remind us that there's only one thing worse than too much politics, and that's too little.

A frequently heard grumble is that politics is too adversarial, with politicians squabbling and arguing with each other 'like children', instead of pooling the best minds for the good of the country. Politics, however, *is* a 'disputatious' (Crick 1995) or 'quarrelsome' (Gilliatt 1987) activity. It is an adversarial business. the configuration and organi-sation of the House of Commons—its opposing front benches separated by two swords' length and one foot—symbolically reminds us so. The cut and thrust of debate is intended to be a more acceptable currency of political discourse than more violent ways of of expressing purposive choice. The party-system has tended to produce a more 'temperate politics' than some of its early observers feared (Humphreys 1992). However, that is not to ignore the reality that the institutio-nalised politics of 'London

SW1', in the case of England, are perceived by apparently large numbers of the population to be of decreasing interest and relevance in their own lives; their belief in the capacity of the institutions of representative democracy to deliver has diminished.

In the political science literature, politics, being about choices, competing preferences and alternative priorities, informs many typical definitions. However, it should be noted that politics is not only about arranging for these more-or-less legitimate differences to be articulated, expressed, heard and debated, but also involves making collective decisions and together agreeing ways forward. Without this second dimension, politics would indeed be a dark and destructive pursuit.

Definitions of politics

- Politics 'considers conflicts of interests and values and how they are or can be conciliated' (Crick 1995: 3).
- 'Political activity is a ...universal phenomenon. It involves disagreements and the reconciliation of those disagreements (Ball and Peters 2000: 27).
- 'People or groups of people who want different things - be it power, money, liberty, etc. - face the potential or reality of conflict when such things are in short supply. Politics begins where their interests clash' (Jones *et. al.* 2001: 8).
- 'Politics may be defined briefly as a process whereby a group of people, whose opinions or interests are initially divergent, reach collective decisions which are generally regarded as binding on the group, and enforced as common policy' (Miller 1987: 391).
- 'Politics is the activity by which groups reach binding collective decisions through attempting to reconcile differences among their members' (Hague and Harrop 2001: 3).
- 'Choice, preference, priorities, they are the currency of politics, and those who translate them into practical policies are politicians' (Wilson and Game 1998: 219).

The business of tourism and leisure throws up practical examples on an almost daily basis. In the wake of terrorist atrocities in New York, Washington and Pennsylvania on September 11, 2001, was it right to postpone golf's Ryder Cup competition? Should motor-racing's Formula 1 circus have raced in Indianpolis or not? At the same time, was it right to switch Glasgow Rangers' European football tie from Dagestan to 'neutral' Poland on account of the former's proximity to war-torn Chechnya? Should the former undis-puted world heavyweight boxing champion and convicted rapist Mike Tyson have been allowed into the UK in 2000 to fight in Manchester? And what about the Miss World context in India in 1996, when protesters from the Indian Forum for Awakening Women announced their intention to set fire to themselves at the pageant as an expression of opposition? What should have been the response of the Indian Authorities to such a clash of culture and values? Should Miss World have been banned? Should the protestors have been permitted to go ahead with deliberate and public self-immolation? Should protestors have been taken into protective custody for 'their own good'? Should the authorities have done nothing and allowed events to take their course? Are there any right or wrong answers at all? Such questions take us to the heart of classical political theory.

In the advanced liberal democracies of the socalled 'free' world, politics tend to be a secular business (Crick 1995). The currency of politics is different from that of religion; there is no holy writ, neither eternal truth nor tablets of stone - only complex problems capable of relatively temporary resolution in terms of shifting political values. Conditions and attitudes change. In this sense, there are no right or wrong answers for at the heart of secular politics lies the 'principle of uncertainty'.

Politics and tourism

The travel and tourism industries, arguably the largest of global business, raise many virtually intractable political issues, such as the balance between development and conservation, the relative distribution of positive and negative external effects, the relationship between host, indigenous cultures and incoming visitors, and long-term sustainability—all at the global, national and local levels. Therefore, given : *(i)* the nature of politics both as an activity and as a field of study, and *(ii)* the nature of the global business of tourism and its consequences, a prominent place for tourism on the political agenda would seem assured. However, this has tended not to be the case (Hall 1994).

'Tourism is widely regarded as the world's largest industry. However, despite the significant role of tourism in national and regional economies, and its social and environmental effects, the political aspects of tourism are rarely discussed in the tourism literature. Given the vast seasonal intra and international movements of people which modern travel represents and the impacts of tourism on many destinations, it must therefore strike the student of tourism that the rarity of academic research on the political dimensions of tourism is somewhat surprising' (Hall 1994: 3).

There are several reasons for this state of affairs. For one thing, governments and politicians tend to play down the intensely political nature of tourism. This is reflected in, for example, their historic reluctance to develop systematically clear policies for tourism (clearly connected with other policy fields such as energy, environment or transport), as well as their disinclination to commission fundamental research (as opposed to collecting visitor numbers or developing marketing strategies). Academics and scholars are also to blame, for they are not inclined to view tourism as a serious subject of enquiry - more to do with holidays than proper, serious work. There are also significant methodological challenges (Hall 1994).

Nevertheless, the hand of the state is ever discernible in the scale, distribution, character and organisation of tourism. Each aircraft flight, or package holiday or overnight hotel stay bears witness to the extent of governmental influence. Take a typical tour operator's brochure from any 'high-street' travel agency, for example. The hand of government is likely to be evident in the choice of available holiday destinations, points of departure, prices, resort information, the use of photographs, textual content, codes of practice, consumer protection provisions, currency regulations, travel advice and so on. Indeed, as discussed in Chapters, tour operations are highly regulated at both the national and European levels. The purpose of this chapter, therefore, is look at the relationship between tourism and government, focusing in particular on the influence of changing 'styles' of government on tourism. the first task, however, is to review the public administration of tourism in the UK (for a detailed account, see Holloway 1998).

Government and Tourism: Aspects of the Administrative Architecture in the UK

In everyday parlance, the term 'government' may be used to convey several different meanings. These include a vague sense of authority, power and order, control by a political party such as the 'Labour Government' or a particular administration, may be as in 'the Blair Government', or a collective of official institutions such as 'government departments' and 'local government'. It may even be used when referring to particular organisations, such as the Ministry of Defence or the Treasury. All of these uses are legitimate. Underlying them all, however, is a deeper meaning, for 'government' conveys a sense of the settled (but not permanent) and agreed formalisation of power and authority which provides a framework within which political discourse can be managed, disagreements can be debated, collective choices made and policy directions set out. In a sense, but not entirely, it's the problem-solving end of politics. Not entirely though, for government policies can themselves cause their own problems. Some would argue, for example, that Mrs Thatcher's economic policies in the 1980s created major problems of social distress and civil unrest whilst, more generally, Dunleavy (1995) has written of the catastrophic unintended consequences of 'policy disasters'.

The United Kingdom is a relatively small centralised (albeit of late increasingly devolved) unitary state. Even so, governmental arrangements for the tourism, leisure and cultural industries are characterised by a high degree of organisational pluralism and institutional fragmentation. Indeed, many governmental bodies are involved in the tourism business, although many of these are not primarily or exclusively concerned with the business of tourism. Therefore, many of the effects of their policies or influence are indirect. Let us take central government as one example.

Central government and tourism

Central government has, for the past couple of centuries at least, exercised significant indirect effects on the development of the tourism industry. For example, nine-teenth century legislation providing for Bank Holidays and paid leave for industrial workers (together with the development of the railways of course) contributed to the development of the Victorian seaside resort. The official promotion of education, literacy and other 'self-improving' pursuits, coupled with the suppression of 'undesirable' leisure activities, such as gambling, drinking or cock-fighting (Henry and Bramham 1989), also shaped the infant leisure and cultural industries. Moreover, nine-teenth century foreign, penal and agricultural policies still exert discernible effects in present day patterns of international tourism, especially in the Visiting Friends and Relatives (VFR) sector. For example, condoning, in the name of agricultural improvement, the clearance of crafting communities in Caithness, Sutherland and elsewhere in favour of the Cheviot sheep (Prebble 1969) was no more an instrument of tourism policy than was British penal policy in the nineteenth century. However, in 'forcibly' relocating British nationals in Australia, Canada, New Zealand, the United States and elsewhere, a significant contribution would be made to the future VFR market. More recently, in the 1980s and 1990s, employment policy, the deregulation and privatisation of the transport sector, as well as the policies of the Europeans Union on consumer protection or monetary integration and the single market, have all had very major consequences for the travel and tourism industries.

Government's first formal support for tourism came about in 1929 when the Department of Overseas Trade made a grant of £5000 to the Travel Association of the Great Britain and Northern Ireland (TAGBNI), successor to the Come to Britain movement (Cooper *et. al.,* 1998). TAGBNI would, in the inter-war years, become the British Travel Association, though still a voluntary as opposed to a statutory body. Apart from continuing grant-aid to this voluntary body, providing extra funds for local authorities which were seaside resorts and a piece of legislation in 1948 relating only to Northern Ireland, nothing too much changed in terms of central government's interest in tourism until 1969 (Harrop and Long 1994). It was in that year that the Development of Tourism Act 1969, was passed.

Hailed as the first piece of comprehensive legislation systematically to address the needs of the tourism industry, the Act provided for the creation of several new statutory boards—the British Tourist Authority (BTA), the English Tourist Board (ETB), the Scottish Tourist Board (STB) and the Wales Tourist Board (WTB)-as well as development grants and an accommodation grading scheme. It was a turning point, heralding as it did the creation for the first time of national arrangements for developing tourism and allocating public funds. However, the Act was articulated against a background of economic crisis and the need to generate earnings and income from wherever; tourism was seen as a major source of 'invisible' earnings and the 1969 Act may have owed as much to this imperative as to a clear commitment to tourism.

This would help to explain one of the apparent paradoxes of the past thirty years. One the one hand, there has been no shortage of central government involvement in tourism, at least not if measured by the number of departments either directly involved. On the other hand, policy has tended to remain general and vague - long on 'motherhood and apple pie', but short on specifics.

Government institutions and tourism

With reference to the first point above (the number of departments involved in tourism), Central Government in the UK has a number of institutional forms, especially:

- The large, well-known Departments of State, such as the Home Office, the Foreign and Commonwealth Office, the Treasury, the Department for Education in its various names and, similarly, Environment and Transport, to name but several. Many of these are relevant to an understanding of the Travel and Tourism business. Some examples might include:

  Foreign Office : conduct of foreign and international relations, travel advice
  Home Office : immigration and security matters
  Environment : the countryside, local government and planning
  Agriculture : countryside matters
  Trade and Industry : hotels, travel agents, business.

Indeed, it would be more difficult to think of Central Government Departments without consequences for tourism than to draw up an inventory of those which do have.

- Secondly, there are the Executive Agencies. These were created after publication of the Ibbs or 'Next Steps' Report in 1988 on management and efficiency in the Civil Service. These Executive, or 'Departmental', Agencies are semi-autonomous organisations which carry out many of the routine, administrative functions of central government - 'freeing-up' the centre to concentrate on policy-making. Well-known examples include the Social Security Benefits Agency and its former sister, the Contributions Agency, now merged with the Inland Revenue. They are by no means all based in London, let alone in Whitehall. Many Agencies are relevant to the business of tourism. These include the UK Passport Agency (set up in 1991); the Meteorological Office (1990); Historic Royal Palaces (1989); the Ordence Survey (1990); CADW Welsh Historic Monuments (1991); and Historic Scotland (1991).

- In addition, the territorial Departments—the Northern Ireland, Scottish and Welsh Offices—traditionally exercised responsibility for tourism in their respective geographical areas until devolution took effect.

In the absence of a dedicated Tourism Ministry, until 1992 responsibility for tourism lay with a designated 'lead' Department. Until 1985, this was the Department of Trade and Industry (tourism means business being the message), when responsibility then passed to the Department of Employment (tourism means jobs). There it remained until the creation of the Department of National Heritage in 1992 and now, the Department for Culture, Media and Sport (DCMS) following its creation after Labour's General Election victory in 1997.

The debate leading up to the creation of the Department of National Heritage in 1992 was an interesting one. It brings us to the second element of our paradox; that is, despite extensive government involvement, overall policy direction remained vague and uncertain. The commons' own Trade and Industry Committee in 1985 commented:

> *The truth is that the Government cannot quite decide what its own role is... The Government minimises the appearance of involvement by reducing policy aims to statements of the obvious but maintains the fact of involvement in the tourist boards and the grants provided through them. The trouble is that this actual financial commitment is then left without there being any clear specific strategy to guide its use* (House of Commons Trade Committee, quoted in Cooper *et. al.*, 1993 : 148).

In the same vein, a retiring Chair of a Regional Tourist Board felt compelled to write in the Board's 1993-94 Report that central government had 'failed to provide the leadership necessary to encourage the development of the tourism industry... there is still no coherent national policy on tourism'.

Reflective of such concerns and criticism, the case for a single, integrated 'Department of Leisure' had gained momentum during the 1980s (Adams 2000; Harrop and Long 1994). It culminated in the creation, after John Major's

General Election victory in 1992, of the Department of National Heritage. In rather rapid succession is Secretaries of State were David Mellor, Peter Brooke, Stephen Dorrell and Virginia Bottomley. Tony Blair, on the back of 'New Labour's' May 1997 General Election triumph, recast it as the Department for Culture, Media and Sport—partly because the word 'heritage' is backward-looking ('heri' in Latin, like hier' in French, means yesterday) and sent out inappropriate messages for the modernising Mr Blair. The Secretary of State for Culture, Media and Sport throughout the Blair government's first term (1997-2001) was Chris Smith. After Labour's return to office in June 2001, he was replaced by Tessa Jowell.

The Department for Culture, Media and Sport is responsible for:

- the arts
- broadcasting
- cultural objects
- film
- the government's art collection
- heritage
- libraries
- the millennium
- museums and galleries
- the national lottery
- new media and information services
- the press
- the royal estate
- sport and recreation
- tourism

The Department for Culture, Media and Sport's overall aim was to improve the quality of life for all through cultural and sporting activities, and to strengthen the creative industries. In doing so, it was expected to:

- bring excitement into the life of the nation and the work of government;
- make things of quality available to the many, not just the few, and
- create the jobs of the future.

On the tourism front, the setting-up of the Tourism Forum in November 1997 was interpreted as signalling a re-positioning of tourism at the centre of the Government's cultural initiatives and in honouring of its promise in *Breaking New Ground,* published whilst still in opposition, to 'implement a committed strategy to assist the development of tourism and hospitality'. In February 1999 appeared *Tomorrow's Tourism,* the Government's strategy for tourism. Recognising tourism as 'one of our most important industries...(because)... it generates wealth, it creates jobs, it promotes entrepreneurship, it provides social and environ-mental benefits, and supports local diversity and cultural traditions' (DCMS 1999: 8), the need for a government strategy for tourism was explicitly acknowledged. Characte-rised by, firstly, diversity and fragmentation, secondly, seasonal and sometimes fickle demand, thirdly, an inadequate understanding of its market and, fourthly, a reliance on infrastructure determined by central and local government in other policy fields, such as transport or planning, the tourism business needs a clearly articulated and joined up strategy (DCMS 1999: 9). Committing itself to work in partnership with the industry towards shared objectives and common targets, the publication of *Tomorrow's Tourism* probably marked the most comprehensive governmental arrangements for tourism since the Development of Tourism Act thirty years earlier. It is a significant attempt to address the policy vacuum for tourism and to deliver on the very least that the industry might reasonably expect of governement, namely the enunciation of a clear overall policy:

> *At the national level, tourism is in the first instance a government responsibility to formulate a tourism policy, which may be translated into a plan... when the role of tourism is defined, the policy provides a statement of the means by which the objectives are to be attained... such... as the administrative arrangements, the respective rules of the private and public sectors and the fiscal arrangements.* (Burkart and Medlik 1992)

Tourism : other institutional arrangements

Despite the complexity of the arrangements described above, there are other relevant items of the administrative 'furniture' to be cited. These ay be briefly summarised as:

- sub-national government
- public bodies
- supra-national government

(i) Sub-national government

In the absence of constitutional guarantees to the regions of the UK, sub-national government has tended to focus on local government. During the past decade, however, the picture has become more complicated. The Conservative government, for example, created Government Offices for the Regions (such as the Government Office for the North East (GONE)). Bringing together the work of some, but by no means all, central government departments on a regional basis, these Offices are involved in local economic development strategies, often with a strong cultural dimension, and the administration of European funds. Additionally, the Blair government's agenda of democratic modernisation has seen the introduction of devolved structures. The Scottish Executive, for example, exercises responsibility for tourism as part of the work of its Department for Enterprise and Lifelong Learning. The organisation of the Scottish Executive does not, however, reflect the configuration of responsibilities of the Department for Culture, Media and Sport for in Scotland, sport, the arts and culture lie within the Education portfolio. Wales now has its own National Assembly and Northern Ireland its Executive. In London, there is an Elected Mayor (Ken Livingstone, who has not always been at one with his own party in national government, as evidenced by disagreement over the future of the London Underground for instance) and a 25 member Greater London Assembly. All English regions have appointed (not elected) Regional Development Agencies and non-statutory Regional Chambers. Fully elected Regional Assemblies for the English Regions remain a possibility. For the student of tourism, the reformed administrative architecture of government beyond Whitehall perhaps serves to compound an already complex picture.

As for local government, there is a comprehensive cover of directly elected, multi-purpose primary local authorities. Again, the arrangements are complex and a review of local government structures in the mid-1990s made the pattern even more complicated than before. In England, Wilson and

Game (1998) drew up a list of 387 principal authorities as follows:

- 34 Non-metropolitan Country Councils, e.g., Northumberland or Hampshire.
- 238 Non-metropolitan District Councils, e.g., Carlisle, Tynedale or The Wrekin.
- 36 Metropolitan District Councils, e.g., Newcastle upon Tyne, Birmingham or Liverpool.
- 46 Unitary Councils, e.g., Stockton, Stoke-on-Trent or Bristol.
- 32 London Borough Councils, e.g., Tower Hamlets, Kensington and Chelsea or Islington.
- 1 City of London Corporation.

In Scotland, 1996 saw a two-tier system of regional and district councils replaced by 32 unitary authorities. Examples include Perth and Kinross. Argyll and Bute or City of Aberdeen. In the same year, Wales similarly adopted a system of 22 unitary authorities, such as Blaenau Gwent, Wrexham or Ceredigion. Northern Ireland has an arrangement of district councils, such as Belfast and Armagh.

In very general terms, local authorities have been the principal public service providers of leisure services in the arts, sport and physical recreation, and tourism (Harrop and Long 1994). They provide an extensive range of facilities, venues and activities, from orchestras to football pitches, ice-rinks to caravan sites and lifeguards. However, their activities relating to tourism fall under two main headings. First are their statutory responsibilities, such as physical planning, development control, inspection and regulation, environmental health or licensing, for example. Additionally, however, they provide many discretionary services, including promotion and publicity, information centres, conferences facilities, heritage attractions and social tourism schemes. For the twenty years, local authorities have engaged in tourism development development as a means of economic regeneration in, for example, Bradford, Glasgow, Sheffield, Sunderland and Wigan. They provide financial support to the Regional Tourist Boards and, in partnership with other agencies, increasingly participate in the development and implementation of tourism development strategies. Recent trends have seen development strategies increasingly integrated into broader economic development or local and regional cultural strategies.

Public bodies

There are many other public bodies which are relevant to an understanding of government and tourism. Sometimes misleadingly referred to as 'quangos', these are part of the 'non-elected' state, including NHS Health Trusts or Learning and Skills Councils. Their members are appointed, not elected.

There are two main types relevant to an understanding of tourism. First, those organisations specifically concerned with the tourism business. Several of these were created by the 1969 Development of Tourism Act, including the British Tourist Authority, the English Tourist Board, the Scottish Tourist Board and the Wales Tourist Board (Adams 2000; Harrop and Long 1994). Focusing on the development of tourism within their particular territorial jurisdiction, these Boards are heavily involved in promotion, marketing and publicising the tourist product. After an increasingly controversial political history, the English Tourist Board was recast in 1999 as the English Tourism Council as part of the new support structure for tourism in England referred to in *Tomorrow's Tourism.* The national Boards and Council work in close partnership with the network of Regional Tourist Boards (Adams 2000).

In addition, there are many other public bodies which are not specifically or primarily concerned with tourism (their principal roles lie elsewhere) but which nevertheless have engaged in tourism development for a number of reasons, or which exert indirect effects. These fall into three main areas:

- arts, culture and heritage;
- environment and the countryside; and
- economic development.

They include the Arts Council, Regional Arts Boards, English Heritage, the Countryside Agency and (in Scotland

and Wales) the Countryside Councils, English Nature and Scottish Natural Heritage, the Forestry Commission and various economic development bodies. The legacy of the Urban Development Corporations, wound up in 1998, is also clearly evident. All are significant elements in the overall picture.

Supra-national government

Last, but by no means least, mention must be made of the work and and influence of the European Union (EU), an example of supra-national government in the form of an economic and political union. Its overall purposes—to restore economic prosperity to a war-ravaged Western Europe after 1945 and to win lasting peace in a world region which had twice within a generation embroiled the rest of the world in almost total warfare - went far beyond tourism. Indeed, no powers relating to tourism were conferred upon the European Commission (and its predecessors) either by the founding Treaty of Rome in 1957 or subsequent Treaties, such as Maastricht. This was not the case with agriculture, fisheries, transport, regional, energy or competition policies, where specific powers were conferred. Nevertheless, the European Union has had major effects in travel and tourism in member states. These can be classified under three headings:

- measures following from the pursuit of the internal market;
- indirect measures from other policy concerns; and
- specific tourism initiatives.

(i) The internal market

In this first category, one might note:

- the role of the Single European Act 1987, in providing for the free movement of goods, persons, services and capital and moving by 1993 towards a frontier-free Europe. This has progressively led to the relaxation and abolition of frontier controls and a relatively passport-free 'Schengenland'.
- deregulation of air transport.
- abolition of duty free sales for travellers between EU member states.

- mutual recognition of training and educational qualifications.
- deregulation of coach transport.
- a Union-wide framework of company law.
- the single currency, or 'Euro'.

(ii) Indirect measures

From other policy commitments include:

- consumer protection initiatives including the package travel directive in 1993.
- denied-boarding compensation (aircraft).
- competition and its effects on civil aviation including transatlantic mergers.
- environmental standards such as bathing water quality.
- cultural tourism, including the European City and Capital of Culture initiatives.

(iii) Specific tourism initiatives

Which include:

- Initial Guidelines on Tourism, 1982.
- European Year of Tourism, 1990.
- Community Action Plan to Assist Tourism, 1991.
- Philcxenia - the proposed First Multiannual Programme to assist European Tourism, 1997-2000.

Competitiveness, quality and sustainability have increasingly become the watchwords of EU thinking.

Towards Governance?

Governmental involvement with the business of travel and tourism is, therefore, complex and multi-layered, extending from the local to the supra-national. This multi-level governance is the outcome of several pressures, including globalisation and Europeanisation. For the UK, there have also been internal pressures which have impacted on governmental arrangements.

Government in the UK has undergone considerable change over the part twenty-five years or so. These changes have not only led to a new operating code in the public services but also to the partial break-up of the unitary state, with powers being devolved from Westminster to the Scottish

Parliament and to the Welsh and Northern Irish Assemblies. These constitution-changing moves have resulted in a further loss of central government control and renewed calls for regional government in England. Some of these have clearly been noted in our review of the administrative furniture. Here, we assess these changes in greater detail and consider some possible consequences of, and for, a 'Disunited Kingdom'.

The Westminster Model

For many years, the Westminster Model provided an organising perspective for understanding British Government, a way of characterising its main features (Rhodes 1997a). Through its longevity, it became the traditional way of thinking about the describing British government. Most lay people would use it unwittingly in any discussion of how the British state functions. Its survival has been perpetuated by the lack of a viable alternative organising perspective.

In the political science literature, the Westminster Model is defined in various ways. Its essence, however, has been concisely captured by Rhodes, who identifies the defining characteristics are focusing on: parliamentary sovereignty; strong Cabinet government; accountability through elections; majority party control of the executive (that is, Prime Minister, Cabinet and the civil service); elaborate conventions for the conduct of parliamentary business; institutionalised opposition, and the rule of debate (Rhodes 1997a: 3).

The Westminster Model's mainstream status has been strengthened by its applicability to other countries which have developed systems of government similar to Britain's. In other words, the Westminster Model has applicability beyond the parliament which gave it its name. The perspective is transferable and portable.

However, the dominance of the Westminster Model is now being challenged. It is argued that it no longer fully or accurately describes the organisation and operation of the state and power in Britain. It is unlikely that the model will ever completely disappear from political science as an organising perspective. It may not accurately capture the move to governance, but will continue to have relevance to understanding the institutions of UK government.

From government to governance

The role and power of the British State has changed. We talk today not of *government* but of *governance.* Governance is about a new way of governing, a changed order. This changed order means a new way of thinking about British government is required, a new way of thinking about and defining the various power relationships. One such way of thinking which has been suggested as overcoming the weaknesses of the Westminster Model is the concept of a 'Differentiated Polity'.

Rhodes (1997a) characterises the Differentiated Polity as 'functional and institutional specialisation and the fragmentation of policies and politics'. He argues that the Differentiated Polity perspective has several advantages over the Westminster Model for conceptualising and understanding the governance of Britain:

- the Differentiated Polity allows fuller appreciation of the limits of the Westminster Model;
- it raises important and distinct questions about government in Britain;
- it identifies and explains the major issues and problem facing policy makers today.

The Differentiated Polity framwork, therefore, has a value beyond academic debate concerning the organisation and management of British government. It is about the state, in its manifest and manifold complexity, affects everyday lives.

For many years, the Westminster Model may have been the dominant perspective. During the past quarter of a century, however, much has changed. The very conception of a public sector, its purpose and role, structures, institutions, resourcing and management practices have all been radically transformed in a process which continues under

Mr. Blair's premiership (Harrop 1999). Although the signs were there to see long before 1979, it was Mrs. Thatcher who set about public service reform with energy and enthusiasm. Partly because of the Westminster Model itself perhaps, the overly bureaucratic state could be lampooned as self-serving, conceited, wasteful, inefficient, disabling, hidebound and insufficiently attentive to the public who, shared and entangled, struggled in deadly web of 'red tape'. Riding the ideological chariot of the 'New Right' into battle, for Mrs. Thatcher the moment was opportune. And after the so-called 'winter of discontent' in 1978-79, there was little popular support for much of the public sector. They may not have liked Mrs Thatcher very much, but they had no affection either for local government, for example.

Contemptuous of the performance of the public sector, Mrs. Thatcher embarked upon her wide-ranging reform agenda. Nothing less than wholesale change would do. Particular emphasis was laid on 'rolling back the frontiers of the state' and lifting the yoke of public bureaucracies from the people, on reducing the burden of public expenditure and making efficiency savings. Clear themes became discernible and a guiding ideological rationale (Rhodes 1997a):

- the large-scale privatisation of public assets (including for example British Airways in 1986 and the British Airports Authority in 1987);
- the marketisation and compulsory commercialisation of what remained in the public sector (including the purchaser - provider split in the National Health Service and compulsory competitive tendering and contracting out in local government);
- the break-up (and in some cases abolition) of public sector bureaucracies and the introduction of alternative delivery systems;
- the introduction and adoption of private sector methods and styles of management;
- de-concentration and devolution of the administrative work of central government (by creating the Executive Agencies, for example);

- a growth in regulation though output control; and
- tighter central resource control.

In the whirl of furious activity, however, not everything was well or carefully thought through. Some of the reforms may have been less than successful because insufficient attention was given to the underlying values and purpose of public services, and the complex challenge of their management. The result was an interesting mix of unplanned, as well as planned, outcomes. The concept of a Differentiated Polity captures something of the unintended, as well as intentional, results of the reforms as the authority of the unitary state diminishes and the ability of central government to control the system is reduced. This may not have been Mrs. Thatcher's intention.

Under Tony Blair the genie of devolution has been uncorked. The result has been the emergence of real policy differences geographically. In Scotland, for example, there are no tuition fees for students in higher education and financial arrangements for care of the elderly are less punitive. Nor do arrangements for the public administration of cultural services reflect those in England. It may be impossible to recork the bottle. 'Balkanisation' of the policy could be unintended consequence of the honourable devolution of power and authority. The balance between freedom and order, always difficult to strike, has shifted.

The consequences of reform

There are several unintended consequences of public sector reform which have important implications for democracy and how the British public is governed, and which also impact on government's management of travel and tourism. The impact of these consequences is augmented by the fact that they will not be easy to undo, meaning that today central government is governing with imperfect control, a situation which looks likely to continue well into the new millennium. The most serious unintended consequences concern accountability, steering and fragmentation (Rhodes 1997b).

Accountability, steering and fragmentation

One of the main objectives of the Thatcher reforms was the break up of public sector bureaucracies, a fragmentation which would free mangers from the constraints of rule-bound administration. However, fragmentation has led to a situa-tion which is harder for the centre to control. Within a framework of networks and 'collaborative governance', may organisations provide public services. The challenge of devising an overall strategy and securing its implementation becomes more difficult for central government. Another stated reason for pursuing a policy of public sector fragmen-tation was to improve accountability. With smaller organisations, the role of individuals and organisations in policy outcomes would be more easily identifiable and, consequently, they could be more easily held to account. However, an opposite outcome may be identified; that is, fragmentation has blurred accountability. The myriad of organisations now involved in the provision of public services means that it is harder to distinguish the precise influence on policy outcomes. The buck stops where? Accountability is as slippery as a bar of wet soap.

Furthermore, the fragmentation of the public sector means that control and steering are major problems facing government. The numbers of interested parties involved in service provision means that the centre cannot clearly control their actions. Moreover, implementing parties will interpret policy to suit best their own purpose. Policy outcomes are, therefore, diluted. This dilution of policy may also result in more policy being generated to plug the gaps in policy outcomes. A vicious circle thus develops. The centre cannot steer the system through traditional means. It is arguable that, under Mrs. Thatcher, these unintended consequences led to a situation of decentralisation to centralise—in other words, in order to control the system, central government had to increase control over resources, thus defeating a main aim of the reform programme. There are no easy solutions to the problems of governance.

As far as the territorial settlement is concerned, the creation of the Scottish Parliament and Welsh and Northern Ireland Assemblies has already moved the UK from the traditional understandings of a unitary state towards disunity. The consequences of these moves are, to a certain extent, dependent on the resultant degree of disunity. It has been argued above that the creation of these devolved structures may add to the problems already apparent in the move from the Westminster Model to a Differentiated Polity. Any further realisation of regionalisation or regionalism through the establishment of regional government in England would necessarily compound the problem.

Regionalisation may ultimately result in the break up of the UK, but what of the standing of the separate emerging administrative units? Scotland may have difficulties in asserting itself in negotiations with the EU and other governments. What chance have the English regions? A more likely outcome is, perhaps, the creation of a regional tier of government in the UK, but then where would this leave Scotland and Wales? Would there be calls for Scottish and Welsh reginalisation? After all, the Highlands and Islands of Scotland may consider its claims for a degree of self-government as valid as that of, say, the South West of England. The ultimate irony, however, would be a situation where the regions of the UK achieved devolved government and found themselves more constrained as a result. The greater the differentiation the greater the integration needs to be to maintain the whole. Again, checks and balances, freedom and order.

Government and Governance, Travel and Tourism

What, then, are the implications of this shift towards governance for travel and tourism?

The UK is no longer the unitary state it once was (perhaps it never was all that united?). Goverment has undergone, and is likely to continue to undergo, great change. The way we think about and explain British government has shifted away from the Westminster Model towards the organising perspective of a Differentiated Polity. Regionalisation is alive, if not always well. The haste to reform has, however, raised new challenges of governance. Publish in haste, repent at leisure was the warning of the wise; reform in a rush and rue the wreckage might be the advice to the legislator. The privatisation of the railways is not the only example—remember dangerous dogs? For tourism policies, what are the implications?

Ironically, in some ways, the history of policies for tourism and travel in the UK displayed many of the features and problems which are now being identified as problematic in the differentiated polity—namely fragmentation, lack of accountability and steering. Undoubtedly, many elements of government and the public sector were relevant to understanding the overall picture. However, the development and implementation of clear policies, systematically connected to other considerations and integrated into other policy fields such as energy, environment or transport, remained weak. The effects of public policy were largely unknown and business lamented the lack of a guiding framework for action. Indeed, various organisations, such as the Tourism Society, have long called for a more cohesive policy framework for tourism.

New Labour's chosen solution, within its general modernisation programme for government, was to think in terms of joined up solutions for joined up problems—joined-up governance, in fact.

The publication in February 1999 of *Tomorrow's Tourism,* its new strategy for 'a growth industry for the new millennium', has already been mentioned in this context. Its raft of recommendations, proposals and action points revolved around a number of key themes:

- to provide a new support structure for tourism in England, including the creation of the English Tourism Council to replace the English Tourist Board;
- to develop and promote quality tourism experiences;

- to provide better information about tourism;
- to promote improved career opportunities including a careers festival;
- to promote the wise growth of tourism through sustainable development; and
- to widen access to tourism, especially for those on low incomes, families, the elderly and the disabled.

One of its provisions was for convening, each March, an annual Tourism Summit of Ministers, officials and senior representatives from the industry. Its papers and proceedings, publicly available, provide a picture of joined-up governance in action. The second Tourism Summit (March 6, 2001) reviewed progress on the initiatives and action points agreed by Ministers at the first Summit. Chaired by then Secretary of State for Culture, Media and Sport, Chris Smith, the Summit participants (16) included another seven Ministers, representatives of the National Assembly for Wales, the Northern Ireland Executive and HM Treasury, as well as the Chairmen of the English Tourism Council, the British, Tourist Executive and senior officers of the British Hospitality Association and the Better Regulation Task Force. The following progress updates were presented:

- *Ministry of Agriculture, Fisheries and Food :*
  - Foot and Mouth disease outbreaks and the effects of restrictions
  - Rural Enterprise Scheme
  - Local food promotion
- *Department of the Environment, Transport and the Regions :*
  - Signage of tourist attractions
  - Spending Review
  - Rural Bus Challenge
  - 'Traveline', the new information system
  - Alternatives to the car for leisure travel
  - 'Waterways For Tomorrow'
  - Bathing Water Directive Standards
  - Rural White Paper
  - Urban White Paper

- *Department for Education and Employment :*
  — Standards in further education
  — Learning Skills Council
- *Foreign and Commenwealth Office*
  — Leave and multi-entry visas
  — UK portable website
  — Sustainable tourism
- *Home Office*
  — Modernisation of licensing laws
  — Sunday dancing
  — Gambling review
  — Easing UK entry procedures
- *Department of Trade and Industry*
  — Small Business Service
  — Knowledge Economy White Paper
  — Best practice forum to strengthen competitiveness through management skills and business procedures.
- Other progress reports were made by HM Treasury, the National Assembly for Wales, the Nothern Ireland Executive, the English Tourism Council and the British Tourist Authority.

New agenda items focussed discussion on resort regeneration, better regulation of hotels and restaurants and the BTA's *First Impressions* survey. The Tourism Summit, in the words of its Chairman, 'had demonstrated its worth in concentrating minds on the needs of tourism', and would reconvene one year hence, although officials would meet more frequently in order to maintain the momentum. 'Joining-up' is not, however, a simple task. One preferred way of going about it is to create co-ordinating organisations and mecha-nisms (the Tourism Summit may be an example of the latter). However, such arrangements may add to the complexity by increasing the number of interests to be joined-up.

There are some possible strategies, however, for overcoming the challenges of governance. These strategies are as applicable to travel and tourism policies as to any other policy area. Stoker (2001) suggests three ways of improving co-ordination in an effective system of multi-level governance:

- the use of contracts or concordats can express joint commitments to spend money and achieve improvements;
- joint budget holding can guarantee co-ordination of policy working; and
- summits or regular meetings of key actors can dissipate conflicts between different levels of government.

He contends that the agenda is not about choosing between these options, but about finding space and scope for them all. The future lies not in establishing exclusive areas of jurisdiction, but in finding ways to co-operate.

Such new ways of governing will not appear, however, without change in the behaviour of key actors. Crucial to New Labour's modernisation programme and prospects for good multi-level governance are the key skills of diplomacy and negotiation. These lie at the root of the new governance and are skills which need to be developed and effectively deployed. Mindsets have to move on. The distance to be travelled may be significant. The travel and tourism busi-ness, however, demands effective policy co-ordination. A complex and fragmented business in a labyrinth of multiple interdependencies, the portfolio cannot be detached from other concerns. Itself a sensitive barometer of economic and political factors, such as economic well-being or safety and security, tourism in turn exerts its own external effects (on the planning process, for example, on transport networks, pollution and congestion, land use, environment or the physical infrastructure such as water supply and sewage disposal to name only a few) and, in addition to its obvious purpose such as offering good holidays, pleasure, relaxation and enjoyment, it can contribute to so many other concerns of public policy, including economic development or regene-ration and social inclusion initiatives. It deserves and dem-ands joined-up governance. The historical baronies of policy making and implementation have not tended to serve it well.

The modernisation of government is generally to be welcomed, but how effective will the emerging arrangements be? The past couple of years have been interesting and challenging ones of tourism. The year 2000 saw a fuel supply crisis, major disruption to rail travel and widespread flooding in the UK. The following year, 2001, was marked by major outbreaks of foot and mouth diseas at home and the terrorist events of September 11 in New York, Washington and Pennsylvania. How well was government able to cope? Were its responses qualitatively improved? That is the acid test of it all for government and the tourism business must make their way together in a real world not always of their own choosing, and one in which there are no easy answers.

4

Organisational Behaviour in Tourism

Introduction

Organisational behaviour is part of the multi-disciplinary field of studying organisations. It explores issues in organisations at the micro level, that is, at the individual and group levels. In other text books, you will also see the terms organisation theory and organisation analysis, both of which, conversely, usually focus on the macro level, or the organisation as a whole. Some commentators argue that these two (the micro and the macro) cannot be separated - understanding behaviour at one level automatically requires understanding of factors at other levels (Rollinson *et. al.*, 1998). However, for the purposes of this chapter, we shall take the first approach; that is, that organisational behaviour looks at behaviour in organisations at individual and group levels.

Why Study Behaviour in Organisations?

There are two main reasons why students of travel and tourism should study behaviour in organisations. First, organisations, in their many forms, are a dominant institution in the modern world. Most people will find that their lives are, to some extent, affected by the existence and behaviour of organisations and so it is important that we try to understand them better. Second, those who manage or aspire to manage in organisations need to understand the factors that influence behaviour in order to help them manage people more effectively. In practice, individuals interact as people who bring their personalities, problems and interests with them into the work situation, and this influences how well they fit into the roles that the organisation gives them.

The rest of this chapter explores four main areas:

- personality,
- attitudes and perception,
- motivation,
- groups and teams.

Personality

Why study personality?

From a managerial perspective, personality is an important issue because it is believed by many that personality is related to job performance and career success (Huczynski and Buchanan 2001). Organisations want certain personality types working for them—for example, people who are committed, conscientious and career-orientated. Knowing about personality helps managers in two ways. Firstly, it helps them to select the appropriate person for the job and the organisation through the use of psychometric testing and, secondly, it helps them to understand the individuals under their management, so that they can manage them and their work environment more effectively.

Definition of personality

Personality refers to the psychological qualities that influence an individual's characteristic behaviour patterns, in a distinctive and consistent manner, across different situations over time (Huczynski and Buchanan 2001). However, whilst personality theory looks at patterns of behaviour that are consistent, this does not mean that personality cannot be flexible. We know that the conscientious, quiet young man in sales can become a rampaging larger lout when on holiday! Behaviour we exhibit depends in part, therefore, on the social context.

There are two main approaches to personality. The first is based on the belief that personality is inherited—it is determined by genes and the biochemistry of our brains. Indeed, some psychologists would even go so far as to say there is a 'criminal' gene. All of this implies that your personality is fixed at birth, if not before, and that life's experiences do little or nothing to alter it. Other psychologists, however, argue that personality is shaped by environmental, cultural and social factors, and that our feelings and behaviour patterns are learned through observing and imitating others. Thus, our personality is flexible and changes with experience.

This ongoing argument between psychologists is referred to as the 'nature versus nurture' debate. Those approaches which favour 'nature' as dictating behaviour are called *nomothetic* approaches; those which believe that it is situational factors which influence our personality are called *ideographic* approaches. The following sections consider these approaches in more detail.

A. Nomothetic Approaches to Personality

The nomothetic approach to the study of personality emphasises the identification of universal personality traits and looks for systematic relationships between different aspects of personality. This approach can be divided into *trait* theorists and *type theorists.*

Traits

A trait is a relatively stable quality or attribute of an individual's personality which influences behaviour in a particular direction. Traits include, for example, shyness, sociability and conscientiousness and trait theorists describe people in terms of a number of personality dimensions.

Catell's 16 Personality Factor Questionnaire

Catell (1965) identifies two types of traits:

- surface traits that are directly observable in behaviour,
- source traits that cannot be observed directly and the existence of which can only be inferred.

He claims that traits are the fundamental factors or building blocks that make up personality (Rollinson *et. al.*, 1998) and his research led him to identify 16 traits that were said to be the fundamental dimensions of personality (see Figure 4.1). Through data, such as ratings by other people of an individual's behaviour, self ratings and objective performance measures, an individual's personality traits can be identified through his questionnaire.

Two points need to be regarding this questionnaire:

1. The sixteen factors are bipolar dimensions of personality. Therefore, whilst an individual can be located somewhere between practical and imaginative, these are two opposing characteristics and not a scale which measures how reserved or outgoing the person is.
2. Each factor is independent of the other factors.

Despite criticisms of being over-simple, Catell's questionnaire is used a lot by organisations for recruitment and selection.

Low score description	Factor	High score description
Reserved, detached, critical aloof sizothvmia	A	**Outgoing, Warm hearted,** easygoing, participating : *affectothymia*
Less intelligent, concrete thinking *lower scholastic mental capacity*	B	**More intelligent,** abstract thinking *higher scholastic mental capacity*
Affected by feelings, emotionally less stable, easily upset : *lower ego stength*	C	**Emotionally stable,** faces reality, clam, mature: *higher ego strength*
Humble, mild, accommodating, conforming: *submissiveness*	F	**Assertive, aggressive,** suborn, competitive: *Dominance*
Sober, prudent, serious, taciturn *desurgency*	F	**Happy-go-lucky,** impulsively lively, enthusiastic : *Surgency*
Expedient, disregards rules, feels few obligations: *weaker superego strength*	G	**Conscientious,** presevering, staid, moralistic; *stronger superego strength*
Shy, restrained, timid, threat sensitive *threctia*	H	**Venturesome,** social bold, uninhibited, spontaneous : *parmia*
Tough minded, self-reliant, realistic, no nonsense : *harria*	l	**Tender-minded,** clinging, over-protected,sensitive : *permsia*
Trusting, adaptable, free of jealousy, easy to get along with : *alaxia*	L	**Suspicious,** self-opinionated, hard to fool *protension*
Practical, careful, conventional, regulated by external realities, proper :*praxernia*	M	**Imaginative,** wrapped up in inner careless of practical matters, bohemian: *autia*
Forthright, natural, artless, unpretentious: *artiessness*	N	**Shrewd,** circulating, worldly, penetrating urgencies: *shrewdness*
Self-assured, confident, serene *untroubled adequacy*	O	**Apprehensive,** self-reproaching, worrying, troubled : *guilt proneness*
Conservative, respecting established ideas, tolerant of traditional difficulties: *conservatism*	Q1	**Experimenting,** liberal, analytical, free thinking : radicalism
Group dependent, a 'joiner' and sound follower *group adherence*	Q2	**Self-sufficient,** prefers own decisions, resourceful: *self-sufficiency*
Undisciplined self-conflict, follows own urges, careless of protocol : *low integration*	Q3	**Controlled,** socially precise, following self-image: *high self-concept control*
Relaxed, tranquil, unfrustrated low ergic tension	Q4	**Tense,** frustrated, driven, overwrought high ergictension

Figure 4.1 : Catell's 16 personality factors

Eysenck's Type Theory

Type theories place people into predetermined categories on the basis of characteristics that are said to give rise to certain types of behaviour. Eysenck (1947) based his 'type theory' on extensive empirical work, which led him to believe that there are two fundamental dimensions of personality:

- Extroversion—Introversion.
- Neuroticism—Stability

These dimensions give four personality types—stable extroverts, unstable extroverts, unstable introverts and stable introverts. These types are sometimes known by the same names used by Hippocrates, when centuries ago, he identified four personality types. As Figure 4.2, demonstrates, each type is associated with a number of specific personality traits.

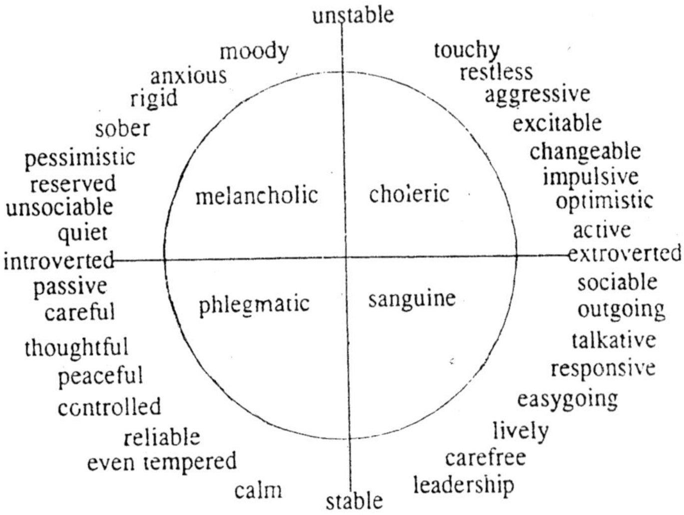

Figure 4.2 : Eysenck's personality types.

Extroverts are generally found to be sociable, outgoing and carefree, but can be aggressive, quick-tempered and sometimes unreliable. Introverts are the opposite. Neurotics can be unstable, anxious and finicky and suffer from lack of self-esteem, whereas stable people show the opposite tendencies.

Eysenck regarded personality as largely inherited; whilst people become diverse and individualistic as they gain a wider experience of the world, their reactions to the experience depend very much upon their personality type. Therefore, hereditary factors are assumed to have a strong enduring influence.

B. Idiographic Approaches to Personality

Unlike nomothetic approaches, the idiographic approach to the study off personality emphasises the uniqueness of the individual, challenging the assumption that we can all be measured and compared on the same dimensions. They deal with the individual as an integral whole and focus on the development of the personality.

The Psychodynamic Perspective

There are common assumptions that underpin all psychodynamic theories:

- the psychological determination of behaviour. That is, mental activity preceds physical activity;
- the unconscious has a prominent role in determining behaviour and, at times, unconscious thoughts can force their way into the consciousness;
- all behaviour is goal directed, although humans are not always aware of what those goals might be;
- adult personality usually results from childhood experiences, so there is a strong emphasis on personality development.

Rather than simply seeking to describe and measure personality, the psychodynamic approach is the only one that seeks to explain in a detailed way how an individual's personality comes to be what it is (Rollinson *et al.* 1998: 70-71).

Freudian Conception of Personality Structure and Dynamic

One of the most famous personality theorists is, of course, Freud. He believed that a person's psyche has three components. They are not 'physical' parts of the brain but, rather, abstract concepts that describe driving forces behind behaviour. These components are also at different levels of depth in the mind:

1. *The Id.* This is the biologically driven component of personality that consists of inherited drives which demand immediate gratification of all that is pleasurable. It is with us from birth and makes no distinction between right and wrong.
2. *The Ego.* This develops out of the Id. It attempts to balance the Id's demands against the reality of the external world, and therefore is the force that keeps the individual together as a whole.
3. *The Superego.* This component reflects the learned rules of society which are absorbed during upbringing. It exerts moral restraint by forbidding certain actions.

Frued (1901) perceived adult personality dynamics as a conflict between the id, the ego, and the superego. In a well-adjusted person, the ego manages to balance the needs/desires/expectations of the id and the superego with the external reality of any given situation. This is a difficult thing to achieve when the id is always driving the person to gratify needs with no thought to the consequences and the superego is constantly driving to resist gratification! If the id or the superego is stronger than the ego, permanent anxieties can be present. These include, for example, 'denial', when the individual refuses to recognise a change which can be harmful and so ignores it, and 'regression', which refers to the ego taking the person back to a form of behaviour that was successful in coping with a similar situation, for instance, bursting into tears being reprimanded at work.

Carl Rogers' Person-centred Theory

Rogers (1951) believes that, in order to understand people, it is necessary to understand how they view themselves and the world around them. Central to his ideas is the individual's concept of self. There is the 'actual' self which the individual believes himself/herself to be and the 'ideal' self—the self as the person would like to be. Rogers argues that most people behave in a way that tries to maintain congruence between what they do and their concept of self and, therefore, if you believe you are sociable and outgoing then you are likely to behave in this way. Thus, the behaviour of individuals can be predicted to some extent by finding out what they think of themselves. However, Rogers also believes that people are always striving for the ideal self, towards 'self-actualisation'. This has important implications for organisations in terms of motivation, as considered later in the chapter.

Implications for organisations of personality

Knowledge of personality is of benefit to the organisation in a number of ways:

1. For recruitment and selection purposes. Nomothetic approaches, which use data from questionnaires to identify different personality traits or types, help organisations to make decisions about who is the best person to join their organisation. Most organisations have their own cultures and accepted patterns of behaviour. Thus, personality differences means some people are likely to fit into an organisation better than others. In addition, jobs differ in terms of the personal charac-teristics that they require and so an individual's person-ality could have an impact on his or her suitability for certain roles.
2. To predict job performance. Again, some personality theories postulate that certain personality types may perform more effectively than other personality types.
3. For counselling/employee welfare purposes. Many organisations today have set up Employee Welfare or Employee Assistance Programmes in order to help employees who may be suffering from work related stress, personal problems, and so on.

Perception

Why study perception?

We all perceive the world around us in different ways; we attach different meanings, interpretations, values and aims to our actions. What we do in the world depends on how we perceive ourselves and our social and physical ennvironment, and on how we perceive our circumstances. Our personal perception of reality shapes and directs our behaviour. Therefore, if we are to understand why someone behaves in a certain way then, first of all, we need to discover how they perceived the conext and their place in it. We need to be able to understand why they perceived things differently in the first place.

Definition of perception

Perception is the dynamic psychological process responsible for attending to, organising and interpreting sensory data. We each have a similar nervous systme and share more or less common sensory equipment so, to this extent, we process and interpret incoming data in a similar way. However, we have different social and physical backgrounds which give us different values, beliefs, knowledge, expectations and, therefore, different perceptions. We do not behave in, and respond to, a 'real world'—we behave in, and in response to, the world as we perceive it. In short we each live in our own perceptual world.

Perceptual sets

A perceptual set is an individual's predisposition to respond in a particular manner. As already stated, perception is an information processing activity—it involves ordering and attaching meaning to 'raw' sensory data. Sensory apparatus is bombarded with vast amounts of information, both internal to us, such as hunger or pain, and external to us from people, objects and events. We are constantly sifting and sorting out this information, making sense of it and interpreting it. The process we go through is influenced by learning, motivation and personality, factors which give rise to expectations which, in turn make us more or less ready to respond to certain stimuli in certain ways and less ready to respond to others.

Perceptual sets and assumptions

Much of perception can be described as classification or categorisation. We categorise people as male or female, lazy or energetic, and so on. These categories are learned - we are not born with neat classification schemes. What also has to be remembered is that what we learn is often culture bound or culture specific. Cultural factors play a significant role in determining how we interpret available information and experience. We tend to select information that fits our expectations and pay less attention to information that does not. When we have complete or ambiguous information we 'fill in the gaps' from our own knowledge and past experience, or what we have 'learned'. This can lead to two phenomena which can give rise to problems in organisations and elsewhere:

(i) Stereotyping

Defined as attributing a person with qualities assumed to be typcial of members of a particular category because the person falls into that category, stereotyping is a bias in person perception. Stereotypes are overgeneralisations. For example, 'Germans are loud and fight over sunbeds on holiday', or 'British holidaymakers just want Blackpool with sun' are both wildly inaccurate generalisations.

(ii) Halo/horns effect

This is a form of stereotyping, when our judgement is based on something that we have noticed about a person, for example, how they dress or how they have behaved in a situation at work. From this we make huge assumptions about the person and their behaviour.

The halo effect is when our assumptions are positive, such as when we assume that a person who dresses smartly must be efficient and well organised. Conversely, the horns effect is a negative one. For example, a person who was five minutes late for the meeting must be lazy, disorganised and not competent in his job. Despite efforts to train interviewers and appraisers in objectively and impartiality, these phenomena are apparent in a number of organisation activities, such as recruitment and selection and performance appraisal (Jacobs and Kozolowski 1985, cited in Rollinson *et. al.*, 1998)

Errors in perception can be overcome by taking more time and collecting more information. Marketing / Customer Service Departments spend vast resources finding out customers' perceptions of their product or service. Direct

Holidays, for example, are currently looking to expand into the Irish marketplace. Their research involves indentifying Irish perceptions of what constitutes a 'good holiday' in order that they can provide a product which appeals. They do not intend to fall into the trap of British: Airways who, in their attempt to incorporate cultural diversity on their flights to Egypt, did not make themselves aware of all the facts. To improve customer service they introduced Arab music, coffee and dates served by multi-national cabin staff on all their flights between London, and Egypt. However, it was not Egyptian music, and Egyptians prefer to drink unit tea. British Airways had, unfortunately, 'stereotyped', categorising all Arabs together rather than perceiving each Arab state as separate.

Definition of attitudes

An attitude can be defined as a persistent tendency to feel and behave in a particular way towards some object (Luthans 1995: 121). Attitudes have the following characteristics:

1. they are held towards something specific that is part of the world of the attitude holder;
2. they reflect the attitude holder's experience of that aspect of his or her world;
3. to a large extent, they are learned from experience and are relatively enduring;
4. since the definition implies feeling and evaluation, attitudes have a bearing on how the individual reacts to the object;
5. because attitudes involve mental processes, they are not tangible objects that can be observed directly and their existence can only be inferred.

Attitudes have three basic components (Breckler 1984 in Luthans 1995) and the more consistent they are with one another, the more stable the attitude.

- The cognitive component, that is, the perceptions and beliefs about the object. For example, a positive attitude a country - Switzerland is clean and well-organised.
- The affective component, or the emotional feelings. Switzerland is inspirational because of its breathtaking mountain scenery.

- The behavioural component, that is, the tendency to act towards the object, in this case Switzerland, in a consistent and characteristic way. For example, going on holiday there every year, encouraging your friends to visit, etc.

Functions of attitudes

Attitudes serve a useful purpose to the individual - they are part of an individual's psychological makeup and develop and change in a response to the person's current needs (Rollinson *et. al.*, 1998). In a work related context, attitudes help predict worker behaviour. For example, if an attitude survey shows that workers are upset by the change in working hours, and the next week absenteeism begins to increase, management may be able to conclude that a negative attitude towards working hours led to an increase in worker absenteeism.

Job Satisfaction

Job satisfaction is one of the work related attitudes that receives the most attention both in the literature and in organisations. There are three important dimensions to job satisfaction:

1. It is an emotional response to a job situation, so it is not tangible.
2. It is often determined by how well outcomes meet or exceed expectations. Therefore, if people feel they are working harder than other people in the department but are receiving fewer rewards, then they will probably have a negative attitude towards work, their superior and colleagues. However, if they feel that they are being treated well then they will have a positive attitude.
3. It represents several related attitudes. Smith, Kendall and Hulin (1969) suggest that there are five dimensions to the attitude all of which reflect responses to the job (Luthans 1995, Rollinson *et. al.*, 1998). These are:
    - *The work itself*—to what extent does the job provide the individual with tasks, opportunities for learning and taking responsibility?

- *Pay*—is the financial reward received adequate and is it equitable compared to what other people receive?
- *Promotion Opportunities*
- *Supervision*—the extent to which the person concerned derives satisfaction from his relationship with his immediate superior. Is the supervisor supportive, both technically and interpersonally?
- *Co-workers*—the degree to which co-workers are technically competent and socially supportive.

Implications of job satisfaction to organisations

Whether or not this is the case, organisations take a great deal of interest in the extent to which people are satisfied in their work because of its potential effects. For example:

1. *Employee Turnover.* Research would indicate that where job satisfaction is high, labour turnover is reduced (Rollinson *et. al.,* 1998).
2. *Employee Absenteeism.* When people are not satisfied in their work, they tend to absent themselves on a more frequent basis. This could be as a result of stress, illness, lack of motivation or because they are looking for jobs elsewhere.
3. *Employee Productivity.* The interest in job satisfaction stems from the fact that, for many years, there has been the assumption that a 'satisfied' worker is a 'productive' worker. However, this debate is ongoing, with some writers believing that rewards play a much greater part in job satisfaction than was first believed (Podsakoff and Williams 1986 in Rollinson *et. al.,* 1998). Another issue is about whether satisfaction leads to performance, or whether good performance leads to satisfaction.

Implications of perception and attitudes for organisations

Managers need to be aware of:

- how perception may influence an individual's behavioural pattern in relation to other people in the organisation, for example, stereotyping, and seek to overcome this through appropriate selection of staff, training, etc.;

Attitudes of Employees in the Cypriot Hotel Industry: A Pilot Study

Since the 1960s, Cyprus has successfully developed into a major, mass tourism destination but now, after many years of growth; the island's tourism industry faces a less certain future. In order to survive and prosper within an increasingly competitive marketplace, there is a need for Cyprus to reassert its reputation for high levels of service and hospitality. This, of course, is dependent upon the co-operation of the workforce, particularly within the hotel industry.

In 1999, a pilot study was undertaken to find out employees' attitudes their work within the hotel industry and towards tourism/tourists. Whilst attitudes towards the tourism industry and working within it were, in general, positive, the findings highlighted a number of implications for management. These were:

- A need for training in order to improve levels of service. It was recommended that this training should not only focus on specific skills such as handling customer complaints, but a total quality approach should be adopted through the development of communication and teamwork to improve customer service.
- A review of remuneration packages. Whilst wage levels within the Cypriot hotel industry remain linked to a national bargaining process, hotel managers were asked to consider introducing a performance-related element into future wage negotiations.
- Job security. Hotel work is often seasonal, which means a lack of job security to many employees. Although this problem is related to the overall characteristics of tourism in Cyprus, the authors of the study believed that attempts could be made by management to work with the tourism authorities and tour operators to develop new products/ markets which might reduce some of the impacts of seasonality on employment.

- How values and attitudes develop in the individual and how these relate to the organisation. In any change situation in the organisation, whether it be changing the organisation's culture, structure or HR systems, all will require a change in attitudes.

- The extent to which the individual's job provides him/ her with what s/he values in a work situation. If not, absenteeism, sickness and eventually leaving the organisation will occur.

Motivation

Why study motivation?

To managers, motivation has great practial significance. Everything that is achieved by an organisation is achieved because of the human activity within it and an organisation's success is dependent upon the extent to which its employees are willing, and able, to channel their energies into performing their tasks. Because of this, managers must know what motivates people and be able to create the conditions which will enable people to perform effectively.

Definition of motivation

Rollinson *et al.* (1998: 148) define motivation as:

> *a state arising in processes that are internal and external to the individual, in which the person perceives that it is appropriate to pursue a certain course of action (or actions) directed at achieving a specified outcome (or outcomes) and in which the person chooses to pursue those outcomes with a degree of vigour and persistence.*

This definition refers to three components of behaviour that has an impact on performance:

- the *direction* of behaviour—what does the person want to do?
- the *intensity* of behaviour—how hard is the person going to try to go in that direction ?
- the *persistence* of behaviour—how willing is the person to keep going in this direction even if there are obstacles in the way?

Theories of motivation

Motivation theories attempt to provide a framework which can predict behaviour, especially behaviour at work. Some focus on how people can be motivated to work harder for the benefit of the organisation whilst others seek to improve an individual's sense of satisfaction and fulfilment at work. At the same time, however, many theories also address the fact that each individual is unique, therefore, not everyone will be motivated in the same way.

A number of next books divide motivation theories up into content and process theories. Content theories are concerned with why do people work and provide a universalistic approach to what motivates. Process identify factors that affect people's willingness of persistence to work.

Three waves of motivation

Watson (1986), however, identifies three categories of motivation theories which he calls 'waves'. The first wave represents the oldest way of thinking, the second more recent, and the third, the most up to date set of ideas. It must be noted that one wave does not replace another. Indeed, Watson (1986: 89) claims that 'the three groupings have little validity beyond the function which they are intended to serve: that of helping the reader find a way through a potentially frightening mass of different ideas and theories'.

Wave 1: people as machines

This wave represents the earliest thinking put forward, which includes the prescriptive approach of Taylorism, or Scientific Management. F.W. Taylor was the first to propose work study, bonus schemes, and time and motion studies, and underpinning his ideas was the belief that employees are economic animals, motivated purely by money, who generally prefer management to do all their task related thinking for them. All management had to do, therefore, was to work out the most efficient way of organising work and then introduce a payment by results system of remuneration so that workers would be motivated to apply themselves to maximum effect to the task in hand and achieve high outputs. This, of course, would produce results which would benefit both the employee and the employer. In this wave, therefore, workers are viewed as machines - both in the manner they are required to work and in the way they are 'fed' with cash in proportion to their output (Watson 1986).

Motivation and retention in call centres

Call centres are in danger of becoming the dark satanic mills of the 21st century as the industry gains a reputation for sweatshop practices and assembly-line methods (Management Today 1999, in Maude 2000: 3).

Maude (2000) researched into what motivates people to work in a call centre for a travel company, and what it is about the job that makes them stay. She believes that, despite the long unsociable hours, the high targets, low pay and weekend work associated with the travel industry, people still find this environment dynamic and attractive to work in. In her report, she puts forward the view that the reputation of call centres, as cited above, stems from organisations operating in industries such as telecommunications where consultants have a specific'script' to keep to and the job is far more repetitive and unchallenging than the job of a sales consultant in the travel industry.

Her findings, however, do not support this view to any great extent. Whilst 'bonuses' and 'incentives' in travel companies appeared to be wider ranging than in other industries, including, for example, education trips, 'travel bank' bonuses for achievement of personal targets each month, free travel insurance and reduced rate travel, employees' opinions were much the same as elsewhere. They felt that the basic salary is too low, targets are unrealistically high, there is inconsistency in incentives and, more importantly, they did not feel valued or recognised by the senior management for good work done.

Maude's (2000) overall conclusion was that:

- The senior management did not meet simple psychological expectations such as praise, recognition and appreciation. Instead, they provided negative feedback and there were repercussions for failure of achievement.
- Reward systems barely met the individual's extrinsic or intrinsic needs.

Wave 2 : People with needs

Under this heading are the approaches of human relations and democratic humanism, schools of thought that attempt to influence managerial practice in terms of improving the human lot, arguing that a human does not become a machine at work whilst existing only as a person outside its doors.

Theorists in this wave emphasis the social needs of people at work and their desire for 'belonging' in some way. They argue that employees' productivity is more affected by thier need to be secure, involved and recognised (intrinsic needs) than by physical conditions or level or monetary reward (extrinsic needs).

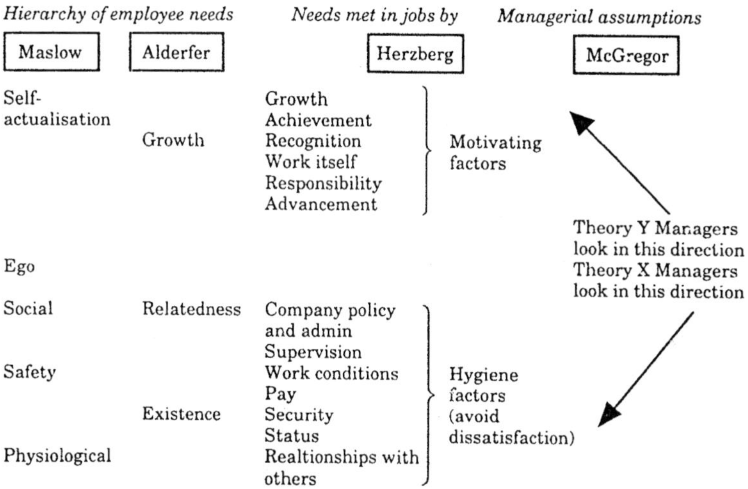

Figure 4.3 : Need-hierarchy based approaches to motivation.

Maslow: Hierarchy of needs (943)

Maslow's basic proposition is that people are wanting beings - they always want more, and what they want depends on what they have. He places their needs in a hierarchy of importance, like a pyramid:

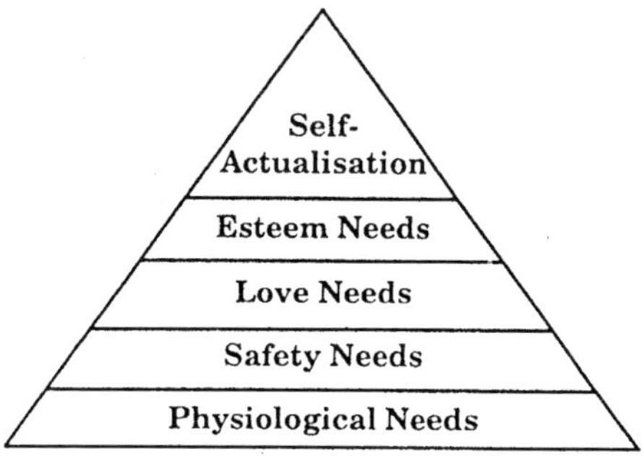

- *Physiological Needs*—food, drink, sex and sensory satisfactions
- *Safety Needs*—security, freedom from pain or harm
- *Love Needs*—Need to belong and affiliate with others
- *Esteem Needs*—prestige, status, and appreciation, sense of achievement
- *Self-actualisation*—the need to reach one's full potential

The pyramid is generally regarded as a fixed order, with individuals progressing up it from the physiological needs to self-actualisation. Once a lower level has been satisfied, it no longer acts as a strong motivator and the next higher level of hierarchy demands satisfaction and thus becomes the motivating influence.

There are, however, a number of problems relating this to a work situation:

1. People do not necessarily satisfy their needs, especially higher level needs, just through the work situation.
2. Individual differences means that individuals place different values on the same need. For example, some people prefer what they see as job security in a public organisation - a tourism department in a local authority—to a more highly paid but less secure job in a commercial tourism organisation.
3. It is unclear which needs lead to which behaviours or which behaviours are determined by which need.

Alderfer's ERG Theory (1972)

Alderfer uses similar ideas to Maslow's, but proposes only three levels: Existence (E), Relatedness (R) and Growth (G). As Figure shows, these approximate to Maslow's levels, although there is an important difference. That is, Alderfer sees needs as lying along a continuum, so that a number of needs are activated or being satisfied at the same time, rather than consequentially as in Maslow's model. Furthermore, he argues that if one set of needs are not being satisfied, the ensuing frustration of satisfaction will force the individual to refocus their efforts on another set of needs.

For example, if you are finding that your work does not give you the opportunities and feeling of self-worth that you need, then you may focus more on your personal relationships outside work.

Herzberg's Two-Factor Theory (1959, 1966, 1976)

Herzberg's research revealed that there are two different sets of factors affecting motivation:

(a) *Hygiene factors,* such as working conditions, salary, status, security and relationships with superiors, which lead to dissatisfaction if they did not meet the expectations of the individual, and

(b) *Motivating factors,* which include receiving recognition, being given responsibility personal growth and achievement.

Evidently, hygiene factors relate to Maslow's lower level needs, whilst motivators relate to his higher level needs. Herberg argues that addressing hygiene factors will prevent dissatisfaction but will not create motivation to work. Therefore, to motivate employees, attention must be given to the motivators. This means designing jobs so that workers themselves take responsibility for planning their work, choosing appropriate methods and so on; in other words, the direct opposite of Taylorism.

McGregor: X and Y theory

McGregor (1957, 1960) identifies two basic styles of management. Theory X assumes that people dislike work and will avoid it if they can, meaning that the manager has to control and coerce people towards meeting organisation objectives. McGregor argues that the theory operates as a self-fulfilling prophecy. That is, it actually brings about the kind of behaviour it assumes to be inevitable, either through an employee's passive acceptance of the situation leading to a lack of initiative and creativity, or becoming resentful and uncooperative (Watson 1986). Theory Y, however, operates under the assumption that people want to take responsibility and that most people are creative and want to take the initiative—they are just waiting for management to give them the opportunity! This means that managers should use a participative style rather than an authoritarian one.

McGregor's theory sets up two extremes of how managers tend to think about employee motivation, and is useful in showing how self-fulfilling prophecies occurring in the motivational area can restrict, or improve, performance.

The theorists in this wave have contributed to the debate about motivation by raising many basic questions about the assumptions managers may have about employee behaviour, or indeed, nature. However, there are drawbacks to this approach:

1. Their psychological universalism infers, to some extent, that cultural and social processes do not have much impact upon an individual's behaviour.
2. More attention is required about how people might want different things from work, or might want different things at different times.

Wave 3: People and Processes

This wave of theory produces a more sophisticated view of human beings and their mental processes. People are not just led by their needs, but are creative and assertive, and they calculate what is worth putting into work for what they will get out of it. These theories are more successful in highlighting the differences between individuals and their differing motivational states. They emphasise the process by which individuals think, calculate and pursue purposes.

Adams: Equity Theory

Adams (1963, 1965) suggests that people balance what they put into their work with what they out of it in the light of what they see other people putting in and taking out of similar situations (Watson 1986: 118). This means that if a reward is perceived as unfair, an individual will balance this out by putting less effort into the situation. However, the reverse has not been proven: that a perceived over generous reward will not motivate the individual to put more effort in, they will merely perceive it as their 'good fortune'.

Vroom: Expectancy Theory

Vroom (1965) suggests that people are influenced by the expected results of their actions. There are five conditions needed before motivation exists. Individuals:

1. Have to believe that the effort make will achieve effective performance.
2. Have to see that appropriate performance will lead to their receiving rewards to perceive the available rewards as attractive.
3. Must have the appropriate skills and knowledge to achieve effective performance.
4. Must have an appropriate perception of the role they are filling. That is, they must be aware of all internal and external factors, such as performance targets or maintaining good relationships with superiors and peers, which influence the extent to which their objectives will be fulfilled.

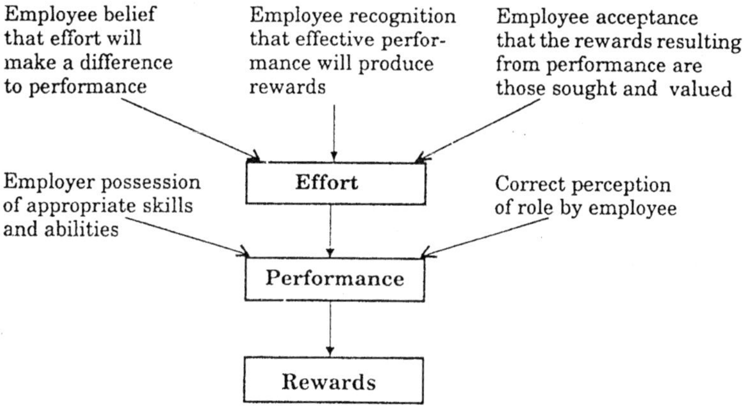

Figure 4.4 : The expectancy view of work motivation.

The advantage of expectancy theory is that it provides a practical framework to managers for analysing work motivation—it provides a checklist of factors and provides the relevant links between them.

Incentive Travel as a Motivation to Employees does it work?

Incentive travel is used by a number of companies to motivate employees. They are generally companies, or departments of companies, that depend heavily on sales and so need to find incentives to motivate staff. That individual who meets or exceeds performance targets is rewarded with an 'extraordinary travel experience' (Society of Incentive Travel 1996) for being such a high achiever.

After money, incentive travel appears to be the most popular reward (Fisher 2000). Reasons given are:

- It offers intrinsic psychological aspects such as relaxation away from the stresses of everyday live.
- It illustrates management's acknowledgement of the achiever's efforts showing that no expense is spared to show appreciation, thus boosting the individual's sense of self worth.
- It has 'trophy value' - the individual is not simply winning a trip but it is also the manner and level of luxury involved.
- Peer recognition boosts self esteem.

According to Ricci and Holland (1992), winning an incentive trip sets the individual amongst the elite group of employees as it is considered an exclusive reward. Incentive travel participation is a combination of basic work motivation ideas, competition, peer recognition, status, self-esteem and fantasy goal fulfilment. Although an attractive theory, however, more recent research suggests the ultimate travel prize is not always a 'satisfactory carrot' (Burleigh 2001: 42). That is, it does appear to increase the motivation of some, but not all, employees. Burleigh's work supports the argument of Holmes and Smith (1987) that travel will only be successful if the reward is perceived to be reasonable to attain and it is attractive to the individual.

Implications for organisations

- Motivation approaches and theories have been considered to give variable insights into the nature of employee behaviour and offer some practical guidance for those involved in the management of employees for enahncing employee performance.

- There is no simple link between motivation and job satisfaction.
- Theories acknowledge to a greater or lesser extent the differences between individuals as to what motivates them, but *culture* has received less attention. Many writers assume that what has been found in developed western countries is likely to be true for any other culture, but organisations also need to think about subcultural differences in motivation, such as gender differences.
- Contemporary theories emphasise the need for the employer or manager to be more than a source of financial rewards and to understand the needs of the workforce, to consider the issue of job design and to enhance the well being of those below him or her.
- No set of theories can be regarded as the whole story; taken together they all have something useful to offer. They provide four general lessons:
  - *(a)* When an employee becomes motivated, this is the outcome of a psychological process. Managers cannot observe this process at work, nor can they apply or supply motivation directly to employees. However, an employee's level of motivation can be influenced to some extent by the manager creating conditions that the individual finds stimulating and encouraging.
  - *(b)* Managers need to be sensitive to variations in individual needs, goals, preferences and abilities - not everyone is motivated in the same way in the same set of organisation circumstances.
  - *(c)* The needs of the individuals can change over time so organisations must be prepared to adapt to those changing needs. Provision of an encouraging work environment has to be kept under constant review.
  - *(d)* Whilst it is not only work that motivates individuals, organisations still need to provide a motivating work experience that gives sufficient diversity, opportunity and challenge to satisfy needs. It is half the battle won.

Groups and Teams

Why study groups and teams?

Most people working in any organisation will spend a lot of their time working in groups, and effective group working is fundamental to the achievement of any organisation's goals and objectives. Therefore, a knowledge of groups and teams, and how they function, is vital for any manager, potential manager, or individual working in an organisation.

Definition of a group

Schein (1980) defined, in psychological terms, a group as any number of people who :

- interact with one another;
- are psychologically aware of one another;
- perceive themselves to be a group; and
- purposefully interact towards the achievement of particular goals or aims.

Formal and informal groups

Groups have tremendous influence over an individual's behaviour whilst an individual's behaviour also has great influence over the group.

Formal groups are those groups that are brought into existence by the structure of an organisation, for example, departments, task groups, command groups. *Command groups* are permanent groups of people all under a single manager who perform similar activities, such as in a call-centre. At Travel Bag, for example, command groups will all be situated in the same room, but one command group will sell holidays to Australia, one to the United States and so forth.

Task groups are temporary formal groups formed for a specific short-term purpose or special project, and they are disperse' as soon as the task is completed; for example, a group of people are brought together to write and print a brochure for a particular destination. The group of people will be from different departments in the organisation, as graphic designers, copy writers, account managers, marketing managers and sales representatives are all required to input their own specific expertise into the project.

Schein (1980) lists six formal functions of groups:

1. They work on complex tasks not easily undertaken by the individual.
2. They are a means of stimulating creativity and generating new ideas.
3. They act as a liaison/co-ordination mechanism which integrates different parts of an organisation.
4. They are there for problem solving purposes where multiple viewpoints are important.
5. The implement decisions so that a common objective or goal can be set for a number of people.
6. They are useful as a socialising device so that a common message, especially with respect to an organisation's culture, can be communicated and reinforced.

Informal groups are not set up by the organisation, but tend to run parallel to formal groups. They exist for a different purpose, however, which is principally to satisfy the social needs of their members. Membership of an informal group is voluntary and joining also involves the consent of existing group members. This means that an informal group can often exert a more powerful influence over an individual's behaviour than a formal one.

The benefits of informal groups are that they:

1. Fulfil the members' social needs, that is, friendship and social interaction.
2. Develop, test and confirm a person's sense of identity and self-worth.
3. Establish and test beliefs, reality, experience and meanings.
4. Reduce feelings of insecurity, anxiety and powerlessness.
5. Achieve mutually agreed informal aims and objectives.

As Rollinson *et. al.*, (1998) argue, it is likely that managers will focus more on the formal groups than the informal groups but, generally, the two complement one another. Even if an individual has not much say in which formal group he must belong to the group can fulfil some of the informal group functions—working on a task, sharing the experiences, implementing decisions can give people a sense of self-worth and accomplishment.

Group formation and development

All groups so through various stages of development from inception to maturity, when they can start to perform effectively. Tuckman (1965) identifies the various stages of group development in his integrative Model.

Stage 1- Forming

The group is a collection of individuals brought together. As a result, they devote a lot of attention to getting to know one another rather than to the task in hand.

Stage 2 - Storming

This stage is characterised by interpersonal conflict; personal agendas and goals surface as people get to know one another and begin to express their views more openly. It is an uncomfortable stage for everyday involved, and concessions need to be made so that the group can move onto the next stage.

Stage 3 - Norming

The rules for a group's way of functioning start to emerge, and group norms are formulated to predict future behaviour, such as keeping to deadlines. Distinct roles start to emerge and signs of co-operation and sensitivity and much in evidence.

Stage 4 - Performing

At this final stage of development, the group becomes capable of effective functioning; task aspects and social aspects complement one another. Members are supportive and trusting, of one another. They are much better equipped to perform their role effectively.

Tuckman added one further stage which is particularly relevant to today's working conditions—that of *adjourning,* when the group is disbanded because people leave or its task has been completed. Adjournment is often accompanied with sadness and a sense of loss.

This particular model is useful for two reasons. Firstly, it provides guidelines to anyone who is starting up a new group and, secondly, it explains why some groups are never effective. Belbin (1981, 1993), however, provides another explanation as to why groups do not always perform as effectively as hoped, or predicted.

Group effectiveness

An effective group is one in which both task and socio-emotive needs are met, and this occurs when individual members occupy compatible roles, Belbin, (1981, 1993) identifies what he believes to be nine key roles in an effective group. The central thrust to his argument is that effective groups and teams seldom consist of people who are of the same type, but of people who have different and complementary skills and expertise. Effective and creative teams require a balanced mix of individual characteristics. If the tasks change then individual roles will change, and if a team is small then people will occupy more than one role.

Definition of a team

Whilst to some people the terms 'group' and 'team' are interchangeable, most theorists make a distinction between the two. Unsworth and West (in Chmiel 2000) believe that a number of conditions must be satisfied before a group of people can be called a team. These are that they:

- have shared goals in relation to their work;
- interact with one another in order to achieve those shared objectives.
- have well defined and interdependent roles; and
- have an organisational identity as a team with a defined organisational function.

Thus, teams go beyond traditional formal work groups by having a collective, synergistic (the whole is greater than the sum of its parts) character. Teams can be formed for any purpose. For example:

- **The plant:** This role requires someone who is creative, imaginative and unorthodox. Plants solve difficult problems, but they ignore details and are too preoccupied to communicate effectively.
- **The Resource Investigator:** Resource Investigators are extrovert, enthusiastic and communicative. They explore opportunities and develop contacts. Sometimes, though they are over optimistic and they lose interest once the initial enthusiasm has passed.
- **The Co-ordinator:** This role requires someone who is mature, confident and a good chairperson. They are able to clarify goals and promote decision making as well as being good delegators. However, they can be seen as manipulative.
- **The Shaper:** Shapers are challenging, dynamic and they thrive on pressure. They have to drive and courage to overcome obstacles, but they can provoke others and hurt people's feelings.
- **The Monitor-Evaluator:** Monitor-Evaluators are strategic and discerning. They see all options and judge accurately. However, they lack drive and the ability to inspire others. They are also overly critical.
- **The Team-Worker:** A role requires someone who is co-operative, mild, perceptive and dynamic. Team-workers listen, build, avert friction and calm the waters. They can also be very indecisive in crunch situations and can be easily influenced.
- **The Implementer:** The Implementer is disciplined, reliable and efficient. They turn ideas into practical actions. However, they can be inflexible and they are slow to respond to new possibilities.
- **The Completer-Finisher:** The Completer-Finisher is painstaking, conscientious but also anxious as they search out errors and ommissions. They always deliver on time and are reluctant to delegate.
- **The Specialist:** This role require someone who is single-minded, self-starting and dedicating. They provide knowledge and skills that are in rare supply. However, they tend to dwell on technicalities and overlook the big picture.

Figure 4.5 : *Belbin's* 9 team roles.

1. *Advice teams*—a team created primarily to provide a flow of information to management to be used in its own decision making, like a committee. It is sometimes responsible for implementing those decisions.
2. *Quality circles*—these teams consist of employees from the same department who meet for a few hours each week to discuss ways of improving their work environment. Quality circles began in manufacturing companies in Japan, but now they are applied extensively in the service industries, government agencies and the voluntary sector.
3. *Cross-functional team*—this is a team composed of employees from about the same hierarchical level but from different work areas or functions within the organisation. They are brought together to complete a particular task, such as quality and customer service improvements, and operate in a similar way to task groups in that they are 'temporary' and individuals remain members of their specific department of function. They are very often used by organisations to implement quality and customer service improvements.

The disadvantages of groups and teams

Whilst there are a number of apparent advantages to group and team-working, as demonstrated above, there are also a number of disadvantages:

Intergroup Conflict

Because an effective and cohesive group has its own norms and values, there is always an inbuilt potential for conflict and, therefore, co-operation between groups cannot be taken for granted. Furthermore, winning can become all important as groups compete with one another for sales targets, customers and so on, so that other groups become the 'enemy'.

Group polarisation (risky shift)

This refers to the tendency of some groups to opt for much riskier decision alternatives than individuals would make. This comes about, perhaps, because of the diffiusion of responsibility that comes with working in a group, the fact that taking risks have some degree of social prestige with the group, and because as the group becomes more accustomed or familiarised with the risky decision as they talk about it, it appears less risky. Furthermore, those most likely to speak out in group decision meetings are often those who have most influence in the group and their suggestions are sometimes adopted without full consideration.

Groupthink

This can be explained as impaired decision making by a group because their desire for being unanimous overrides examining the consequences of a decision. The concept was developed by Janus (1972) after researching into the invasion of Cuba 1961. Historical evidence revealed that John Kennedy and his group of expert advisors were driven by seeking group consensus when making and important decision rather than basing it upon information and reality. As a result, the invasion failed (Unsworth and West, in Chmiel 2000).

Implications for organisations of groups and teams

- Organisations should not feel threatened if informal groups emerge. They are created to meet the socio-emotive needs of the individuals, which formal groups cannnot always do.
- Organisations need to be aware that it takes time for a collection of individuals to develop into an effective group. If the organisation tries to hurry the process in a way that leaves some of the issues at one stage unresolved, the eventual effectiveness of the group can be seriously impaired.
- Organisations need to be aware that group effectiveness can crucially depend on an appropriate mix of different but complementary roles.
- Whilst there are a number of advantages to groups, organisations should also recognised that there are potential problems in highly cohesive groups. This includes intergroup conflict and impaired decision making.

Conclusions

This chapter has attempted to give an overview of some of the main theories which help us to understand aspects of individual and group behaviour. Individuals come together within an organisation to achieve some common purpose, but the way that these individuals are 'organised' and how the organisation 'treats' them will affect their perceptions of that organisation and the work that they do and, subsequently, their behaviour within that organisation. Therefore, managers have to be aware of a number of issues. Firstly, they have to realise that the environments in which people live and work influence their behaviour. If the external changes, then the needs of the people will change will it, and so must the organisation's capability to meet those needs by creating a stimulating and rewarding working environ-ment.

Secondly, managers must understand that all people cannot be 'managed' in a similar way. Whilst some individuals may respond to the 'carrot and stick' approach of scientific management, others place far greater importance on feeling valued for the work that they do. Managers, therefore, need to be sensitive to the variations in individual needs, goals, preferences and abilities in order to get the best out of their people.

5

Functions of Human Resource Management

The Role of Human Resource Management

Definitions

There are a number of definitions of human resource management. Most simply, it may be described as getting the right number of the right people into the place at the right time. Although a succinct statement, this nevertheless sums up a lot of the activities of human resource management in any business or organisation, including those in the travel and tourism sector. The emphasis on the 'right number' refers to human resource planning and its attempts to relate the number of people employed to the amount of work to be done. The need to have the 'right people' shows the need to have well-designed recruitment and selection procedures to choose people who will fit into the organisation. However, that is not the end of the story, as these people must then receive appropriate training and coaching to help them develop their skills.

Mention of the 'right place' and the 'right time' again refers to human resource planning, but it goes further. Recruitment and training, together with performance management, must be used to develop individuals so that they have the ability to make a worthwhile contribution when the time comes for promotion or their is a need for reorganisation. This requires forward planning in an attempt to foresee the directions in which the organisation will have to move.

Another definition suggests that the key purpose of human resource management is to 'enable management to enhance the individual and collective contributions to the, short and long-term success of the enterprise' (Personnel Standards Lead Body 1993).

The human resource management cycle

There has been considerable discussion of the concept of 'strategic human resource management' (Fombrun *et. al.*, 1984). One of the main features of the concept of human resource management is that it is a coherent approach, as demonstrated in Figure 5.1:

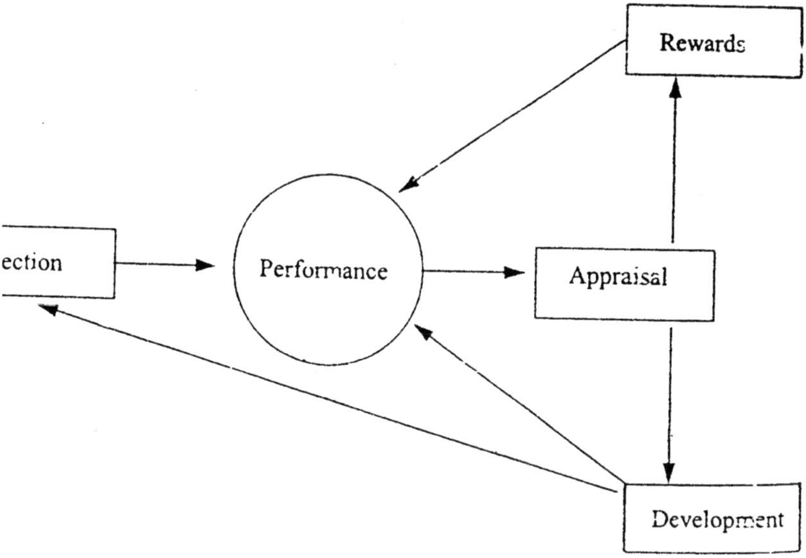

Figure 5.1 : The human resource management cycle.

This model provide the outline structure of this chapter: an organisation, whether in travel or tourism or any other industry, must plan how many people it requires of what types and then select the best people. Having selected them, they must use a variety of techniques to ensure they obtain the necessary development. This will include providing training to ensure they perform effectively, appraising them to establish their development needs, and rewarding them appropriately to ensure they are motivated to achieve the necessary level of performance.

Human Resource Planning

Definitions

Human resource planning is an essential feature of human resource management. Indeed, the above the definition of human resource management, getting the right number of the right people into the right place at the right time, could also be used as a definition of human resource planning as it includes the key concept of matching the number of people to the amount of work to be done. Thus, human resource planning can be treated in its widest sense of making the best of the human resources available to the organisation.

There are number of other definitions of human resource planning, perhaps one of the most helpful being a strategy for the acquisition, utilisation, improvement and retention of an enterprise's human resources (Department of Employment 1974). Let us examine this definition in more detail:

- A strategy implies a relatively long term plan which has been devised bearing in mind other aspects of the organisation's operations.
- Acquisition refers to recruitment and selection, and then subsequent promotions and transfers.
- Utilisation means that having employed a group of people, they must be used in an efficient manner to attain high productivity.
- Improvement refers to training and development, and also to performance appraisal as a means of identifying training needs.
- Retention means that the organisation must provide work organised in a way to motivate that staff, with adequate financial compensation and opportunities for promotion.

It is evident from the above that human resource planning incorporates much of what is considered to be the subject matter of human resource management. Thus, it is a product of the techniques of human resource management designed to match the demand for staffing with the supply available.

The need for human resource planning

In the current financial climate, most organisations are having to become increasingly cost-conscious. At the same time, in an increasingly competitive industry such as travel and tourism, organisations are faced with the need to improve efficiency, which in turn means maximising the return on all available resources, whether these be financial or human. Organisations will usually set themselves a number of goals in relation to their staffing. There is a tradition in the travel industry of high levels of seasonal, part time, casual and female labour and these groups tend to be associated with high labour turnover. This can cause particular problems for the human resource planner who needs to ensure the right number of people are employed, as too many means an unneccessarily high wage bill, whilst too few may mean that sales targets cannot be met. They need the right balance of people, with neither too many managers compared to the number of workers, nor an inexperienced workforce without adequate supervision and leadership. The skills of the staff must be in balance so that the range of jobs can be covered.

These goals can be placed in two categories. The first is to ensure that there is the right number of the right people to do the job efficiently now. The second looks to the future to ensure that there will be the right number of the right people in a few years time, even though it is not known what the exact requirements may be five years hence.

Atkinson (1984) introduced the concept of the 'flexible firm', and suggested there were three kinds of flexibility:

- **Functional flexibility,** so that employees have multiple skills and can be moved between a range of jobs.

- **Numerical flexibility,** by the use of part time and temporary contracts so that the numbers of employees can be easily increased or decreased in line with the demand for labour.
- **Financial flexibility,** which provides for pay levels to reflect the state of supply and demand in the external labour market.

The concept of the flexible firm involves employing a core of permanent, full time, relatively well paid and well trained staff, supported by peripheral workers who move in and out of the labour force in line with demand. The peripheral workers can have a range of different types of contract; for example, Lunn Poly employ part timers who can be asked to work anywhere between 4 and 37 hours a week, although the average is around 18.

There is, then, an evident need for organisations to carry out human resource planning. However, it has been observed that there are so many problems to overcome, and so many uncertainties in the local, national and international environment, that it is pointless spending a lot of time and effort on an activity which so frequently produces the wrong answers. In particular, the travel and tourism industry has a number of features which can make predicating staffing needs very difficult. For example, the demand for holidays can be affected by a range of factors, from weather conditions to the strength of sterling, while industrial action by air traffic controllers and political unrest generally have an impact somewhere in the world each year. This may make the task more problematic, but does not mean it should not be attempted at all!

Stages of human resource planning

It is possibly to identify a number of stages in human resources planning:

- Assessing demand—this involves looking at the objectives the organisation is trying to achieve overall, and then assessing the number of people it will require.
- Assessing supply—this involves taking an inventory of the number and type of people employed today, and then

making a projection of how the position is likely to change in future years.

- Balancing supply and demand—there is likely to be a disparity between the number of people available and the number of people needed.
- Human resource planning—this involves determining the necessary actions so that the supply of labour matches the demand for labour.

An organisation must satisfy three conditions if the above stages are to be carried out effectively:

(i) Human resource planning must be fully integrated with corporate planning

It is impossible to make decisions about staffing requirements unless decisions have also been made about the products and services the organisation will offer in the future. Decisions must also be made about the human resource policies of the organisation, for example, in terms of the levels of training to be offered and the salary levels to be paid.

(ii) Comprehensive human resource records and statistics must be available

It is impossible to forecast the level of staffing available unless there are accurate and up-to-date records and statistics available. Human resource planning requires both information on individual employees, and also statistical information on trends in the labour force, such as the number of people leaving over a year.

(iii) The organisation must define its objectives

The organisation must decide the period over which the forecast should be attempted, and also the degree of accuracy and detail which it requires. There will be certain areas which are critical to the success of the organisation, and on which the human resource planner should concentrate attention.

For example, a travel agency chain may set itself the target of increasing the number of travel shops by 5 per cent in the next 12 months, or a tour operator may decide to enter the cruise market, or a theme park may decide to build a number of new rides and a hotel. All of these decisions require resources to make them happen, whether capital, material or human, and planning to ensure that things happen at the right time.

However, staffing requirements are expressed not only in terms of quantity, but also in terms of type and quality. Thus, it is insufficient to say we need 10 people to fill 10 posts; they must have the knowledge and experience to be able to do the 10 jobs. This implies a need to conduct a 'skills audit' to discover the skills and abilities of the existing staff and an analysis of the job descriptions of the vacant posts to ensure that the people are recruited.

Human Resource Forecasting

An organisation has to predict the number of people it will need in the future. These people are only available from two sources: those people who are currently working within the organisation, and those people currently outside the organisation. Whilst seemingly obvious, this indicates clearly the two which the human resource planner must investigate.

(i) Within the Organisation

This requires an analysis of the skills and experience of current employees, their length of service, training potential, and also their personal preferences. Some assessment of the likelihood of them leaving the organisation must also be made.

(ii) Outside the Organisation

This requires an analysis of the availability of people with specific skills outside the organisation. Even in times of high unemployment, certain occupational groups will still be in great demand. Some assessment must also be made of the likelihood of the organisation being able to attract the people it will require.

Assessing Staffing Supply

The purpose of human resource planning is to estimate the size of any future shortages or surpluses in particular skill groups so that action can be taken if necessary. In order to succeed at human resource planning, it is essential to have an accurate picture of the organisation's existing labour resources and then to assess the extent by which this stock will have been reduced by labour turnover by the end of the forecast period. At the same time, an assessment must be made of the extent to which the future requirements for labour will be available.

Internal supply

Human resource records should record the number of staff in different categories, their age, sex and length of service. Records must be kept of the absence levels of staff in specific occupations and also on the turnover of staff. It may be helpful to conduct exit interviews to establish the reasons why staff are leaving the organisation. The information gained will allow predictions to be made about the numbers of days likely to be lost through absence, and also how many staff are likely to leave the organisation. The age and length of service of employees may also affect future wastage rates. Younger employees are more likely to leave the organisation than older employees, and people who have a longer length of service are less likely to leave than those who have only been with the organisation for a shorter period of time.

External supply

An estimate must be made of the supply of labour outside the organisation. This is based on the total population figures, but also on the numbers in particular age groups, for example schools leavers or university graduates. The educational system will also determine the numbers available with particular qualifications at a range of levels; for example, over the last ten years there has been a tremendous increase in the number of travel and tourism graduates in the labour market. There are also social factors which influence the number of people available, such as the availability of child care provision.

Effect of new technology

It has been said that Britain is undergoing a second Industrial Revolution, brought about by the increased availability and sophistication of computers. New technology has an impact both on the demand for different products and the methods used to provide different goods and services. For example, within the travel industry there has been a move towards 'ticketless' travel which has reduced the commission available to travel agents. The availability of new machinery can either be used to increase the output from the same number of staff or to maintain the output level with a smaller number of staff. However, increased automation may also call for different skills from employees and may also change the way in which work is organised. This is already happening in travel agencies, where some employees are mainly booking clerks, entering details in a computer, while others are able to make full use of the available technology to provide high quality advice on a range of destinations.

The human resource plan

The next step is to draw up a plan to ensure that the demand for labour will be met by the appropriate level of supply. More specifically, it will specify future recruitment requirements, training and development to be undertaken, and any necessary redundancies. The process of forecasting future labour requirements may also indicate areas in which improvements in productivity could be made.

Perhaps the most important point to remember about human resource planning is that even detailed human resource plans are useless in themselves. Their only value lies in providing the manager with information to make decisions. If the figures show that absence or labour turnover is rising in a particular department, then action must be taken to find out the reasons why so that further action can be taken to reduce it. Monitoring is vital so that any change in the actual position compared to the fore cast position will be noticed and then action can be taken either to change the trend or to change the forecast. The result of this may be to modify long term plans, policies or objectives.

Recruitment and Selection

The previous sections on the role of human resource management and on human resource planning have stressed the need to select the 'right people', and this is achieved by using recruitment and selection techniques. The CIPD publish a Code of Practice (1995) on Recruitment which 'aims' to promote and maintain high standards of professional practice by encouraging recruiters to adhere to best practice'. The Code contains advice and guidance on a range of aspects, including ensuring equality of opportunity.

It is helpful to divide the process into four distinct stages and examine each one in turn:

Recruitment:

1. Assessing the job,
2. Attracting a field of candidates.

Selection:

1. Assessing the candidates,
2. Placement and follow up.

Assessing the job

The first question to be asked is 'Do we need to fill this vacancy?' In the current climate, where many organisations are attempting to reduce their numbers by natural wastage, the answer to this question may well be 'no'. However, if the question is not asked at all then there is no opportunity to examine the work done by the post-holder in an attempt to see whether it could be reorganised in a more efficient manner. One technique which may be helpful in examining the work done is job analysis which is an analytical study of a job to determine the essential component factors.

The job analyst will ask four basic questions to determine what a job involves:

- what the job holder does,
- how the job holder does it,
- why the job holder does it,
- what does the job involve.

Job description

The information about a job will normally be presented in the form of a job Description. This will detail the organisational position of the job in terms of department, location, who the post-holder reports to, and which posts they are responsible for. The job description will also outline the resources available to the post-holder and any specific constraints. The main part of the job description comprises a list of the duties and responsibilities involved in the job, together perhaps with some indication of the amount of time spent on individual activities. There has been a move away from detailed job descriptions in some organisations as it is felt they can inhibit flexibility. However, there is still a need for some indication of the personal competencies which are necessary to perform a particular job. Armstrong (1999: 280) draws a distinction between work-based or occupational competencies, which refer to what people should be capable of doing and the standards that people are expected to attain, and behavioural or personal competencies, which are the personal characteristics of individuals which they bring to their work roles.

Person specification

When all the above information has been collected, it will be possible to determine the knowledge and skills required to perform the job successfully. A popular classification of human attributes which can be useful in compiling a person specification is Rodger's Seven Point Plan. The purpose of the Plan is to set a standard under a range of headings against which individual candidates may be measured. The Seven Point Plan covers:

- Physical make up (e.g., clear speaking voice)
- Attainment (e.g., academic and other achievements)
- General intelligence (e.g., other evidence of mental ability)

- Special aptitudes (e.g., foreign languages)
- Interests (e.g., physical, mental or social)
- Disposition (e.g., preference for working in a team)
- Circumstances (e.g., where they live and how far they have to travel to work).

When preparing the person specification, requirements should be stated under each heading. The temptation will often be to draw up an over-idealised specification, perhaps requiring GCSE Maths when really an understanding of how to calculate percentages would be sufficient. It may be helpful to consider those attributes which are essential, those which are desirable and those which are undesirable and would automatically disqualify any individual who possessed it. An example of the latter may be an applicant for a position of regional sales manager who has a conviction for driving while under the influence of alcohol.

Attracting a field of candidates

There are three main sources of recruitment: internal sources; external agencies; and advertisements.

Internal Sources

There may well be somebody already employed in the organisation who could perform the job competently. Indeed, some organisations have an agreement with their staff that all vacancies should be advertised internally to give existing staff a chance of promotion. However, there should be a balance between bringing in people with new ideas from outside the organisation and offering promotion prospects to existing employees. An advantage of promoting existing staff is that their abilities are well known whilst their knowledge of the organisation should allow them to make a more immediate contribution in their new job than an outsider.

External Agencies

There are a range of different agencies, some of which are Government-funded and others which are operated privately. Job Centres are located in most suburban shopping centres and provide a basically free service to both employers and job seekers. They tend to concentrate mostly on manual and clerical jobs, although they provide specialised services for particular groups, such as disabled workers and the long term unemployed. Careers Services are particularly useful for school and college leavers as they have close links with educational institutions. Private agencies frequently specialise in certain fields, such as travel and tourism, or in particular areas of the market, such as secretarial staff, IT staff, drivers or temporary workers. These agencies charge the employer for their services.

Advertisements

Most organisations will use advertisements at one time or another, and they can form a substantial part of recruitment costs. They must be written very carefully and be placed in the appropriate place at the right time if they are to prove cost-effective. The aim of recruitment advertising is to produce a compact and well-qualified field of candidates who are motivated to accept the job. This implies that sufficient candidates must apply to offer a reasonable selection, but not so many that they present an administrative burden. The candidates should meet the requirements of the person specification, and they should have obtained a favourable impression of the organisation.

It may be helpful to state in the advertisement that a copy of the job description will be sent with the application form. This will give potential candidates a much better idea of what the job entails and enable them to decide at an early stage if they feel that the job is not what they are looking for. This will save the employer administrative time and expense in dealing with applications which will not lead to an appointment. It also recognises that recruitment is a two-way process and that the candidate needs to have the information to select a suitable employer in the same way the employer selects a suitable candidate.

Application Forms

A well designed application form will request the information which is required in a systematic manner. A specific item of information will be in the same position for each candidate which should allow speedier comparisons. There should be sufficient space in which to write the required information. Many application forms for more senior positions require the candidate to state at some length why they feel their experience and qualifications make them a suitable contender for the job.

Assessing the candidate

The first two stages should have produced a shortlist of qualified candidates. The subsequent selection stage, using a range of selection methods, then involves deciding on the most suitable. The most common selection method is the interview which may be supplemented by selection tests, group methods, and references.

Selection tests

A range of tests are available which are designed to assess various attributes. These include tests of practical skills, such as filing or typing, and verbal and numerical abilities. There are also psychometric tests designed to provide information on personality characteristics. Many of these must be administrated by a trained psychological to facilitate interpretation of the results.

Group selection methods

These involve bringing a group of candidates together and giving them tasks to do. This is often used to recruit tour operators' overseas representatives, where their ability to get on well with other people and be able to present material clearly and concisely can be assessed. They may be given a topic to discuss, be asked to deliver a 'welcome talk', or sell excursions. Trained observers watch each individual's contribution and make an assessment of their personal skills and their ability to work with a group of people. These exercises may be time-consuming, but properly used can obtain information which would be very difficult to obtain using other methods.

References

The purpose of a reference is two-fold. Firstly, it is designed to obtain, in confidence, factual information about a prospective employee and, secondly, it may ask for opinions about their character and their likely suitability for the post in question. Some people argue that references rarely supply any useful information, while others argue that they provide a valuable safety net. They are probably most useful when they ask for specific information on starting and leaving dates, salary history, and sickness record.

Selection interview

The interview is trying to find an answer to two simple questions: can they do the job, and will they do the job? At the same time, however as well as trying to select the best candidate for the job, the interview is also trying to persuade the candidate to accept the job. The majority of candidates will be unsuccessful but it is, nevertheless, important that they too receive a favourable impression of the organisation. That is, there may be a temptation in times of high unemployment to feel that it is less important to try to sell the job because it is a buyer's market. However, if the organisation is trying to recruit the best people for the job, those people are likely to receive offers from other organisations as well. Thus, it is equally important to convince the candidate that the job is right for their as to assess whether they are right for the job.

Research has shown that interviews can produce very poor selection decisions-most people only have to look around their own organisations to see evidence of this. Better results can be obtained if the interview has been trained, and if they carry out adequate preparation prior to the interview. The interview room itself should be free from interruptions and arranged for either a formal or an informal interview as appropriate. A one-to-one interview may be conducted fairly informally around a coffee table but a panel interview involving three or more interviewers may dictate a more formal seating plan.

One-to-one interviews

A single trained and experienced interviewer may well produce the best results. The candidate is likely to be more relaxed in this situation and the conversation will, therefore, flow more easily. The main problem, however, is that the organisation then relies on the judgement of one individual who may be biased in certain directions. This type of interview is more common in the private sector.

Panel interviews

These can vary in the number of interviewers, although they have been known to enter double figures. The smaller the numbers, the more likely they are to be effective as large numbers are very difficult to control. The panel members should agree beforehand on their respective roles and they should be carefully controlled by a chairperson. The advantages of a panel interview are that the people involved can share the responsibility for making the decision and that experts in particular areas can ask questions on their own specialism.

During the interview

At the start of the interview, the interviewer should try to create a rapport so that the candidate begins to relax and settle down. Typically, the interviewer may ask about the candidate's travelling arrangements, how well they know the area or some other non-threatening topic of conversation. Inexperienced interviewers tend to ask. "Did you find us easily?" and then launch straight into the interview. It is well worth taking more time to relax the candidate, particularly if they are young or obviously nervous. The interviewer will often tell the candidate a little about the organisation and the specific job applied for. Care must be taken not to talk for too long as the candidate will probably be nervous and unable to easily absorb the information.

The actual questions should then be put to the candidate and the interviewer should carefully listen to the answers. This can be quite difficult in practice, as the inexperienced interviewer will tend to be thinking about how to ask the next question rather than listening to the answer from the last one. Thus, a useful technique is to follow up each question with at least one supplementary question designed to probe what the candidate has just said.

Different techniques are useful in different situations. Leading questions will usually provide little information as to the candidate's true feelings, whilst multiple questions can lead to confusion. Generally speaking, open questions are more useful than closed questions as they encourage the candidate to talk. One technique which can produce reasonably consistent and reliable results is the 'behaviourally situated' interview. This technique is based on the belief that the past performance is the best predictor of future performance. The candidates are asked pre-prepared questions such as:

- describe a situation where you used yourr influencing skills to achieve a successful result, or
- describe a situation where you had to overcome difficulties to complete a task.

The questions are chosen to reflect the type of situations which are likely to be crucial to effective job performance. It is important that the interviewer should really probe to discover exactly what the candidate did to achieve the outcome.

It has been suggested that the interviewer should talk for no than 30 per cent of the time because while they are talking are not learning anything. It may be helpful to take notes as a reminder of the answers, particularly if a number of candidates are to be seen at the same time. The candidate should also be given the opportunity to ask any questions they might have and then the interview should be brought to a close. The interview should be told when they can expect to receive any information and also how to claim their expenses if appropriate. Each candidate should feel that they have had a fair hearing and have been given sufficient information so that they can make their own decisions as to whether they would like to do if were offered. It is much better that a candidate refuses a job offer because they feel the job is unsuitable rather than accepting, only to leave the organisation after a short period of time.

After the interview

Any notes which have been made during the interview should be written up immediately afterwards, before the next candidate is seen. The selection decision is then made by comparing all the available information on a candidate with the requirements of the job. It may be helpful to use some form of rating scale based either on the Seven Point Plan or on the specified criteria for the job as a systematic means of recording information on each candidate. If a number of interviewers have seen the same candidate there may be some fairly lengthy discussions before a measure of agreements can be reached. Candidates who are unsuccessful should be informed promptly and courteously.

No matter how carefully the recruitment and selection procedures have been carried out the new employee will still need assistance if they are to become fully effective as quickly as possible. The administrative details must be handled competently and the new employee must receive appropriate induction training. Even an experienced operative will require training in the particular procedures to be adopted in their new organisation, as well as needing information on the organisation itself and such practical matters as stationery supplies and when they will be paid.

Training and Development

Training is of vital importance if the organisation is to ensure that it has the right people available at the right time. It should be considered as an investment in the organisation's most valuable resource, the people it employs However, in times of financial difficulty it is often one of the first activities to be curtailed. In the past, a lot of training has undoubtedly been carried out for its own sake rather than helping the organisation to meet specific objectives. The aim then should be to ensure that training is designed to meet specific needs.

Potential Benefits of Training

Training is provided to:

- Provided specific skills—it can be easier to train your own staff in essential skills rather than relying upon the labour market to provide them.
- Improve performance and productivity—teaching the best methods of working can increase the quantity and quality of the output.
- Reduce wastage—employees who make mistakes are wasting both time and perhaps materials.
- Reduce accidents—the correct method will also be a safe method.
- Reduce labour turnover—employees who are unsure about what they are supposed to be doing and who receive complaints because they make mistakes are more likely to be absent or to leave the organisation.
- Individual advancement—employees will improve their personal position by acquiring new skills.

Many employees have a probation period during which their performance is closely monitored and they receive training and feedback on how well they are adapting.

It is sometimes said that training is designed to effect a change in three main areas, namely, knowledge, skills and attitudes. Knowledge-based training is sometimes called education as it involves the assimilation of a number of facts, for example, the codes used for different airports. Skills-based training will enable the trainee to do something at the end of the training, for example, type at 40 words per minute. Training designed to change attitudes can be the most difficult, such as encouraging a calm and patient response when faced with an irate and demanding customer.

Although all training will be directed towards bringing a change in knowledge, skill or attitudes, or a combination of them, it is possible to identify particular types of training:

Induction training

This can fall into two categories. Firstly comes the introduction to the organization which every new employee will need. The second part involves initial training related to the specific job they will be required to do.

Skills training

This is an extension of the induction training and is designed to enable employees to perform all parts of their job competently.

Management training

This may be carried out within the organization, or by attendance on external courses, and is designed to encourage the skills required to manage other people.

There will be wide range of training needs of any organization and only a limited amount of money available in the budget. In these circumstances, decisions must be made as to which activities take priority so that the training provided will be both relevant and cost-effective. The best way of achieving this is by drawing up a training policy which has the support of the highest level of decision makes within the organization. Decisions have to be made about the staff and resources which are to be devoted to training, as these in turn determine the actual the staff and resources which are to be devoted to training, as these in turn determine the actual training carried out.

Training cannot be carried out in isolation; it must be integrated with the other activities of the organization. Thus, if the policy is to recruit school leavers and then train them, the resources must be available to do this. If the organization is installing new machinery or expanding into new markets then the staff must be trained in the necessary skills. Training is simply one more method of helping the organization to achieve its overall objectives.

The Training Cycle

If training is to be carried out in the most efficient manner, it is important that it is approached in a systematic fashion. There is a Four Step Approach, the Training Cycle, which can be applied to all types of training at all levels.

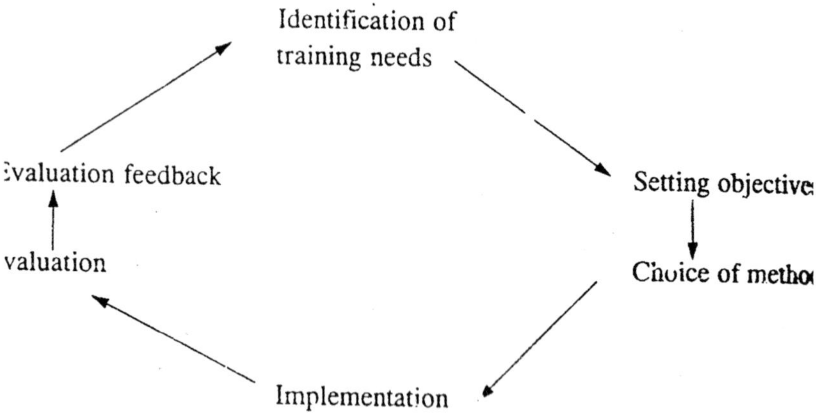

Figure 5.2 : The systematic training cycle.

Identify Training Needs

It seems obvious to say that it is necessary to find out what training people need before giving them any training yet, in many organizations, this does not happen. People are sent on training courses because their colleagues have been sent on the same training course, rather than because the course is actually right for them.

In order to determine an individual's training needs, it is necessary to carry out a training needs analysis. Examine their job description to see what they are required to do and then interview the individual and their supervisor to see what they can do already. The difference between the two is called the Training Gap and it is here that training should be directed. There are also other ways of deciding what training needs to be done and these are more suitable for deciding what training requires to be done on an occupational or departmental level and on the organizational level. Training may be related to.

(ii) Set the objectives for training

Training may be related to:

- Changes in legislation: this can involve changes in policies, practices or procedures.
- Changes in equipment: people must be trained to operate and maintain the new equipment.
- Changes in product: there may well be new techniques involved.
- Productivity figures: these may indicate where improvements can be made.
- Accident figures: high numbers of accidents may indicate training should be given in safe working practices.
- Wastages figures: large amounts of spoiled materials may indicate a need for training.
- Customer complaints: those may indicate where things are going wrong.

Labour turnover: people who are finding it difficult to do their jobs are more likely to leave the organization.

A word of caution is necessary, as there may be an assumption that training can solve all problems. It is true that training may be able to help in all of the above examples, but it will be only of limited assistance if the problems basically stem from obsolete equipment and poorly-designed procedures.

(iii) Plan the training

Once decisions have been made about who needs what training, then further decisions must be made about how this is to be achieved. In particular the following questions must be answered:

- WHO: who will carry out the training?
- WHERE: where will the training take place?
- WHAT: what specific knowledge, skills and attitudes will be included?
- WHEN: when will be the date, time and duration of the sessions?

Having answered these questions, then arrangements must be made for the people, equipment and rooms to be made available as required.

On-the-job and off-the-job training

There is sometimes an assumption that training only takes place in a classroom away from the job. In reality, people learn most about their job by actually doing it. Effective learning takes place when people are given an opportunity to practice particular skills and are then given feedback on their performance. It may well be that a short period of off-the job training can best be followed by guided practice on-the-job, by somebody who has been trained in instructional techniques.

(iv) Evaluate training

Most organizations will have carried out the previous three steps, to a greater or lesser extent, when arranging a training programme. However, in many cases little or no attempt is made to systematically evaluate the training with the attention of feeding back these results to future training programmes. It is so wonder that training is one of the first areas to be cut back if there is no data available on the extent to which it is helping the organization to achieve its overall objectives.

Evaluation can be carried out at different levels and thus provide answers to different questions:

- Did the training achieve what it set out to do?
- Were the original objectives appropriate?

The success of a training programme can also be measured at different points in time:

- Reaction evaluation: this involves asking the trainees to assess how much they learned and whether they 'enjoyed' the training. This is the most common form of evaluation, but is of limited usefulness.
- Learning evaluation: this involves testing the employees at the end of the course to see if they have achieved the objectives. To be fully effective, a test should also be given prior to the course to ensure that the learning is a result of the course.
- Performance evaluation: this involves making an assessment of the performance of the trainee when they have returned to their job to see if they are implementing their training in practice.

- Organisational evaluation: this is the ultimate test which is designed to show whether the organization as a whole is performing better as a result of the training.

It will be clear that the most valuable information relating to the impact on the organization is the most difficult to obtain and is most affected by external variables. Thus, although British rail invested a great deal of money in their 'Charm Schools' which were designed to improve the social skills of their staff, it is impossible to say whether this alone contributed to increased passenger revenues. However, it undoubtedly led to a reduced number of complaints about the attitudes of certain members of staff, which could in itself be considered to be sufficient justification for the training.

The cost involved in training must be carefully controlled to ensure both that the most cost-effective methods are being used and that benefits to the organization outweigh the money spent on training. It is only by monitoring the situation closely that the organization will be able to maximize the benefits of an investment in training. At the end of the day, training must be seen to be producing the desired results in terms of contributing to the overall organizational objectives.

Performance Appraisal

In every organisation, there is a need regularly and systematically to take stock of current manpower. The aim is to assess people's performance in existing jobs and their potential for future jobs. The technique used to achieve this is performance or staff appraisal. Properly conducted, performance appraisal can achieve the following:

- It gives line managers the opportunity to assess the employees' strengths and weaknesses.
- It gives employees the opportunity to assess their current position within the organisation, and to review their personal future.
- It provides the opportunity for action to be taken to provide training and development which will enable the individual to more closely match the requirements of the job.

The importance of the word 'action' must be noted. Undoubtedly the most frequent criticism of appraisal scheme is that much talking is done and many forms are filled in, but nothing actually happens as a result.

In essence appraisal entails one individual sitting in judgement on another. Many managers dislike the idea of 'Playing God' and employees may be reluctant to receive criticism, particularly if they feel the organisation itself is making it difficult for them to achieve their goals. Some organisations try to shift the focus of appraisal so that the manager helps the employee to identify their own strengths and weaknesses and from there pinpoint their own training and development needs. The success of this sort of approach will depend on the relationship which exist between the manager and the employee.

Staff appraisal ranges from intermittent, informal and often ill-informed discussion between managers and individual members of staff, to highly formal appraisal procedures, based on extensive sets of forms and laid down times, rules, and frequency of assessments. Generally, an important point is that any decisions made as a result of the appraisal process should be based on sufficient, relevent and objective information.

Value of Performance Appraisal

Appraisals are not an end in themselves, but a means to an end. Research has shown that appraisal schemes aim to achieve one or more of the following purposes:

- to improve current performance;
- to identify future potential; and
- to link pay realistically with performance.

It is, of course, very difficult for any one scheme to successfully achieve all of the above. For example, if one is attempting to improve current performance, this assumes a fairly frank discussion about strengths and weakness. However, if the employee is aware that a future pay increase rests upon their performance during an appraisal interview, they are likely to be less forthcoming about their weakness and concentrate on their strengths.

A similar distinction can be drawn between schemes which aim to improve current performance, and those which aim to identify future potential. The former will require detailed discussions with the employee in order to review past performance, set performance targets, and motivate the employee to achieve these. However, the latter objective requires less discussion with the employee as the information required to identify 'high flyers' can perhaps be more readily obtained from other sources.

Designing a Scheme

When designing the scheme, early consideration must be given to the categories of staff which it is appropriate to include and whether it will be necessary to incorporate different aims and procedures as a result. Some organisations only include white-collar staff in their scheme, or white-collar staff between certain levels.

Acceptability of scheme

The scheme must be designed to suit the needs of the organisation and must have the full support of senior management. It must also be acceptable to line managers, employees and the trade unions, if appropriate. Trade unions have a traditional mistrust of appraisal schemes as they feel it allows scope for management to show favouritism. To achieve acceptability the scheme must be fully explained to all parties, training must be given to the managers involved, and the system should be designed to involve a minimum of bureaucracy.

Performance and Reward

If a decisions has been taken that pay increases will in some way be linked with an assessment of performance rather than using an incremental payment scheme, then this process should be separate from the process used to help the individual improve their current performance. The reasons for this are set out below:

- A full and frank exchange of views becomes less likely.
- It may be better to link pay with some objective measures rather than a manager's subjective judgement.
- Managers may avoid differentiating between their staff and give everyone the same increase.
- Those disadvantages may at least be minimised by separating the two processes in time and also preferably in paperwork and procedures.

The appraisal interview

This forms the basis of the scheme and is conducted at regular, usually annual, intervals. It is not intended as a substitute for day-to-day management, so feedback, both positive and negative, should be given as appropriate as near as possible to the specific events. Its purpose is to take an overview of the last year's performance and from there plan and appropriate course of action for the future. This is done by taking into account both the needs of the organisation and the personal preferences of the individual.

The interview can be seen as rather threatening by the employee, so care must be taken to ensure a genuine two-way flow of information. If handled well, the employee can leave the interview feeling that there has been an opportunity to discuss in detail their hopes and problems, and feeling that action will be taken to sort out specific issues. On the other hand, if handled badly, the employee may feel resentful because the manager did not listen to the comments and opinions expressed and used the interview as an opportunity to criticise.

Objective setting

The most effective interviews usually involve the evaluation of performance against pre-set targets which had been jointly set by the manager and employee. There may be the disadvantages that the interview concentrates on only a limited part of the job as a result. The main advantage is that results-oriented appraisal is likely to be more impartial and therefore may be more acceptable to the parties involved.

Paperwork

It has already been said that appraisal is a means to an end but, if an organisation produces elaborate documentation, then the completion of the forms themselves is seen as being increasingly significant. If managers are unconvinced about the usefulness of the exercise, or feel uncomfortable about the process, they may conduct the interview at a superficial level in order to complete the form.

Certain basic information will be required, such as the job description for the post, any statements of objectives agreed previously, plus basic human resource information on the employee. In addition, the following types of forms may prove helpful:

- Self-appraisal form: used by the employee prior to the interview to assist them in thinking about their own performance.
- Free written report: either a blank sheet of paper, or including a number of headings, which encourage the managers to comment as they see fit without being over-constrained.
- Comparative rating form: the manager is asked to rate the employee on a number of scales covering different aspects of job performance.
- Combination report: this combines rating scales with an opportunity for more descriptive comment.

Whichever forms are used, simplicity in design and ease of use are vital factors to be considered.

Employee Rewards

The notion of 'reward' includes both financial and non financial benefits which are given to the employee. The financial rewards include basic pay, commission, overtime, and bonuses. However, some organisations also provide other benefits, sometimes known as indirect pay, in the form of pensions, life assurance, health assurance, and subsidised loans. Annual holidays are not strictly remuneration but are also regarded as a benefit Non-financial benefits may include recognition as an 'employee of the month', or the opportunity to attend training courses.

An employee reward system 'consists of an organisation's integrated policies, processes and practices for rewarding its employees in accordance with their contribution, skill and competence and their market worth'. The purpose of a reward system is to attract, retain and motivate staff, and its success can be measured by how well it achieves these things. Both the employer and the employee have different requirements from a reward system and sometimes these may in conflict with each other. The employer will, in general, want to minimise the expenditure on wages, whilst the employee will want to maximise their earnings. The employer will want as much work as possible, at the appropriate quality, while the employee will want stable earnings. The employee will want to feel they receive a 'fair' reward for their efforts compared with other people in the organisation and with similar jobs outside.

The level of pay in any organisation is determined by a combination of a number of factors. These include the external value of the job as determined by market forces, the comparative value of jobs within the organisation, sometimes determined by job evaluation, the value of the person as measured by performance appraisal or other measures and , in some cases, the influence which can be exerted by trade unions. There is generally believed to be a certain balance between supply and demand so that people who have skills which are in short supply will be able to command more than those who have skills which are easily obtained elsewhere. This is one of the reasons why pay is low in the travel in and tourism industry, as many of the jobs require relatively low skills levels and therefore replacement staff can be found easily.

A number of people in the industry receive a form of bonus or commission dependent upon the sales which they receive. This can take a number of forms, such as $X per booking or passenger, or the opportunity for top sales people to 'win' a holiday. It can also take the form of a bonus paid to everyday depending on the sales or profit made by the whole organisation. The idea is to relate the efforts of the worker or the team of workers to a reward. The major variable is the ratio of effort to earnings: in some schemes this is set so very little effort can produce proportionately high earnings whereas in others a lot of effort can produce a small increase in pay.

The human resource management approach would look at the extent to which the payment system matches other parts of the overall human resource strategy and the extent to which it contributes to the overall corporate strategy. For example, an organisation which was trying to provide a high quality service should not have a payment system which only rewarded the quantity of output. Alternatively, an organisation should not only reward individual achievement if the employees need to work together as a team in order to perform the job effectively.

The reward system is a very powerful expression of what the organisation values and is prepared to pay for and it plays a significant part in the communication of the organisation's values, performance, standards and expectations.

6

Law and Tourism

Introduction

This chapter is divided into two sections. the first describes briefly the English legal system and is intended to provide a basic understanding of the legal framework within which the travel industry must operate. The second gives a broad outline of some of the most important areas of law that are of particular relevance to the package travel industry.

The English Legal System

The purpose of this first section is to explain the sources of English law and, in particular; to differentiate between civil and criminal law. In other words, it explains where laws come from and the different kinds of law that exist.

Sources of law

Broadly speaking, there are two sources of law in England—legislation and case law. Legislation is law made by Parliament and is the collective name for what are also known as Acts of Parliament or statutes. Case law is law made by the courts and is also known as the common law or judicial precedent.

(a) Legislation

An act of Parliament, or a statute, is a law which has been passed by Parliament after being subjected to a rigorous scrutiny by both the House of Commons and the House of Lords (often after an equally rigorous consultation process outside Parliament). This process includes a formal introduction into one House by means of a first reading of what is then known as bill. Then there is a full scale debate on the merits of the bill during the second reading. After the second reading the bill goes through the committee stage where it is looked at in some detail—often clause by clause. Finally, it is returned to the floor of the House where, after a report stage, it receives its third reading. Then the bill is sent to the other House where it undergoes a similar process. If it survives all this it then receives the royal assent and becomes law.

Parliament only has time to deal with about 70 or 80 new statutes a year. Examples of statutes passed in recent years that have had a direct bearing on the regulation of the travel industry include the Trade Descriptions Act 1968, which concerns false trade descriptions, and the Consumer Protection Act 1987, which is about misleading price indications. Further examples are the Unfair Contract Terms Act 1977 and the Misrepresentation Act 1967.

(*b*) Delegated legislation

Apart from Acts of Parliament, another very important form of legislation is delegated legislation. For a variety of reasons, including lack of time, lack of technical expertise of the need for speed, Parliament often delegates the making of legislation to an inferior body-usually a minister but sometimes a local authority. Much law is therefore made without proper Parliamentary consideration and is usually done by way of an enabling Act—an Act of Parliament which contains a power enabling a minister, or whoever, to make delegated legislation.

One example of delegated legislation of direct relevance to the travel industry is the Civil Aviation (Air Travel Organisers' Licensing) Regulations 1995, otherwise known as the ATOL Regulations. These Regulations provide that tour operators who offer air-inclu-sive package holidays must be licensed and boned by the CAA. Although they were first passed in 1972 they have been amended on a number of occasions. However, the most important example of delegated legislation relevant to the travel industry is the Package Travel, Package Holidays and Package Tours Regulations 1992. In this instance, the enabling Act is the European Communities Act 1972 which was passed when the UK joined the EEC and provides that European legislation can be enacted in the UK by means of delegated legislation. This was how the EC Directive on Package Travel, Package Holidays and Package Tours 1990 became part of English law.

(c) European legislation

Increasingly, much English law comes from Brussels rather than Westminster and it is necessary, therefore, to give a brief explanation of the types of legislation that we are subject to as members of the European Union.

(i) **Treaties:** The European Community Treaty (the Treaty of Rome), as amended by Treaty on European Union (the Maastricht Treaty) and the Treaty of Amsterdam, are all primary sources of European law and are directly applicable in the UK by virtue of the European Communities Act 1972 s.2(2). This means that they create rights in English law without the necessity for legislation by *Parliament.*

(ii) **Secondary sources:** These include Directives which in general are not directly applicable in the UK unless Parliament gives effect to them by statute or delegated legislation. As explained above this is how the Package Travel Regulations came into being. Regulations are a form of European legislation which, in general, are directly applicable.

Occasionally, European secondary sources of law are regarded as being directly applicable without Parliament having implemented them by means of domestic legislation. For instance, if the UK had not complied with its European obligations by bringing the Package Travel Directive in force by 31 December, 1992, the Directive would nevertheless have been directly applicable in the UK. What this means is that a UK citizen who was adversely affected by the failure of the UK government to bring the EC Directive into force could *sue the government* for the losses caused by the failure. Thus, if a tour operator had become insolvent before the Government had implemented the requirements about security, the consumers harmed by this failure could claim compensation from the Government. This situation actually arose in Germany in 1993, as illustrated by the following case.

Dillenkofer and others v Germany. A German tour operator became bankrupt before the German government had implemented the Directive. German consumers who lost out as a result sued the German government to recover their money. The European Court of Justice held they were entitled to be compensated by the government which had failed to implement those provisions of the Directive which would have protected consumers in the event of a tour operator's insolvency.

Note that the Directive is directly applicable against the state - known as vertical applicability - but it does not create rights as between individuals (horizontal applicability).

(d) Case Law

A large part of English law is to be found not in statues but in case law—decisions made by the judges in individual cases which create *precedents* which are then *followed* by other judges. A system of *binding precedent* (otherwise known as stare decisis) has evolved, whereby once a court has decided a case then the rule or principle that it establishes is binding in later cases. The rule that the case establishes is also known as *ratio decidendi*—the reasons for the decision. The judge in a subsequent case has no choice in the matter, he *must* follow the previous *ratio* no matter how much he disagrees with it. The reason for this is to establish consistency in the law. If a judge could decide a case according to whatever principles he chose then it would be difficult for anyone to know where they stood in any particular situation.

It could be argued that a disadvantage of such as system is that lacks flexibility and, consequently, the law is unable to grow or adapt to changing circumstances and unjust decisions are perpetuated. However, the system in general does posses sufficient flexibility to overcome the problems of excessive rigidity. Firstly, it is possible for a court higher up in the hierarchy of courts to *overrule* a previous decision of a lower court. For instance, the Court of Appeal can overrule decisions of the High Court, and the House of Lords can overrule decisions of the Court of Appeal. (A case is *overruled* when a court in a later case decides that the ratio of the first case is wrong. A case is *reversed* when a court to which that case is appealed decides that the decision of the lower court was wrong.) Note that it is higher courts that bind lower courts, not *vice-versa.*

Secondly, a subsequent court can *distinguish* the decision of a previous court and refuse to follow it. To distinguish a previous case is not to disagree with the principle or rule that it lays down but simply to say that the sufficiently different to justify coming to a decision which is not based on that principle. For example, the case of *Jarvis v Swans Tours* [1973] 1 All ER 71 establishes that in holiday cases a plaintiff is entitled to damages for distress and disappointment. But how far does this principle extend? *Hayes v Dodd* [1990] 2 All ER 815 decided that, where a contract is not for the purpose of providing peace of mind or freedom from distress, damages for distress and disappointment are not recoverable. So what about a 'flight-only' contract to a holiday destination? Is this to be decided according to *Jarvis* or *Hayes?* It would be possible for a judge, if he so wished, to distinguish the facts of such a case from either *Jarvis* or *Hayes* - giving him the freedom to decide the case as he saw fit. This would not require him to ignore or overrule these decisions—merely to say that the factual situation he is dealing with does not fit comfortably within the principles established by those cases and therefore need not be followed. One County Court case does address just this issue.

Lucas v Avro [1994] CLY 1444. The plaintiff had bought 'flight-only' tickets from the defendants. The return flight returned almost 24 hours later than the plaintiff expected because of a mistake on the ticket. Avro admitted breach of contract and paid damages of £165 for hotel, taxi and telephone expenses and loss of earnings. However, the plaintiff also claimed damages for distress and disappointment. It was held that, as the contract was not one to provide either freedom from distress or to provide peace of mind, such damages were not recoverable.

It remains to be seen whether the reasoning in this case will be adopted by the higher courts.

Finally, it is possible, if all else fails, for legislation to be passed to overrule inconvenient or unjust precedents. This is effectively what the Package Travel Regulations have done to large parts of the common law relating to package holidays. For instance the decision in *Wall v Silver Wing Surface Arrangements* (1981, unreported), a High Court decision which was followed in a number of County Court cases, laid down that a tour operator was not liable to clients who were injured on holiday by the negligence of the hotel they were booked into. Now, Regulation 15 of the Package Travel Regulations provides that a tour operator is responsible for the negligence of suppliers.

Civil and criminal law

Broadly speaking, the criminal law is concerned with offences that are regarded as being sufficiently serious or anti-social that, when they occur, the state should intervene to maintain order to protect citizens who may be unable or unwilling to protect themselves. This intervention will usually take the form of an individual being prosecuted by the State in a criminal court and, if the *defendant* is found *guilty*, then *punishment* such as a fine or imprisonment will be imposed. This clearly applies to 'traditional' crimes such as murder, manslaughter, arson, rape or theft, but the criminal courts also deal with large numbers of 'regulatory' offences, such as parking on double yellow lines or failing to label the contents of processed food properly. These are not criminal offences in the traditional sense but, in order to regulate a complex modern society, it has become necessary to categorise such activities as criminal and to impose criminal penalties simply in order to ensure that the traffic on our roads can flow freely or we can eat food confident in the knowledge that it is properly labelled.

A number of statutes that impact heavily on the travel industry fall into this latter category, including the Trade Descriptions Act 1968, the Consumer Protection Act 1987 and many of the provisions in the Package Travel Regulations 1992 relating to the provision of information. Lord Scarman has said of the Trade Descriptions Act:

> "....it is not a truly criminal statute. Its purpose is not the enforcement of the criminal law but the maintenance of trading standards. Training standards, not criminal behaviour are its concern.".

The civil law, on the other hand, is largely concerned with disputes between individuals. Two of the most important areas of civil law are contract law and the law of torts, in which the dispute will often resolve itself into a situation where a *claimant,* formerly called a *plaintiff* (the person with the grievance) is *suing a defendant* in a civil court. If the defendant is found *liable,* then the will endeavour to find a *remedy* - usually financial compensation called *damages* but, occasionally, an *injunction* or an award of specific *performance.*

Frequently, the same set of facts can give rise to both criminal and civil liability. For example, if a tour operator describes a hotel in a misleading fashion, such as stating that the hotel has a children's swimming pool when it doesn't this may give rise to a criminal prosecution under s.14 of the Trade Descriptions Act 1968 or Regulation 5 of the Package Travel Regulations. It may also give rise to a civil action for breach of contract or misrepresentation. If the misrepresentation was deliberate, then this amounts to the tort of deceit. The tour operator may end up paying both a hefty fine for the criminal offence and substantial damages for the civil liability.

Package Travel Law

Building upon the overview of the English legal system, this second looks at those aspects of the law, both civil and criminal, that have most bearing on the package travel industry. More specifically, it considers, those parts of the law that govern the relationship between tour operations and their clients. Some of this law, such as the of contract, is of general application in that it applies to all business but some, such as the Package Travel Regulations 1992, is specifically aimed at the travel industry.

This section covers four main areas:

- The civil liability of tour operators as defined by the Package Travel Regulations (PTR).
- The law of contract and its relation to the Package Travel Regulations 1992.
- Tour operators' criminal liability under the Package Travel Regulations, the Trade Descriptions Act 1968 and the Consumer Protection Act 1987.
- The protection the law gives to consumers when their tour operator becomes insolvent.

The liability of hotels, airlines, railways, ferry operators, coach operators and other travel industry business who do no come within the ambit of the Package Travel Regulations are not covered here as they fall outside the scope of this chapter.

Civil liability: the Package Travel Regulations 1992

Scope of the Regulations

The purpose of the Regulations is to regulate conventional package holidays, such as two weeks of sun, sea and sand in the Mediterranean and other similar arrangements. On this everyone is agreed but, unfortunately, the scope of the definition of a 'package' in Regulation 2 is so wide that it goes far beyond conventional package holidays. There is an amazing variety of travel and holiday arrangements over which fierce arguments rage about their inclusion in the definition of package, such as overnight ferry tips to the continent; business travel; holiday camps and caravan sites; 'tailor-made' packages put together by travel agents; sleeper accommodation on the newly privatised railways; holidays provided by local authority social services departments for their pensioners; and activity holidays provided by schools or local education authorities. Interestingly, the Association of British Travel Agents (ABTA), the main trade association, has issued guidelines on the scope of the Regulations which disagree fundamentally on the extent of the definition.

We are concerned here with examining the scope of the definitions in the Regulations with a view to determining what falls within the Regulations and is subject to its regime and what falls outside and remains regulated solely by the common law.

(i) The definition of 'package'

The Regulations define 'package' in the following manner:

> 2(1) *'Package' means the pre-arranged combination of at least two of the following components when sold or offered for sale at an inclusive price and when the service covers a period of more than twenty-four hours or includes overnight accomodation:*
>
> (a) transport;
>
> (b) accomodation;
>
> (c) other tourist services not ancillary to transport or accomodation and accounting for a significant proportion of the package. and
>
> (ii) the submission of separate accounts for different components shall not cause the arrangements to be other than a package;
>
> (iii) the fact that a combination is arranged at the request of the consumer and in accordance with his specific instructions (whether modified or not) shall not of itself cause it to be treated as other than pre-arranged.

Thus, for there to be a package there has to be :

- a pre-arranged combination
- sold at an inclusive price
- consisting of two of the following:
  — transport
  — accomodation
  — other tourist services

At the margins, all these terms cause difficulties. For instance, is a 'fly drive' package caught by the Regulations because it is only two forms of transport? Or what about package put together by travel agents? Are they 'pre-arranged' combinations? Does the term 'other tourist services' include services for businessmen? Despite the fact that the Regulations are now several years old, many fundamental questions like this remain unanswered. However, the vast majority of holidays sold by major tour operators, like Thomson, Airtours, JMC and First Choice, undoubtedly fall within the Regulations.

(ii) Upon whom is liability imposed?

The regulations impose liability on 'the organiser' and 'the retailer'.

1. The Organiser

> *2(1) 'Organiser' means a person who, otherwise than occasionally, organises packages and sells or offers them for sale, whether directly or through a retailer.*

The test here is how frequently the organiser arranges packages, not, as in other consumer protection legislation. whether the organiser acts in the course of a business. The definition will clearly catch conventional tour operators but, importantly, it will also catch most travel agents in its net. If 'tailor-made packages' are regarded as 'pre-arranged', then it will be very rare indeed that a travel agent can say that he does not 'otherwise than occasionally' put a package together. In this context it is important to note that the term organiser cuts across the more conventional terms of principle and agent. That is, to be an organiser it is not necessary to be a principle and, by the same token, an agent is not precluded from being an organiser simply because he is an agent; the criterion is whether a person 'organises' a package, not whether they act as principal.

The chief significance of being labelled an organiser is that the liabilities are much greater that those of a retailer. The organiser is responsible for the performance of the whole package but the retailer's liabilities are much more narrowly defined. There are also additional criminal offences for organisers to fall foul of.

2. The retailer

2.(1) 'Retailer' means the person who sells or offers for sale the package put together by the organiser.

The definition clearly covers the activities of travel agents. Under the Directive, member states had the option of imposing liability on either organisers or retailers or both for failures in the package itself. It is generally believed that the Regulations do not impose such extensive liabilities on retailers but they do make them subject to the provision of information regime (Reg. 5 and possibly also Regs 7 and 8) and they incur civil liability under Reg. 4 for providing misleading descriptive matter. However a recent case has imposed liability on a travel agent.

Hone v Going Places (2001, Court of Appeal). The claimant, who was on a package holiday, was injured during an emergency evacuation of an aeroplane following a bomb scare . Both the tour operator which organised the holiday and the airline which provided the flights were bankrupt and not worth suing so the claimant sued the travel agent through whom the holiday had been purchased. During the purchase of the holiday the travel had not made it clear that they were only acting as an agent for the tour operator; they had given the impression that they were the principles selling the holiday. The Court of Appeal held that they would be treated as 'organisers' because they had held themselves out as such. (Note that although the travel agents could be sued as organisers they were ultimately not liable because the court said that there was no failure to take reasonable care of the claimant.)

As previously stated, a travel agent who puts a package together and sells it in his own name falls within the definition of organiser rather than retailer and is, therefore, subject to the more stringent liabilities in the Regulations. Similarly, the agent who packages extra elements with a conventional packages is likely to be classified as an organiser rather than a retailer.

(iii) In whose favour is the liability imposed?

The Regulations impose civil liability on the organiser and, in some cases, the retailer, in favour of 'consumers'.

> *2(2) ... 'consumer' means the person who takes or agrees to take the package ('the principal contractor) and elsewhere in these Regulations 'consumer' means, as the context requires, the principal contractor, any person on whose behalf the principal contractor agrees to purchase the package ('the other beneficiaries') or any person to whom the principal contractor or any of the other beneficiaries transfers the package ('the transferee')*

Traditionally in English Law, only a party to a contract is entitled to take the benefit of it. In other words, there have been doubts as to the extent to which members of a client's family who are named on the booking form but who may not be party to the contract would be entitled to the benefits of the contract. All 92 and *Wooder v wimpey* [1980] 1 All ER 571. The problem also extends to members of a party where one person has made the booking on behalf of others.

However, the definition of 'consumer' in the Regulations, making what amounts to a revolutionary change to a long established rule of English law (which still applies to all but package holiday contracts) goes some way to eliminating these problems. Furthermore, if a consumer transfers his booking to another person, as he is sometimes entitled to do now under Regulation 10, the transferee stands in the same position as the original consumer.

Contract

(a) Making the contract

A contract can be defined as a *legally binding agreement.* Legally binding simply means that it is an agreement recognised by the law which can be enforced if necessary by the courts. Briefly, the elements of an enforceable contract are that:

- the parties have come to an agreement;
- the agreements is intendent to be legally binding;
- each party has provided the other with consideration;
- the contract is in the right form; and
- the parties each have the legal capacity to make the contract.

Apart from the first of these requirements, we can dispose of the other elements briefly because they do not cause much problem in holiday contracts. However, it is important to look at how agreement is arrived at in more detail.

Intention: as far as intention to create legal relations is concerned, in general most commercial transactions are intended to be legally binding and certainly a contract between and individual and a tour operator for the provision of a holiday would be enforceable.

Consideration: consideration means that each party has given something or done something of value for the other. Consideration is the price one party pays to enforce the promise that the other party has made. So, in a holiday contract, the consideration provided by the consumer is the price he pays, or promises to pay, for the holiday. The tour operator's consideration is his promise to provide the holiday in exchange for the price.

Capacity: if a party does not have the legal capacity to make a contract, it is not binding on him. Persons falling into this category would be drunks, the insane and minors. The former two categories are of marginal legal importance and as for minors they do not in practice create problems for tour operators.

Form: some contracts must be in the right form. As far as package holiday contracts are concerned, the Package Travel Regulations 1992 provide in Regulation 9 that all the terms of a contract must be reduced to writing and a copy given to the consumer before the contract is made, unless this is impracticable. Even where it is impracticable to do it before the contract is made, a copy must be provided to the consumer in every case. If this is not done, the consumer has the right to cancel the contract.

Offer and acceptance

Turning now to *agreement,* before there can be a legally binding contract the parties must have reached an agreement. Lawyers break down the process of agreement into two parts. One of the parties must have made an *offer* to the other party which the other party has *accepted.* An offer can be defined as a statement by one party he is prepared to be bound by the terms of his offer if the other party accepts his offer. An acceptance is an unquivocal agreement to the terms of the offer. An offer must be distinguished from an *invitation* to treat. An invitation to treat is where a party sets the ball rolling by indicating that he is prepared to consider offers from the other party. In other words, he is not yet prepared to commit himself to making a firm offer but he wishes to enter into negotiations. In a package holiday context, the tour operator usually makes an invitation to treat when he publishes his brochure. In effect, he is saying that he has holidays available for sale and if members of the public come forward and make an offer to buy a holiday then the tour operator may then accept the offer.

In this process of offer and acceptance, there are a number of other rules:

- an offer can be withdrawn at any time before it is accepted but the withdrawal of the offer must be communicated to the other party before it is effective.
- an offer will lapse after a stated time, or after a reasonable timer or after it has been rejected.
- a counter offer amounts to a refusal to the offer, which then lapses.

- silence does not amount to consent; for example, the statement 'I will assume we have a contract unless I hear to the contrary' will not bind the other party, even if they do not reply.

(b) The contents of the contract

As part of the bargaining process, before a contract is concluded the two parties will make a variety of statements to each other, either orally or in writing. Some of these statements may end up as part of the contract and some may not, and those which end up as part of the contract may vary in importance. This section is concerned with how to classify these statements. It is important to be able to do this because the rights of the parties clearly depend upon whether a statement is part of the contract or not, and if it is, the relative importance to be attached to it.

(i) Terms, representations and mere puffs

The task of classification is complicated by the fact that English law distinguishes between three different types of statement. Firstly, there are those statements which end up as *terms of the contract* which, if broken, give the victim a straightforward action for *breach of contract.* These are the things which the other party has promised you will get. In a package holiday context, it will be a term of the contract, for instance, that it is a four state hotel, that the clients will get a balcony and private facilities, that there are three pools and two bars, that it has a children's club, and so on. Generally, these are all statements which are printed in the brochure and are what the operator has *contracted* to provide.

Secondly, there are statements which *induce* the other party to enter into the contract but do not become terms of the contract. These are known as *representations* and, if they are *false,* they give rise to an action for *misrepresentation.* An action for misrepresentation is not as straightforward as an action for breach of contract and the remedies available may be inadequate in some circumstances. Often it is difficult to distinguish between a term and a representation but, for example, it would probably only be a representation if an operator, having described the hotel, then went on to describe the resort as having a 'wide range of shops'. The operator is contracting to provide an hotel with particular facilities but then, in order to encourage the client to enter into the contract, he makes other statements which will influence the client's decision but which do not form part of the contract. If the resort turns out not to have a wide range of shops, the client can sue for misrepresentation but not for breach of contract.

Thirdly, there are statements which have no legal force at all. These are known as 'puffs' or 'mere puffs' and a victim of such a statement has no redress at all. In one case, *Hoffman v Intasun (1990,* High Court, Unreported), the plaintiff tried to make out that because of the extravagantly worded statements made at the beginning of 'Club 18-30' brochure, the defendants, Intasun, had *contracted* that they owed her an especially high standard of care. The judge rejected this approach. He decided that the satements had no contractual effect at all. This is what he said:

> "I am asked to say that because of the advertising—what lawyers call "puff"—in the early part of the brochure, the Defendants were undertaking to give an especially high standard of care. That is an argument that I reject. Puff is Puff, and if that is what lawyers call it, lay people have their own expressions for it which are perhaps less flattering. Everybody knows that travel agents (sic) set out to create an atmosphere on paper of a wonderful holiday and marvellous value for money. It cannot possibly be said that a visitor to the Tyrol can sue the travel company for breach of contract if he fails to have any respiratory defect in regarding the breathtaking views of the mountains there - and so on. I look for example at how the Club reps are described on page 8 of the brochure. Mr Eccles (counsel for Intasun) in his opening drew my attention to it specifically saying that the reps were the life and soul of the party, hard working, good timing, trouble shooting, guitar playing, beach partying, smooth operators. I do not know if Miss Gail Tarburn [the Intasun rep] can even play the guitar and I am certain that it could not form any part of a breach of contract if she cannot."

Much of the advertising hype that goes into the front of brochures falls into this category, with satements that make the holiday sound good but do not amount to specific contractual promises. Examples are to be found in most borchures—'picturesque villages set amidst glorious scenery'—'quality hotels'—'the number one choice for families'—'the holiday of a lifetime'—'the most beautiful locations around the Mediterranean'—'hand picked accommodation'—'a luxury cruise around the glittering Caribbean', and so on.

Thus, not only do terms have to be distinguished from representations, they both have to be distinguished from mere puffs.

(ii) Conditions, warranties and innominate terms

Terms can be classifieds into either *conditions or warranties.* A condition is a major term of the contract which if broken provides the victim of the breach with not only a right to damages but also the right, if they wish, to terminate the contract altogether. A warranty, on the other hand, only gives rise to an action for damages. There is no right to terminate the contract for what is regarded as a breach of a minor term of the contract. There is also an intermediate form of term - called an *innominate* term - which cannot immediately be classified as either a condition or a warranty. Its classification depends upon the nature and severity of the breach.

(iii) Express and implied terms

Terms can be further classified into *express terms* and *implied* terms. An express term, as its name suggests, is one which is expressed in some way, either in writing or orally. An implied term is one where the term is not expressed but can nevertheless be implied into the contract. Terms can be implied either *in fact* or *in law.* The following travel law case, decided before the Package Travel Regulations were passed, revolved around the issue of implied terms and illustrates the problem vividly.

Wall v Silver Wing Surface Arrangements (1981, Unreported), A party of holidaymakers were injured in a hotel fire in Tenerife. They had been unable to escape down the fire escape because the hotel owners had padlocked the gate at the bottom. In the contract between the clients and the tour operators nothing was expressly stated about safety at the hotel but the clients alleged that there was an implied term in the contract that they would be reasonably safe in using the hotel for the purposes for which they had been invited to be there. Ultimately the court held that there was no such term but it had to make a difficult choice between protecting the interests of the clients by implying a term relating to their safety and the interests of the tour operator by not extending its liability to all the components of the package.

(iv) The Package Travel Regulations and the Classification of Terms

The classification of terms in a package holiday contract is no longer simply a matter for the common law, but is heavily affected by the Package Travel Regulations. For instance, Reg. 6 states that all the particulars in the brochure (whatever that means) are implied warranties. On the face of it this has two major effects. Firstly, it potentially upgrades just about every statement in the brochure to at least a term of the contract - representations and puffs alike. Secondly, it appears to classify all statements as minor terms of the contract.

As far as this second effect is concerned, closer examination of the Regulations shows that this is not entirely so. For instance, Regulation 9 explicitly states that it is an implied *condition* that certain information must be supplied to the consumer before the contract is made. In addition, there are other regulations which have the same effect. Reg. 12 permits a consumer to withdraw from the contract if significant alterations have been made to the contract before departure and Reg. 14 effectively gives the consumer the right to terminate a contract if, atter departure, a significant proportion of the services cannot be provided.

(v) Exclusion clauses

One very important type of term, which will be looked at in more detail in a subsequent section, is the exclusion clause—also known as an exemption clause or an exception clause. These are clauses where one party to the contract endeavours to escape liability for breach of contract by inserting a clause into the contract excluding his liability.

(vi) Liability under Regulation 15

Until 1992, the position at common law was that tour operators were not liable for the defaults or negligence of their subcontractors (or suppliers as they are often called). This was the issue which was at the heart of the *Wall* case referred to above. Although it had been the fault of the hotelkeeper that the fire escape gate had been padlocked, no blame could be attributed to the tour operator in the case. On the contrary, the judge said that the tour operator was a reputable company that had acted properly throughout. It had selected a modern hotel and monitored it for safely and there was nothing more that could reasonably be expected of them.

In practice, this approach meant that because most of a package is made up of elements subcontracted to others—airlines and hotels—much of what went wrong with a package could not be made the legal responsibility of the tour operator. This often left clients either without a remedy or the difficult task of suing a foreign hotel or airline. However, regulation 15 of the PTR changes all that. It provides:

> 15*(1) The other party to the contract is liable to the consumer for the proper performance for the obligations under the contract, irrespective of whether such obligations are to be performed by that other party or by other suppliers of services but this shall not affect any remedy or right of action which that other party may have against those other suppliers of services.*
>
> *15(2) The other party to the contract is liable to the consumer for any damage caused to him by the failure to perform the contract or the improper performance of the*

contract unless the failure or the improper performance is due neither to any fault of that other party nor to that of another supplier of services, because :

(a) the failures which occur in the performance of the contract are attributable to the consumer
(b) such failures are attributable to a third party unconnected with the provision of the services contracted for, and are unforeseeable or unavoidable, or
(c) such failures are due to :
   (i) unusual and unforeseeable circumstances beyond the control of the party by whom this exception is pleaded, the consequences of which could not have been avoided even if all due care had been exercised;

   or

   (ii) an event which the other party to the contract or the supplier of services, even with all due care, could not foresee or forestall.

The effect of this is that if part of what the tour operator has promised to the client is to be performed by subcontractors, the tour operator is nevertheless held responsible if things go wrong unless he can prove one of four things:

- It was the consumer's own fault.
- It was the fault of a third party unconnected with the contract.
- It was caused by *force majeure.*
- It was caused by some other event which the tour operator couldn't predict or avoid.

(c) Misrepresentation

In the previous section, we saw that some pre-contractual statements did not become terms of the contract but were only *representations.* If these representations turn out to be false. Then the victim may have an action misrepresentation. To succeed in an action for misrepresentation it must be established that:

- One party to the contract
- Made a false statement of fact

- To the other party to the contract
- Which induced the other party to the contract to enter into it

Statement of fact

Statements of opinion, or intention, or statements as to the future are not statements of fact and are therefore not actionable. Thus, if a tour operator prints in his brochure a statement that all clients will be accommodated in twin rooms with ensuite bathrooms and he fully intends to fulfil this promise (and has contracts with hotels to substantiate his statement), then he cannot be sued for misrepresentation if, for instance, the hotelier lets him down and his clients are all accommodated in single rooms with no bathrooms. At the time the statement was made it was neither true nor false, merely a statement of intention. It would be different, however, if the tour operator had never intended to fulfil his promise. In those circumstances, he would be making a false statement (albeit implied) about his intention to fulfil the contract. In the words of one judge "The state of a man's mind is as much a fact as the state of his digestion."

Inducing the contract

The victim of the misrepresentation only has a remedy if he can show that the statement induced the contract. If the statement had no effect upon his decision to make the contract, it is not actionable. Thus, if an 85 year old booked a holiday at an hotel where the tour operator's brochure indicated that water sports were available, when in fact they were not, he would not be able to claim for misrepresentation unless he could show that the statement influenced him to book the holiday—which seems most unlikely.

(i) Types of misrepresentation

Once it has been established that a misrepresentation has been made, it is necessary to determine what type of misrepresentation it is. This is because the remedies for misrepresentation are determined according to the type of misrepresentation. There are three types of misrepresentation.

- *Fraudulent misrepresentation*—where the representor made the statement knowing it was false or was reckless as to its truth.
- *Negligent misrepresentation*—where the representor made the statement honestly believing it to be true but reasonable grounds for that belief.
- *Innocent misrepresentation*—where the representor made the statement honestly believing it to be true and having reasonable grounds for that belief.

Putting it more broadly, the difference between the three types depends on whether the person making the statement acted carelessly or innocently.

(ii) Remedies for misrepresentation

There are two remedies for misrepresentation, damages and rescission. Rescission is a drastic remedy which involves calling the contract off altogether and restoring the parties to the position they were in before the contract was concluded. It is available for all types of misrepresentation automatically but can be lost in certain circumstances, such as by lapse of time, by affirmation or if the parties cannot be restored to their original position because for instance the subject matter of the contract has been consumed. This would apply in a holiday case if the clients only discovered the misrepresentation when they arrived in resort.

For fraudulent misrepresentation, damages are awarded at common law because a fraudulent misrepresentation amounts to the tort of decit. For negligent misrepresentation damages are awarded under s.2(1) of the Misrepresentation Act 1967. There is no right to damages for innocent misrepresentation except in one case. Under s.2(2) of the Misrepresentation Act the court has a discretion to award damages in lieu of rescission if it thinks it just to do so. Thus, if a represented has a right to rescind the contract for innocent misrepresentation, he may be awarded damages instead—but only if he has not lost his right to rescind for other reason, such as lapse of time.

(d) Regulation 4

Regulation 4 creates a statutory right to compensation for the consumer that cuts across the traditional boundaries of the common law. It imposes civil liability on both organisers and retailers if they supply misleading information. It states:

> *4(1) No organiser or retailer shall supply to a consumer any descriptive matter concerning a package, the price of a package or any other conditions applying to the contract which contains any misleading information.*
> *4(2) If an organiser or retailer is in breach of paragraph (1) he shall be liable to compensate the consumer for any loss which the consumer suffers in consequence.*

There is liability if the plaintiff can show that :

- a tour operator or travel agent,
- supplied,
- to a consumer,
- a brochure,
- that contained misleading descriptive matter,
- concerning a package or its price,
- and the consumer suffers as a consequence.

The liability is imposed for supplying misleading descriptive matter. The implication here is that it will cover written matter but not oral statements. The word *matter* suggests something tangible. It will obviously cover borchures and other brochure-like leaflets and it would most probably extent to videos of holiday destinations. It probably does not extend to window displays or window cards because the requirement is that the matter be supplied to the consumer and it cannot be said that such matter is supplied to the consumer. Press advertisements are a different matter. It is a moot point whether it can be said that the operator or the retailer have supplied the matter. It comes in a paper or journal supplied by a publisher or newsagent.

The other qualification is that liability is only imposed where the consumer, as a result of the misleading information, suffers in consequence. For the consumer to show that as a consequence of the descriptive material he suffered loss, there will have to be some evidence of cause and effect. He will have to show that he relied upon the information, otherwise how can it be said that he suffered loss as a consequence? In this respect, it is similar to an action for misrepresentation.

A significant point is that the travel agent, as well as the tour operator, could incur liability, thus making them strictly liable for brochure errors they might know nothing about - and with no defence. The only way to combat this liability is to ensure that the agency agreements they have with operators contain indemnity clauses. Whether they do may very well be a matter of bargaining power.

(e) Exclusion clauses

In this section, we will look at the extent to which it is possible for a party to exclude his liability for breach of contract. In other words, can a party who is in breach of contract escape liability by relying upon a term in the contract stating that in the event of a branch he will be under no liability?

As far as tour operators are concerned, the legal obstacles that have been created mean that, for all practical purposes, they are unable to exclude their liability to consumers and can only limit their liability in very restricted circumstances. Both the common law and statute have combined to produce this situation.

(i) Common law

Although the judges bulked at striking out exclusion clauses simply on the grounds that they were unreasonable, they nevertheless created a number of hurdles before an exclusion clause could be relied upon.

Notice: for an exclusion clause to be effective it has to be incorporated in the contract. Failure to do so means that it cannot be relied upon.

Olley v Marlborough Court Hotel Company [1949] 1 KB 532. A guest had valuables stolen from her room because of the negligence of the hotel. The hotel relied upon an exclusion clause on the bedroom wall to avoid liability. It was held that the contract for the room had been made downstairs at the reception desk at which time the guest had no notice of the exclusion clause. It was held that the clause was ineffective as it had not been incoporated into the contract .

Construction: if the words used by the party trying to escape liability do not cover the kind of breach that occured the clause will not help them.

Spencer v Cosmos, The Times, December 6th, 1989; LEXIS, CA. The plaintiffs had been expelled from their hotel for alleged rowdy behaviour. They sued their tour operator for breach of contract. The tour operator could not prove that the plaintiffs had been rowdy. In their defence they argued that an exclusion clause in their contract protected them even against wrongful expulsions. It was held by the Court of Appeal that "... the clause does not even set out to exclude claims in contact for failure to provide the services comprised in the holiday" and they permitted the plaintiffs' claim.

(ii) The Unfair Contract Terms Act 1977

The Unfair Contract Terms Act 1977 (UCTA) regulates exclusion clauses in most types of contract, not simply holiday contract. It has the effect of making some exclusion clauses void altogether and many others valid only if they can satisfy a reasonableness test. The main provisions are found in sections 2 and 3.

Section 2 provides:

> *2(1) A person cannot by reference to any contract term or to a notice given to persons generally or to particular persons exclude or restrict his liability for death or personal injury resulting from negligence.*
>
> *2(2) In the case of other loss or damage, a person cannot so exclude or restrict his liability for negligence except in so far as the term or notice satisfies the requirement of reasonableness.*

Thus, if a tour operator negligently causes death or personal injury to a client, this cannot be excluded at all.

Even if the damage is not death or personal injury, for example, loss or damage to baggage, this liability can only be excluded if the tour operator can establish that it would be reasonable to exclude this liability - which might prove difficult.

> *Thompson v LMS* [1930] 1KB 41. The plaintiff was injured when she stepped down from a train which had pulled up short of the platform. The defendants escaped liability because their exclusion clause had been incorporated into the contract by means of a notice on the back of her ticket. The case was decided in 1930. Today, the railway would be found liable because s.2(1) of UCTA would prevent them from relying on an exclusion clause which protected them against negligence causing death or personal injury.

Section 3 provides:

> *3(1) This section applies as between contracting parties where one of them deals as consumer or on the other's written standard terms of business.*
>
> *3(2) As against that party, the other cannot by reference to any contract term -*
>
> *(a) when himself in breach of contract, exclude or restrict any liability of his in respect of the breach, or*
>
> *(b) claim to be entitled -*
>
> *(i) to render a contractual performance substantially different from that which was reasonably expected of him, or*
>
> *(ii) in respect of the whole or any part of his contractual obligation, to render no performance at all, except in so far as (in any of the cases mentioned above in this subsection) the contract term satisfies the requirement of reasonableness.*

A holidaymaker will benefit from the protection of this section if they can demonstrate that :

- either they dealt as consumer, or
- they dealt on the other party's written standard terms of business, and
- they suffered from one of three types of exclusion clause:
  - — one which excludes or restricts the liability of the other party, or

  - one which the other party claims entitles him to offer a substantially different kind of performance, or
  - one which permits the other party not to perform at all, and
- the tour operator cannot prove the term is reasonable.

The first and third types of exclusion clause are relatively straightforward to understand. The second is illustrated by this case:

> *Anglo-Continental Holidays Ltd v Typaldos Lines (London) Ltd.* (1967) 2 LIoyd's Rep. 61. The plaintiffs were travel agents who had booked a party onto the defendant's ship, Atlantica, for a cruise to Israel. With less than two weeks to go, the defendants substituted a much inferior ship, the Angelika, and an equally inferior itinerary. The plaintiffs cancelled the cruise, refunded their clients' money and sued the defendants for breach of contract. The defendants relied on an exclusion clause which stated: "Steamers, Sailing Dates Rates and Itineraries are subject to change without prior notice". The case was decided at common law in favour of the plaintiffs but today it would be decided under UCTA and the decision would probably be the same. The defendant's would not be permitted to substitute an inferior ship and itinerary because this would be substantially different from that which was reasonably expected'.

Deals as consumer: this is further defined in section *12.* It covers persons who do not make the contract in the course of a business contracting with someone who does make it in the course of a business. Thus, it would cover holidaymakers contracting with tour operators but not business who purchase packages. Note that the definition of consumer in this legislation differs from the definition in the PTR and in other consumer protection legislation, such as the Consumer Protection Act 1987, which will be examined later.

Dealing on written standard terms of business: this simply means that the business relying on the exclusion clause uses a standard set of terms and conditions on which to contract. Given that most tour operators have a set of such terms, then most people who contract with them will get the benefit of s.3.

The rationale for both s.2 and s.3 is to offer protection to those classes of contractor who find themselves at a disadvantage or where the ability to negotiate is virtually non-existent-private individuals and those who have to contract on someone else's pre-printed terms and conditions.

(iii) The Package Travel Regulations

The provisions in the PTR relating to exclusion clauses are to be found in Reg. 15. Reg.15(5) contains a blanket prohibition on exclusion clauses.

> *15(5) Without prejudice to paragraph (3) and paragraph (4) above, liability under paragraphs (1) and (2) above cannot be excluded by any contractual term.*

However, there are two major exceptions found in Reg. 15(3) and (4).

Reg. 15(3) provides

> *15(3) In the case of damage arising from the non-performance or improper performance of the services involved in the package, the contract may provide for compensation to be limited in accordance with the international conventions which govern such services.*

There are international conventions covering carriage by air (The Warsaw Convention), carriage by sea (The Athens and London Conventions) and carriage by rail (The Berne Convention). Under these conventions, the carriers are entitled to limit their liability for death and injury and loss or damage to baggage to relatively modest sums. However, under Reg. 15(1) and (2), the tour operator is responsible not only for the actions of themselves but also their suppliers, such as air and sea carriers. The immediate practical effect of this would be that if, say, an airline carrying a tour operator's clients crashed, the airline could limit its liability but the tour operator could not. Thus, the main burden of comprehension would fall on the tour operator rather than the airline, even though it would be the airline that actually caused the crash. To redress the balance, the PTR permits the tour operator to limit his liability in the same way that the airline (or cruise line, or railway) could. Of course, this will only happen if the tour operator incorporates an appropriate term in his contracts. It does not happen automatically.

Reg. 15(4) provides

> *15(4) In the case of damage other than personal injury resulting from the non-performance of improper performance of the services involved in the package, the contract may include a term limiting the amount of compensation which will be paid to the consumer, provided that the limitation is not unreasonable.*

Fortunately, most complaints about package holidays are 'quality' complaints that do not concern death or personal injury. In those circumstances, the PTR permits tour operators to limit their liability to sums which are 'not unreasonable'. Tour operators take advantage of this provision in two different circumstances. Firstly, they often print tables of compensation to cover situations where they make major changes before departure. The compensation offered rises as the date of departure approaches. The amounts vary from operator to operator but often the sums are quite derisory and would quite clearly fail the test, leaving the tour operator exposed to a larger claim. Secondly, there is often a 'catch-all' clause stating that the tour operator limits its liability to a maximum of, say, twice the price of the holiday. Such a sum would, in fact, compensate consumers for all but the most disastrous of holidays and, given that the legislation permits the operator to *limit* his liability (i.e., it envisages that the tour operator will be able to escape paying full compensation in some circumstances), this would probably be regarded as a reasonable sum.

(iv) The Unfair Terms in Consumer Contracts Regulations 1994

Unlike UCTA and the PTR, the Unfair Terms in Consumer Contracts Regulations (UTCCR) cover not only exclusion clauses, but also terms which are simply unfair.

In this respect, the UTCCR is much wider than the other two. For instance, if I promise that you will be accommodated at a four star hotel but insert a clause into the contract saying that I will not be liable to you if you are accommodated in a lower rated hotel then I am *excluding* my liability. On the other hand, if I say that in the event of you wishing to cancel your holiday you must pay 100% cancellation charges no matter how long before departure it is you cancel, then I am not excluding my liability but imposing a term on you which is unfair. The UTCCR covers both type of term but UCTA and the PTR only cover the former.

To gain the protection of the UTCCR it has to be established that

- a consumer
- made a contract with a supplier
- which contained unfair terms
- which were not individually negotiated

Consumer: this term is defined to cover any natural person who makes a contract for purposes that are outside his business (Reg.2(1)). Thus, business and companies are outside the protection offered by the Regulations.

Supplier: this means anyone supplying services in the course of a business (Reg. 2(1)). Tour operators would fall within the ambit of this definition.

Unfair terms: these are terms which contrary to the requirement of good faith cause a significant imbalance in the parties' rights and obligations to the detriment of the consumer (Reg.4(1)).

Individually negotiated: terms which have not been individually negotiated are subject to the Regulations. This correspondents to the requirements in UCTA relating to written standard terms of business.

Illustrative terms: Schedule 3 to the Regulations contains an 'indicative and illustrative' list of terms which may be regarded as unfair. Contained in this list are examples of standard exclusion clauses which would also be caught in most cases by UCTA, but one type of term that is potentially unfair which is listed in the Schedule is a clause 'requiring any consumer who fails to fulfil his obligation to pay a disproportionately high sum in compensation'. Tour operators are in the habit of requiring consumers who cancel their holidays to pay cancellation charges, usually on a sliding scale that rises to 100 per cent as the date of departure nears. Some of these scales might be open to attack under the UTCCR on the grounds that they are disproportionately high.

Consequences of finding a term unfair: if a term is unfair then it is void and the tour operator cannot rely upon it.

The role of the Office of Fair Trading (OFT): the OFT is given powers under the legislation to investigate unfair terms in contracts drawn up for general use and in appropriate cases he may bring an action for an injunction against the person using the term to have it restrained. Currently the OFT is in the process of investigating cancellation clauses in tour operators contracts.

Terms which reflect other legislation: one drawback for consumers wishing to employ the UTCCR against tour operators' contracts is that, under Reg. 3(1) and Schedule 1, the Regulations do not apply where the contract incorporates a term which is there to 'comply with or which reflects' other legislation. However where contract terms go beyond what is permitted in this other legislation the UTCCR can be invoked. The OFT has already used its power to require airlines to amend their standards conditions of carriage where they have not complied with the Warsaw Convention and they have made numerous requests for tour operators to change their terms and conditions.

(f) Remedies

If one party to the contract breaks it, then the other party is entitled to a remedy. The usual remedy in contract is damages, that is, financial compensation designed to put the victim of the breach in the same position as if the contract had been performed (*Robinson v Harman* (1848) 1 Ex 850). However, package holidaymakers also benefit from a range of other remedies created by the PTR which are in addition to damages and are not available in other areas of contract. These include the right to be offered an alternative holiday if, before departure, the tour operator makes a substantial change to the holiday booked, and the right to be repatriated if the tour operator cannot provide what he promised.

(i) Damages

In order to compensate the consumer for breach of contract, three heads of damage are recognised

- Damages for difference in value.
- Consequential loss.
- Damages for distress and disappointment.

Damages for difference in value: where the tour operator has provided a holiday which is worth less than the holiday he contracted to provide, the holidaymaker is entitled to the difference in value. A straightforward example of this principle is the following case.

> *Mcleod v Hunter* [1987] CLY 1162. The tour operator promised a luxurious villa but what they provided was a cramped apartment. The court assessed the difference in value as £439. This was in addition to damages for distress and disappointment.

Consequential loss. when the breach of contract results in the holidaymaker having to expend further sums in order to rectify the breach, damages for consequential loss can be claimed. Sometimes these damages are referred to as out of pocket expenses.

> *Harris v Torchgrove* [1985] CLY 944. The court awarded £40 damages for parking expenses because the promised parking at the apartment was not available and a further £300 for the cost of extra meals taken in restaurants because the apartment had no oven and the fridge was 'eccentric'.

Note that difference in value claims and consequential loss claims cannot be combined to give double compensation. For instance, if a tour operator promises full board but no evening meals are provided, the consumer cannot claim both the difference in value between half board and full board and also the out of pocket expenses for purchasing restaurant meals in the evening.

Damages for distress and disappointment: Holiday contracts are almost unique because in appropriate cases the courts will award damages for distress and disappointment caused by a breach of contract. Such damages are not available generally in the law of contract. The rule was established in the following case.

> *Jarvis v Swans Tours* [1973] 1 All ER 71. The plaintiff booked a holiday in the Tyrol at Christmas. He was promised a 'house-party' atmosphere; 'gemutlichkeit'; fondue parties; yodler evenings; afternoon tea and cakes; etc. The hotel was virtually deserted, the skiing was very restricted, almost none of the services were provided and the hotel proprietor spoke no English. The Court of Appeal awarded the plaintiff £125 damages on a holiday that cost £64. Lord Denning said, "In a proper case damages for mental distress can be recovered in contract ... One such case is a contract for a holiday, or any other contract to provide entertainment and enjoyment. If the contracting party breaks his contract, damages can be given for the disappointment, the distress, the upset and frustration caused by the breach.

The rationale behind the decision is that where the purpose of the contract is to provide peace of mind and enjoyment then such damages can be claimed, but not for everyday commercial transactions where the provision of pleasure is not the essence of the contract.

Mitigation of loss: A victim of a breach of contract cannot simply sit back and collect damages. They must take reasonable steps to mitigate their loss and failure to do so can mean that they will lose their damages. In holiday cases, one of the simplest ways to mitigate your loss is to complain to the tour operator or its representative who may then be able to put things right. Reg. 15(9), in fact, requires tour operators to put a term into their contracts obliging consumers to complain at the earliest opportunity if they have a problem.

> *Czyzewski v Intasun* (1990) County Ct. Unreported. The plaintiff complained of an 'offensive' toilet. After several unsuccessful attempts to repair it the hotel offered him an alternative room but for some reason he declined to take it and remained in his room for the rest of his holiday. The court awarded him only £50 damages based on the limited amount of time he would have had to spend in the room if he had accepted the alternative.

(ii) Remedies for pre-departure changes

Under Regulations 12 and 13, a consumer is entitled to remedies other than damages. These Regulations provide

12 In every contract there are implied terms to the effect that

(a) where the organiser is constrained before the departure to alter significantly an essential term of contract, such as the price (so far as regulation 11 permits him to do so), he will notify the consumer as quickly as possible in order to enable him to take appropriate decisions and in particular to withdraw from the contract without penalty or to accept a rider to the contract specifying the alterations made and their impact on the price; and

(b) the consumer will inform the organiser or the retailer of his decision as soon as possible.

13(1) The terms set out in paragraphs (2) and (3) below are implied in every contract and apply where the consumer withdraws from the contract pursuant to the term in it implied by virtue of regulation 12(a), or where the organiser, for any reason other than the fault of the consumer, cancels the package before the agreed date of departure.

13(2) The consumer is entitled -

(a) to take a substitute package of equivalent or superior quality if the other party to the contract is able to offer him such a substitute; or

(b) to take a substitute package of lower quality if the other party to the contract is able to offer him one and to recover from the organiser the difference in price between the price of the package purchased and that of the substitute package; or

(c) *to have repaid to him as soon as possible all the monies paid by him under the contract.*

13(3) *The consumer is entitled, if appropriate, to be compensated by the organiser for non-performance of the contract except where -*

(a) *the package is cancelled because the number of persons who agree to take it is less than the minimum number required and the consumer is informed of the cancellation, in writing, within the period indicated in the description of the package; or*

(b) *the package is cancelled by reason of unusual and unforeseeable circumstances beyond the control of the party by whom this exception is pleaded, the consequences of which could not have been avoided even if all due care had been exercised.*

Thus, under Regulation 12, if a consumer can establish that a tour operator has

- altered significantly
- an essential term

he has the choice of either

- withdrawing from the contract, or
- accepting the change with a rider to the price.

Presumably, if there is such a major change, then the consumer will withdraw unless the tour operator offers enough by way of compensation. If the consumer does withdraw, or if the operator cancels the holiday for any reason other than the consumer's fault, then the consumer is entitled to the following choices:

- a substitute holiday of equivalent or superior quality, or
- a substitute holiday of inferior quality plus the difference in value, or
- a full refund, and
- compensation, except where the contract was cancelled for *force majeure* or because of lack of minimum numbers.

(iii) Remedies for post-departure changes

where problems arise with the holiday after departure this is dealt with by Reg. 14 which provides

14(1) *The terms set out in paragraphs (2) and (3) below are implied in every contract and apply where, after departure, a significant proportion of the services contracted for is not provided or the organizer becomes aware that he will be unable to procure a significant proportion of the services to be provided.*

14(2) *The organizer will make suitable alternative arrangements, at no extra cost to the consumer, for the continuation of the package and will, where appropriate, compensate the consumer for the difference between the services to be supplied under the contract and those supplied.*

14(3) *If it is impossible to make arrangements as described in paragraph (2), or these are not accepted by the consumer for good reasons, the organizer will, where appropriate, provide the consumer with equivalent transport back to the place of departure or to another place to which the consumer has agreed and will, where appropriate, compensate the consumer.*

Thus, if the consumer can show that

- A significant proportion of the services are not to be provided, or
- The tour operator becomes aware that they cannot be provided the tour operator must,
- Make suitable alternative arrangements for the continuation of the holiday, or
- If it is impossible to make alternative arrangements transport the consumer home again,
- And, in both cases, compensate the consumer where appropriate.

Criminal liability

This section of the chapter is concerned with the criminal offences that a tour operator might commit. There are three pieces of legislation that are relevant, the Trade Descriptions Act 1968 which regulates false trade descriptions, the Consumer Protection Act 1987 which regulates misleading prices, and the Package Travel Regulations which regulate both descriptions and prices. The offences are usually tried in a magistrates' court where the maximum penalty is £5,000 per offence but, in extreme cases, an offence under these provisions could be tried in the Crown Court before jury and the maximum penalty would be an unlimited fine. The offences fall into a category of criminal offence labelled as regulatory offences; that is, they are not concerned with traditional types of criminal behaviour but are intended to improve trading standards.

(a) The Trade Descriptions Act 1968

Section 14 of the TDA sets out two offences:

14(1) It shall be an offence for any person in the course of any trade or business—

(a) to make a statement which he knows to be false; or

(b) recklessly to make a statement which is false;

as to any of the following matters, that is to say—

(i) the provision in the course of any trade or business of any services, accommodation or facilities;

(ii) the nature of any services, accommodation or facilities provided in the course of any trade or business;

(iii) the time at which, manner in which or persons by whom any services accommodation or facilities are so provided;

(iv) the examination, approval or evaluation by any person of any services, accommodation or facilities so provided; or

(v) the location or amenities of any accommodation so provided.

To put it another way, for the prosecution to succeed it must prove that the tour operator:

- made a statement,
- in the course of a business,
- relating to one of the categories in section 14 (for example, the facilities or the accommodation),
- that was false,
- and the statement was made knowingly or recklessly.

In the course of a trade or business: most tour operators, when they sell holidays, are doing so in the course of a trade or business. As with most busines, there will be those who only participate at the margins and there are those who organize holidays for groups of friends and, therefore, questions may be raised as to whether they are acting in the course of a business. However, for most tour operators, this is not an issue.

The statement must fall within the categories listed in section 14: only if a tour operator makes a false statement falling into one of the categories listed in Section 14 can a prosecution succeed. The list, however, is quite comprehensive and most of the statements that a tour operator makes in a brochure would be covered by the list. For instance, *Herron v Lunn Poly* SLT 2 was a prosecution under s.14(1)(b)(i) for a false statement relating to the provisions of any services, accommodation or facilities. That case concerned an hotel and its facilities which were incomplete when the clients arrived. *R v Clarksons* 57 Cr App R 38 was prosecution under both s.14(1)(b)(iii) for a false statement as to the time at which any services are provided. (See also *R v Avro plc* (Court of Appeal, 14th January 1993)).*R v Sunair* 1 WLR 1105, included a count for contravenings. 14(1)(b)(v) relating to the location and amenities of any accommodation provided. The prosecution concerned the non-availability of promised facilities.

The statement must be false: clearly, a statement that the hotel is only 100 metres from the beach when, in fact, it is 500 metres is a false statement and a tour operator would be rightly convicted, but some statements are much more difficult to label as true or false.

> *Thomson Travel Ltd v Roberts* (1984) 148 JP 666. A tour operator published a brochure which described and hotel as having a 'beach'. The so-called beach was man made construction consisting of an area of sand approximately 51 yards long and 17 yards wide retained behind a concrete wall bordering the sea. Access to the sea was the ladders down to water level at which point the depth of the sea was equivalent to the shallow end of a swimming pool. Before it could be decided whether the tour operator had made a false statement about the beach the court had to decide what was meant by the word 'beach'. Only after deciding that what existed at the hotel could not be described as a beach could the court then go on to say that a false statement had been made about a beach.

It has also been held that statements as to future intention are not capable of being either true or false. At the time they are made they are merely promises which may or may not be fulfilled. Given that much of a tour operator's brochure consists of promises as to the future, this has caused some difficulties.

> *Sunair v Dodd* 2 All ER 410. A tour operator published a brochure describing the facilities at an hotel as "all twin-bedded rooms with private bath, shower, WC and terrace". Clients who read the brochure in January 1969 and made a booking on the basis of the brochure description discovered, when they arrived at the hotesl in the summer, that their rooms did not have balconies. At the time the brochure had been published the tour operator had a contract with the hotel for rooms with twin beds and balconies. It was held by the Divisional Court that what the brochure statement meant was that the tour operator was offering to supply rooms with twin beds and balconies and as this was a statement as to future intention it could not be classified as a false statement when it was published. The tour operator was therefore not guilty.

Note, however, that the situation would have been very different if the tour operator had had no contract with the hotel for the rooms described and no intention of providing such rooms. In that case there would have been a false statement—as to the state of mind of the tour operator.

The statement must have been made knowingly or recklessly. To secure a conviction, the prosecution must establish that the statement was made knowingly or recklessly, that is, they must prove a state of mind. In legal terms, they must prove *mens rea* – a guilty mind. Case law, however, has developed to a stage where it can be said that the offence approaches strict liability, that is, liability without fault.

> *Wings v Ellis* AC 272 A tour operator published a brochure which described an hotel as having air-conditioning. This was false but, at the time the brochure

was published, the tour operator did not know this. As soon as they discovered the false description, they issued errata to all existing clients and told all sales staff to bring the false description to the attention of new clients when they booked. Despite these precautions, a client managed to book a holiday without being informed that the hotel had no air-conditioning. Thus, the position was that the tour operator knew that the statement was false but it did not know that the statement was being made. If they had done so, they would have seen to is that the statement was corrected. On appeal to the House of Lords, it was held that *wings* a were tightly convicted. The offence in section 14(1)(a) is to make a statement which we he knows to be false, and this is what *wings* had done. Thus *wings* were convicted even though it might be said that they were not at fault – they were doing their best at the time to avoid committing the offence.

Wings was case under s. 14(1)(a) involving knowledge. The following case, which is not a travel case but where the principles are the same, involves a s.14(1)(b) offence which requires recklessness. Again, it shows that the case law imposes a liability much stricter than one would suspect when first reading the statute.

MFI Warehouses Ltd. v Nattrass 1 All ER 762. The defendants published an advertisement which contained a false statement. The advertisement had been drafted by a director and approved by the chairman. The latter had considered the advertisement for about 5-10 minutes but had not specifically considered whether it contained any false statements. On appeal to the Divisional Court, it was held that the defendants had recklessly made a false statement. Recklessness is actually defined in the Act in the following terms "a statement made regardless of whether it is true or false shall be deemed to be made recklessly..." Literally this meant not having regard to the truth of the statement, which is what had happened. The chairman had not thought about the falsity of the statement.

Who must make the statement? An offence under the TDA requires the prosecution to prove a state of mind – knowledge or recklessness. However, most defendants will be companies who have neither minds nor bodies. The laws solves this problem by requiring the prosecution to establish that one of the 'directing minds' of the company, for example, a director or managing director or company secretary, had the requisite state of mind.

> *Airtours v Shipley* Divisional Ct. Unreported. The defendants had published a brochure which stated that a hotel had a pool when it didn't. They were found not guilty on appeal because they demonstrated that the 'directing minds' of the company had not acted recklessly. They had established a 'due diligence' system which established that they had had regard to the truth or falsity of the statement in the brochure.

(b) The Consumer Protection Act 1987

The Consumer Protection Act is concerned with misleading prices. Section 20 creates two offences: giving a misleading price indication (s.20(1)); and giving a price indication which subsequently becomes misleading (s.20(2)).

Section 20(1) provides

20(1) Subject to the following provisions of this part, a person shall be guilty of an offence if, in the course of any business of his, he gives (by any means whatever) to any consumers an indication which is misleading as to the price at which any goods, services, accommodation or facilities are available (whether generally or from particular persons).

Section 20(2) provides

20(2) Subject as aforesaid, a person shall be guilty of an offence if—

(a) in the course of any business of his, he has given an indication to any consumers which, after it was given, has become misleading as mentioned in subsection (1) above; and

(*b*) some or all of those consumers might reasonably be expected to rely on the indication at a time after it has become misleading; and

(*c*) he fails to take all such steps as are reasonable to prevent those consumers from relying on the indication.

Thus, for the prosecution to succeed under s.20(1), they must show that :

- a person in a course of a business of his,
- has given a misleading indication,
- about the price, or
- the method of calculating the price,
- of goods, services, accommodation or facilities,
- to a consumer.

And, under s.20(2), the prosecution must show that

- a person in the course of a business of his,
- has given an indication of the price or its method of calculation,
- which has subsequently become misleading, and
- some consumers might still be relying upon the original indication, and
- he has not taken reasonable steps to correct the indication.

A person in the course of a business of his: as with the TDA, the CPA is only aimed at offences committed in the course of a business. The difference between the two is that, under the CPA, the offence can only be committed by someone acting in the course of a business *of his*. The importance of this is that employees cannot be prosecuted under the CPA whereas they can be under the TDA.

Misleading indication: this is defined very widely in s.21(1) and s.21(2). It would include, for instance, not making it clear that supplements and tax had to be added to the price in the pricing panel; not explaining that prices were based upon two sharing a room; not making clear that under-occupancy supplements were payable; and, not making it clear that insurance was a compulsory extra.

Consumer: this term is defined in s.20(6) as being any person who might wish to be provided with the services otherwise than for the purposes of a business of his. Thus, purchasers of business travel would not be protected but ordinary members of the public would. Note that no purchase has to be made - it covers any private individual *who might wish* to purchase the services.

(c) The Package Travel Regulations 1992

The PTR contain a number of criminal offences but the most important is to be found in Reg. 5. It covers both misleading descriptions and misleading prices. It provides:

> *5(1) Subject to paragraph (4) below, no organiser shall make available a brochure to a possible consumer unless it indicates in a legible, comprehensible and accurate manner the price and adequate information about the matters specified in Schedule 1 to these Regulations in respect of the packages offered for sale in the brochure to the extent that those matters are relevant to the packages so offered.*
>
> *5(2) Subject to paragraph (4) below, no retailer shall make available to a possible consumer a brochure which he knows or has reasonable cause to believe does not comply with the requirements of paragraph (1).*

The prosecution must, therefore, establish in relation to tour operators that

- an organiser,
- has made available a brochure,
- to a possible consumer,
- which does not indicate adequately, accurately, legibly or comprehensibly,
- information listed in Schedule 1.

In relation to travels agents, the prosecution must establish, in addition, that the travel agent knew or had reasonable cause to believe that the brochure did not comply.

Schedule 1 to the Regulations lists the following information:

1. The destination and the means, characteristics and categories of transport used.
2. The type of accommodation, its location, category or degree of comfort and its main features and, where the accommodation is to be provided in a member State, its approval or tourist classification under the rules of that member State.

3. The meals which are included in the package.
4. The itinerary.
5. General information about passport and visa requirements which apply for British citizens and health formalities required for the journey and the stay.
6. Either the monetary amount or the percentage of the price which is to be paid on account and the timeable for payment of the balance.
7. Whether a minimum number of persons is required for the package to take place and, if so, the deadline for informing the consumer in the event of cancellation.
8. The arrangements (if any) which apply if consumers are delayed at the outward or homeward points of departure.
9. The arrangements for security for money paid over and for the repatriation of the consumer in the event of insolvency.

The effect of Reg. 5, taken in conjunction with Schedule 1, is to ensure that *if* a tour operator publishes a brochure, then it must contain certain information that relates to the most important elements of a package holiday. Note that there is no requirement that a tour operator must publish a brochure.

A possible consumer: as with the CPA, there is no need for the prosecution to show that a purchase had been made by a consumer, simply that a brochure had been made available. Thus, simply displaying an inaccurate brochure would be sufficient. Note that the definition of consumer in the PTR is different from that in the CPA. 'Consumer' in the PTR covers anyone who agrees to take the package and, thus, it extends to packages bought in the course of a business.

Adequately, accurately, legibly, comprehensibly: legibly presumably means that if the print cannot be read by someone with good eyesight, then it does not comply with the Regulation. Comprehensible means that it can be understood, thus obscure and overly legalistic language will be penalised. Accurate is a word that is currently causing problems to tour operators who have adopted a practice called 'fluid pricing' (i.e., where they print a price in a brochure which is a maximum price but then indicate that discounts are available for early bookers). It is argued that the price is not accurate because a consumer cannot ascertain in advance from the brochure what price he will pay. Adequate means that there must be enough information on which the consumer can make an informed choice.

Knowledge or reasonable cause: a travel agent is in a different to a tour operator. For a tour operator, the offence is one of strict liability; that is, the prosecution do not have to prove fault to prove their case, However, with travel agents the offence, as with the TDA offences, requires *mens rea,* a 'guilty mind'.

(d) Defences

All the offences we have looked at, under the TDA, the CPA and the PTR, have defences. Some are specialised and only apply to the particular legislation, but there is one which is of general application. This is known as the 'due diligence' defence. It appears in slightly different terms in each piece of legislation but essentially it has the same effect whatever the legislation. Reg. 24 of the PTR provides:

> *24(1) Subject to the following provisions of this regulation, in proceedings against any person for an offence under regulation 5,7,8,16, or 22 of these Regulations, it shall be a defence for that person to show that he took all reasonable steps and exercised all due diligence to avoid committing the offence.*

The corresponding provision in the TDA is found in s.24 and in the CPA at s.39. The essence of the defence is that tour operators will escape conviction if they can establish that they were not at fault, because they took all reasonable precautions and exercised all due diligence to avoid committing the offence. Note that the burden of proof is on the tour operator rather than the prosecution and that the burden is difficult to discharge, as illustrated by the following case.

Buckinghamshire CC v Crystal Holiday Ltd (1993) Div. Ct. Unreported. The defendants published a brochure in which they stated that there was a golf course at a particular resort. In fact when the borchure was originally published the golf course was only in the course of construction but everyone confidently believed that the course would be open by the time the season started. Unfortunately because of bad whether the golf course did not open on time. The defendants were prosecuted under the TDA for making a false trade description. Their defence failed because the prosecution pointed out they could have prevented the commission of the offence simply by changing the wording of the brochure to say that they expected the golf course to be open at the beginning of the season. The judge said, "... it seems to me that once one is able to identify a precaution which one can properly be described as a reasonable precaution which was not taken, such as the different wording ... being put in the brochure in this case, then that really is the end of the case so far as (the defence) is concerned."

Nowadays, most tour operators have adopted 'due diligence' systems to ensure that the information in their brochures is thoroughly checked before it is published. In the *Airtours v Shipley* case referred to above, this is what saved them from conviction. Note, however, that the due diligence system was used in that case to prove that Airtours had not acted recklessly under s.14(1)(b) rather than as a due diligence defence under s.24 of the TDA. Technically there is a difference but the effect was the same.

Protection against insolvency

Expenditure on the average family holiday usually ranks as one of the two or three largest items of expenditure in the family's annual budget. In the vast majority of cases, the money has to be paid in advance to the tour operator. The obvious danger with this is that, if the tour operator becomes insolvent, consumers will lose their money. The problem is exacerbated if the clients happen to be abroad at the time. Prior to 1992, there were various voluntary and statutory schemes in place to protect consumers if this happened. Thus, if a consumer booked an air package holiday they were protected by the Air Travel Organisers' Licensing (ATOL) scheme which required air package tour operators to take out a bond to be paid out to clients in the event of the tour operator's insolvency. ABTA also operated a scheme whereby their members whether air package operators or not, were also required to have bonds to protect their clients. However, the protection was not universal and it was possible for a client to book a holiday with a non-bonded operator and lose their money. Many bus tour operators fell into this category.

Now, the PTR requires all tour operators to be able to provide evidence of security for the return of pre-payments and for repatriation. The Regulations provide that this can be done in a number of ways:

- by bonding,
- by insurance,
- by establishing a trust fund.

If a tour operator chooses to protect his clients by bonding, then the level of the bond is determined by whether or not the tour operator is a member of an 'approved body' which has reserve fund or not. The bonding level is higher for approved bodies with no reserve fund to make up the shortfall if the bond is insufficient. Approved bodies are organisations such as ABTA and AITO. Arrangements falling within the ATOL scheme are automatically covered by the new requirements.

Because bonds and insurance are relatively expensive to acquire many smaller, particularly domestic tour operators, are attracted by the possibility of trust funds. These work by having the pre-payments paid into a trust fund and only paid out again once the holiday has been completed. The arrangements for policing these schemes are weak and there is a real possibility of fraud associated with them.

7

Financial Management for Travel and Tourism

Introduction

Although the travel and tourism industry covers a diversity of different organizations, including tour operators, airlines, hotels and travel agencies, financial management is important to all of them. Financial management is that part of the total management function concerned with the effective and efficient raising and use of funds.

Finance, like physical resources, has a large number of competing uses, is scarce but can be obtained at a price, and is bought and sold in markets. Financial management is concerned with managing this scarce resource so as to ensure that:

- Finance is obtained at the least possible cost and
- Finance is used in the most profitable ways

The Scope of Financial Management

Financial management can be seen as a function of management concerned with managing the financial aspects of a company's activities, just as the marketing function and personnel functions, for instance, are concerned with the managing of products and the managing of people, respectively. Financial management encompasses a broad range of activities including :

- Financial planning, control and reporting;
- Budgeting;
- Treasury management.

Of these, this chapter will focus specifically on treasury management, as this area of financial management has a considerable significance for most companies operating in the international travel and tourism industry.

Treasury Management

Over the last two decades, increasing attention has been paid to the Treasury aspect of financial management. It has become a specialist aspect of financial management with a professional body, The Association of Corporate Treasurey, founded in 1979.

The increasing internationalization of business and the extreme volatility of exchange rates (following the breakdown of the previous fixed rate regime in the early 1970s), together with volatility of interest rates, has forced many businesses to concentrate resources and attention on this aspect of their business. Since travel and tourism is the most international of business, treasury management is of particular impor-tance.

Treasury management is concerned with the management of a company's cash so as to ensure:

- The right amount of cash is available;
- In the right place;
- In the right currency;
- At the right time.

In managing the company's cash in such a way, Treasury management is about minimizing risks, (such as minimizing exposure to movements in foreign exchange and interest rates and minimizing the financing costs of the business), and maximizing returns, specifically, maximizing the returns on surplus funds. Since maximizing the returns entails taking risks, decisions have to be made which require compromising some degree of profitability in return for a reduction in risks.

The role of treasurer

The role of treasurer or treasury manager is still developing but, in broad terms, it can include any corporate activities or services directly associated with banking and the financial and currency markets. Indeed, many companies (and most in travel and tourism) may not have a treasurer or a treasury department as such. The responsibilities may be split across several departments or operations, or carried out by outside financial institutions or consultants.

In most cases, however, whether treasury management is centralized or decentralized, is carried out internally or is delegated to outsiders, some degree of management of cash activities takes place and overall responsibility is vested in one person, if not the treasurer, the financial director.

Arguably, this area of management is poorly understood and managed by many travel and tourism companies, particularly small and medium sized enterprises.

The relevance of treasury management to travel and tourism

The importance of treasury management can be attributed to two particular factors that affect the industry:

Managing Foreign Exchange

The industry operates internationally producing international flows of funds in various currencies. Tour operators and airlines typically have a very large exposure to movements in foreign exchange rates, almost certainly far larger than for most companies of a similar size engaged in other areas of the economy, for instance, manufacturing companies. The very purpose of these companies implies that they are international in their activities, thereby leaving them exposed to international risks associated with foreign exchange transactions.

So for instance,

(a) a French airline may:
- sell tickets in many currencies
- buy its fuel and aircraft in US dollars
- pay most of its staff and report its profits in French francs (or euros).

(b) similarly, a British outbound tour operator may:
- receive most of its income in sterling
- buy aircraft fuel and pay leasing costs in US dollars
- pay its staff in sterling
- pay its hoteliers and other suppliers in various currencies, including euros and US dollars.

Cash Management

The industry is highly seasonal, which usually leads to a highly seasonal pattern of cash flow. At certain times of the year, companies may have large cash balances and, at other times of the year, many companies need to borrow money in order to maintain payments to suppliers (creditors). The industry is also cyclical in nature, in that cash flows are very responsive to changes in the general level of economic activity.

In terms of cash management, tour operators and travel agents are typically low margin business, deriving important parts of their income not from operating profits (through the selling of holidays), but from interest income derived from investing cash surpluses they may be holding at certain times of the year.

So, for instance, a British tour operator may:

- receive revenue from customers before the company has to pay its suppliers
- invest this revenue to produce interest income
- view the interest income derived as a major source of the company's profitability.

We will now look in greater detail at these two important aspects of treasury management.

Foreign Exchange Management

The profitability of any company that trades internationally is affected by changes in foreign exchange rates. As Lockwood (1989) states:

> *As a large part of the travel and tourist industry is concerned with persuading and assisting people to cross national boundaries and thus to buy goods and services priced in a foreign currency, the identification and management of exchange rate exposures is vital to the profitable operation of a travel and tourist business.*

Thus, foreign exchange management is very significant for many travel and tourism businesses. The lack of stability caused by the continual changes in exchange rates between currencies creates uncertainty. Specifically, uncertainty is created as to:

- what foreign income will be worth when it is received
- what payments will cost when they have to be made, and also
- what the value of foreign assets and liabilities might be in the future.

The overall foreign exchange position of a company may be complicated as illustrated by the position of British Airways. The British Airways Annual Report and Accounts for 1998-99 states that:

> *The group does business in approximately 140 foreign currencies, which account for approximately 60% of Group Revenue and approximately 40% of operating expenses. The Group generates a surplus in most of these currencies (i.e. revenue are greater than costs). The principal exceptions are the US dollars and the pound Sterling in which the Group has a deficit arising from capital expenditure and the payment of some leasing costs, together with expenditure on fuel, which is payable in US dollars and the majority of staff costs, central overheads and other leasing costs, which are payable in pounds Sterling.*

British Airways, consequently, has a highly complex foreign exchange position, but it is imperative to the profitability of such a company that this exposure to foreign exchange rate movements is recognized and managed appropriately.

In all cases, risk attributed to foreign exchange rate movements arises out of uncertainty about the future exchange rate between two currencies. This risk would be minimized if it were possible to predict future rate movements. Unfortunately, however, it is not possible to do so with any degree of accuracy and for a company to try to do so can be financially dangerous. Therefore, given that foreign exchange rates cannot be predicted, another option might be to pass on to the customer the effects of any adverse movements in exchange rates and, hence, the company would incur no impact. In most cases, however, the highly competitive nature of the travel and tourism business prevents higher costs being passed on to the customer in this way. For instance, if Spain as a destination increased in price as a result of an appreciation of the Spanish peseta or euro, (making Spanish hotel costs more expensive to foreign customers), over time customers might switch to say Turkey as a cheaper alternative.

Furthermore, because many tour operators now have to 'no surcharge guarantees' it effectively means that increased costs resulting from adverse foreign exchange rate movements cannot be passed on to the customer. At the same time, even if 'no surcharge guarantees' are given, passing on increased costs can be difficult, as the Association of British Travel Agents (ABTA) Code of Conduct requires members to absorb unforeseen costs up to 2 per cent of the original holiday cost. Similarly, although the European community Package Travel Directive allows tour operators to impose surcharges to pass on the increased costs arising from adverse movements in currency (or fuel) rates, the directive stipulates that a maximum surcharge of 10 per cent can be levied, with any increase over and above this level having to be absorbed by the operator.

Clearly, then, it is prudent to manage these risks, although it is common in the industry for the risks to be ignored, especially by smaller companies. We can identify three different types of foreign exchange risk or exposure a company may be faced with.

Transaction exposure

Transaction exposure arises 'because the cost or proceeds (in home currency) of settlement of a future payment or receipt denominated in another currency may vary due to changes to exchange rates'.

Transaction exposure relates to the foreign exchange exposure where contracts have already been entered into. When a company has counteracted to receive or pay an amount of money in a foreign currency at some time in the future, a risk is incurred. The specific task is that adverse exchange rate movements between now and the time of the eventual cash receipt/payment which will increase the amount to be paid out or decrease the amount to be received.

For example, a UK tour operator selling holidays to America would receive its income in pounds Sterling, but has to make payments to hoteliers and other suppliers in US dollars. In order to make the payments, the company would at some stage have to convert sterling into US dollars. This would entail a risk that the US dollar might rise in value (appreciate) against sterling, thereby making the payments more expensive in sterling terms. Assume, for instance, the company had costed its hotel beds in its American programme at a rate of $1.70 to the pound (i.e. 1 pound buys 1.70 US dollars), and that the total cost to purchase the required bed spaces was $1,700,000. The cost in sterling to the company would be $1,700,000/1.70 = £ 1,000,000. Now if the rate subsequently fell to $1.60, the cost would increase to $1,700,000/1.60 = £1,062,500.

Translation Exposure

Buckley states that 'translation exposure arises in the consolidation of assets, liabilities and profits denominated in foreign currency in the process of preparing consolidated account'. The concept is also known as *accounting exposure*.

For example, if a UK hotel company purchases a hotel in Australia, it acquires an asset priced in Australian dollars. Each year, when the balance sheet of the business is prepared, the value of the hotel would be translated into sterling at the prevailing rate on the balance sheet date. The hotel might therefore be worth less in sterling terms as shown in the balance sheet of the company.

In general, the management of translation exposure receives less active management attention than the management of transaction exposure. It might be argued that such an exposure is not a real exposure, since the asset itself remains unchanged; that is, the company still owns the same hotel. However, if at any time the company wishes to sell the hotel and want to realize its value through the repatriation of the proceeds to the host country, then the revenue received will be affected by the prevailing exchange rate. Therefore, to give a true and fair picture of the current value of assets and liabilities, it is necessary for them to be re-valued in the balance sheet of a company.

Consequently, under UK accounting convention (Statement of Standard Accounting Procedure 20), translation exposure is seen as a potential risk that might be incurred and is reported through a movement in reserves on the balance sheet. All foreign assets and liabilities are translated into domestic currency at the rate of exchange ruling on the balance sheet date (the *Closing Rate Method*) or the average rate throughout the year (the *Average Rate Method*).

Economic exposure

Economic exposure (sometimes referred to as political exposure) arise from the effect of adverse exchange rates movements in future cash flows where no contractual arrangement to receive or pay money has yet been made. This kind of exposure is longer term in nature and often difficult to quantify exactly and forecast accurately.

For instance, suppose a specialist tour operator operates most of their programme to one country, such as The Gambia, then the company will have an economic exposure to that country and its currency. In some cases, the political and economic circumstances are very uncertain and if, for example, the government should be replaced in a violent way, (as occurred in The Gambia in 1994), customers will be reluctant to book holidays to that country, thereby severely limiting the revenues of the specialist tour operator.

Another example of such a risk might relate to the effect that relative exchange rate changes have on demand. For instance , if the value of the euro appreciates versus sterling whereas the value of the Turkish lira falls, it may well lead over time to reduction of demand for Greek holidays among British customers and an increase in demand for competing Turkish holidays. Consequently, a company selling Greek holidays would suffer a fall in revenues.

Thus, movements in foreign exchange rates lead to a number of different problems or exposures for travel and tourism companies. These exposures can be dealt with in a number of ways, the most obvious way being to avoid the exposures altogether, either by trading in domestic markets only or by passing the exposure over to suppliers or customers. However, these alternatives are seldom possible in international travel and tourism and so other management methods have to be employed in order to reduce the risks.

The Management of Transaction Exposure

The first step in managing transaction exposure is to identify the magnitude and the timing of the risks involved. An exposure occurs as soon as the commitment to buy or sell in a foreign currency is taken and a company needs to build up and overall picture of these commitments in order to work out total transaction exposure. This information can then be presented on an exposure summary.

To demonstrate how we can show the risk and how that risk can then be managed, we will consider a simple example using a fictitious UK tour operator, Stateside Travel. The major part of the business of Stateside Travel is selling package holidays to the USA to British customers. The operator also has a smaller operation selling British holidays in America. This produces both payments and receipts in US dollars. Table 7.1 shows a summary of Stateside's total transaction exposure for US dollars. A similar table would be produced for each currency for which an exposure exists.

Table 7.1 : Stateside Travel—US $ transaction exposure ($000's)

	Mar	*Apr*	*May*	*Jun*	*Jul*	*Aug*	*Sept*	*Total*
Payments	(600)	(900)	(1100)	(1250)	(1350)	(1500)	(900)	(7600)
Receipts	50	100	100	(150	200	250	50	900
Net Cash Flow	(550)	(800)	(1000)	(1100)	(1150)	(1250)	(850)	(6700)
Cover	300	600	800	(900)	950	1000	700	5250
% Cover	55	75	80	82	83	80	82	78
Net Exposure	(250)	(200)	(200)	(200)	(200)	(250)	(150)	(1450)

In this example, Stateside has a large amount of US dollar payments (because it has to pay its American suppliers) than receipts. These payments, therefore, have to be met using funds from elsewhere. In other words, the company has at some time to purchase US dollars with sterling and thus has US dollar exposure.

There are a number of methods that could be used to manage such an exposure. These include:

(a) Matching (sometimes termed 'netting')

The company could develop an American source of income to offset against the payment. That is, it could use US receipts to directly make US payments. The company could do this by developing its American sales of UK holidays, the effect of which would be to equalize receipts and payments, payments being made from the money derived from receipts. Since in such a case no foreign exchange purchases would be necessary, the company can be said to have covered its exposure. However, such a position is difficult for a company to achieve, at least in the short term, because different products grow at different rates.

(b) Forward foreign exchange contracts

A forward foreign exchange contract allows a company to:

- Arrange to enter into a binding contract with a bank.
- To buy or sell at a specific future date, an agreed amount of a foreign currency.
- At a rate of exchange that is determined 'now', that is, when the forward contract is made.
- The rate agreed will be linked to the current or spot exchange rate, with an adjustment made (the premium or discount) for forward value.

Forward contracts allow a company that knows it will have to buy or sell a foreign currency at a date in the future to make the purchase or sale at a predetermined rate of exchange. The company will, therefore, know in advance either how much local currency it is likely to receive (If it is selling foreign currency from the bank), or how much local currency it must pay (if it is buying foreign currency from the bank). The contract is entered into now for an agreed date in the future (the maturity date) at which time the currencies are actually exchanged. Note the premium or discount is added or deducted from the spot rate and represents an adjustment for the interest rate differential between the two currencies.

Taking out forward cover by means of forward foreign exchange contracts is by far the most common method of covering known transaction exposures. There are, however, costs involved with forward contracts. In some cases, banks demand collateral of up to 20 per cent of turnover in order to agree to transact forward contracts with smaller companies. Also, if the foreign currency is trading at a premium to the home currency, it makes it more expensive to buy in the future than the current prevailing spot rate. However, the fact that foreign costs and receipts are known exactly in advance is an important benefit in that uncertainty is removed. Furthermore, knowing in advance the costs of foreign currency purchases or the revenues to be received as a result of foreign currency sales can allow a company to put these details into its calculations when formulating brochure prices. The company, therefore, protects itself against the risk of adverse currency movements between the time it makes the forward contract and the time the foreign currency actually needs to be delivered or received at some future date.

This can be illustrated by referring again to the Stateside example. At the start of the season, Stateside has estimated that in June, for instance, payments exceed receipts by $1.1 million. That is, there is a net exposure of this amount in June. There are three ways in which this shortfall can be met:

(i) The company could purchase the necessary US dollars now and retain them on deposit earning interest until required. This necessitates the immediate availability of sterling to pay for the US dollars and ties the money up in a foreign currency until it is needed.

(ii) The company could leave the transaction until the US dollars are required in June. This would, however, leave the company open to the risk of an adverse movement in exchange rates. If, for instance, the US$/£ rate is now $1.75 (in late February when the forecast cash flow was drawn up) and this rate it is assumed is maintained until

June, the US dollars would cost the company 1,100,000/1.75 = £628,571. If, however, the rate between US dollars and sterling fluctuates, so the rate had moved to say $1.55 (quite possible in the timescale), the US dollars would cost 1,100,000/1.55 = £709,677, that is, an additional cost of £81,106. In an industry such as travel and tourism, where 10 per cent profit margins are commonplace, an adverse rate movement such as that outlined above of some 13 per cent could completely eradicate all profits.

(iii) The company could arrange a forward foreign exchange contract with a bank. The bank would, for instance, arrange to sell US dollars to the company at US$/£1.74 on 1st June. This transaction would cost US $ 1,100,000/1.74 = £632,184, that is, £3,613 more than if the current or spot exchange rate had been applied. However, in this case the company would have paid for the certainty that, whatever the prevailing rate might be on 1st June, it could nevertheless purchase its requirements at the agreed rate and that no funds need to be transferred until that date.

Forward cover is, however, an acceptable means of covering exposure only where there is a reasonable degree of certainty as to the size and timing of foreign currency receipts and payments. Nevertheless, it is usually taken out on the basis of forecasts which will almost certainly turn out to be wrong (especially given the volatility of travel and tourism demand). Therefore, in order to deal with this problem and to introduce a degree of flexibility, other ways have been developed to cover foreign exchange exposure, most notably foreign currency options.

(c) Foreign currency options

A foreign currency option can be described as a method by which the buyer has the right, but is not obliged, to buy or sell a certain quantity of a currency at a specified rate of exchange *(the exercise price)* within a certain limited time or at the end of that period. Thus, the primary difference between a currency option and a forward contract is the absence of the obligation to buy or sell the currency once the option contract is entered into. This facility gives the contract a greater degree of flexibility, since if cash flows fail to materialize, then the contract can be allowed to lapse without being exercised; that is, no currency is exchanged. Additionally, if rates move in a favourable direction, then the contract can also be allowed to lapse. The company can take advantage of the favourable rate through the purchase of the currency needed at the time it is required.

The increased flexibility of foreign currency options also makes them more expensive than forward contracts but, in industries such as travel and tourism that often have highly volatile and unpredictable cash flows, the increased flexibility may be highly desirable for atleast a part of the cover taken out.

In the Stateside example, the cover taken out (whether in the form of forward contracts or options), is shown. The difference between the net cash flow and the cover represents the proportion of the cash flow remaining at risk from exchange rate movements. For instance, in the example, Stateside needs to pay $1,100,000 in June of which $900,000,or 82 per cent, has been purchased (forward contracts and options), leaving $200,000 at risk from adverse currency movements.

The meaning of the risks arising from transaction exposure, often referred to as *hedging* the risk, can be illustrated by looking at the approach of two companies, British Airways and Thomson, as shown in Figure 7.1.

The Management of Translation Exposure

Translation exposures are different to transaction exposures in that they represent potential changes in the profitability of a company. Only when assets are sold or when liabilities are settled do these risks directly affect profitability. However, translation exposure can lead to very large changes in the size of a company's reserves and so most companies attempt to manage the total size of their translation exposure in some way.

The most common method of managing translation risks is by *matching* currency assets and liabilities, so that a company has equal amounts of assets and liabilities denominated in a particular foreign currency. As a result, the assets and liabilities are translated at the same rate and, consequently, the effects of a revaluation of assets and liabilities offset each other. If, for example, Hilton decided to build a hotel in Germany (an asset) the company, might may finance it by borrowing in local currency, namely euros. The euros borrowing, which would be a liability on the balance sheet, would be translated into pounds sterling for the accounts at the same rate as the hotel. Consequently, an increase or decrease in the viable of the hotel is offset by a corresponding increase or decrease in the value of borrowings. Also, the stream of earnings from the hotel can be use to repay the interest on the loan.

British Airways

The broad spectrum of currencies in the business, many of which are linked in their movements to the US dollar and the pound sterling, gives the Group a measure of protection against exchange rate movements and reduces the overall sensitivity of the Group's results to exchange rate fluctuations. Nonetheless, the Group can experience adverse or beneficial effects. For example, if the pound sterling weakened against the US dollar and strengthened against other major currencies, the overall effect would be likely to be adverse, while the reverse would be likely to produce a beneficial effect.

The Group seeks to reduce its foreign currency exposure arising from transactions in various currencies through a policy of matching, as far as possible, receipts and payments in each individual currency. Supples of convertible currencies are sold either immediately *(spot)* or forward for US dollars and pounds sterling.

Source: British Airways Report and Accounts (1998-99)

Thomson Travel Group

A substantial proportion of the Group's revenue are demoinated in sterling. However, the Group's UK air inclusive holidays activities, a majority of the Group's costs are denominated in currencies other than sterling, notably US dollars, Spanish presets. Greek drachmas and, in the future, euros (following the introduction of the European Monetary Union). A strangulating of these currencies impacts upon profitability. Each season Thomson Travel Group enters into forward contracts to 'hedge' its estimated costs in foreign currencies and at April 1998 had hedged its estimated costs up to the end of the summer 1999 season.

Figure 7.1: Managing foreign currency transaction exposure at British Airways and Thomson.

Airtours

The group net assets in currencies other than sterling are hedged to reduce effect of currency movements on the Group's sterling balance sheet. The group's policy is to minimise this effect primarily through matching the currency assests with centrally held currency liabilities by using. Currently foreign exchange contracts an dept.

Figure 7.2 : Managing foreign currency translation exposure at Airtours.

Another method of managing translation exposure could be through the use of forward contracts. The method of management is often viewed as being inappropriate, since contracts have to taken out for a specified period of time, (the maturity of the contract), whereas the assets or liability that is to be covered by the contract may have no known maturity date. That is, it is not known when the asset will be sold or the liability will be settled, and the risk realised.

The Management of Economic/Political Exposure

Since economic or political exposure is difficult to measure and forecast, it is also difficult to manage effectively. Such risk can, of course, be avoided entirely if a company declines to trade internationally, but this is rarely an option in travel and tourism.

The main method of managing the risk that can be employed is through diversifying the product and, thus, spreading the potential risks. A company will normally seek to have a balanced portfolio of products that cover different countries and currencies diversifying products in such a way lessens exposure to any one country or currency. If, for instance, in the case of a company that sold holidays to Croatia, the company also sold holidays to other parts of the Mediterranean, only part of the business would be affected if hostilities were to break out in Croatia.

In managing the economic risks, British Airways Annual Report and Accounts states that exchange rates can affect demand for services, especially form lesisure travellers whose decision whether and where to travel may alter a result of exchange rate movements. While it is not possible to quantify this effect, British Airways does monitor exchange rate movements in an attempt to antipate likely changes in the pattern of demand'.

Foreign Exchange Risk Management Strategies

Different companies implement very different strategies for dealing with the various risks described. The reasons for these differences on how to manage the risks stem, fundamentally, from management attitudes to taking risk. Some company managers as *risk averse* in their attitudes to taking risks, in that they will attempt to cover all foreign exchange exposure, Conversely, other managers may accept risks, duty to either a lack of understanding or to a readiness to speculate in the hope of gaining increased profitability from favourable foreign exchange rate movements.

Three strategic options can be considered by management in relation to taking our cover against foreign exchange exposure:

(i) Doing nothing

A firm my be unaware of the risks or the opportunities for reducing the risks. This may well be the case, for instance, with small tour operators who may worry about the operational aspects of the business to the exclusion of the financial risks. Attentively, the firm may take the view that exchange rates will remain unchanged or move in its favour. Effectively, such a firm would be said to be speculating.

(ii) Covering everything

This is the only way to avoid all risk, but the total costs involved in terms of commissions to banks, premiums and collateral may be substantial. However, once the cover has been taken out, and the costs are known, they can then be included as part of the calculation for working out holidays costs.

(iii) Selectively cover

By hedging only a proportion of the total risk, total costs can be reduced, for example, 70 per cent of transaction exposure.

This strategy, covers the majority of the risk whilst leaving some room to benefit from favourable exchange rate movements should they occur. It also allows for errors in forecasting.

Cash Management

Travel and tourism companies make profits from their operations, such as selling accommodation, holidays, airline tickets and so on. However, they also drive substantial revenue from investing the cash that they receive from their customers. Indeed, in some cases, it represents the major source of income to companies in the industry.

Cash management is concerned with the investing of cash surpluses and financing of cash shortages. During the course of trading, companies often generate *surplus* cash for which there is no current requirement. This cash surplus can be invested in order to obtain income in the form of interest receivable. At other times, however, even the most successful of companies may encounter periods of cash shortage during which cash has to borrowed and interest paid. The task of a *cash management* is to manage the cash in such a way so as to maximise the amount of interest receivable and minimise the amount of interest payable.

All companies have a need to hold cash or have the ability to borrow cash. Cash is used to pay creditors (suppliers) which for a tour operator, for instance, might include airlines, hotels, ground handing agents, and travel agents. This cash expenditure is used to provide a service, such as a holiday, to coustomers. The service is sold to debtors (customers) who pay cash to the company. This cash flow cycle is illustrated in Figure 7.3.

The Importance of cash management in travel and tourism

An important feature of travel and tourism products is that, usually, a full cash payment is received for the product before it is provided. For instance, the holiday business generates substantial positive cash flows as passengers traditionally pay in advance, while the holiday companies themselves pay their suppliers in arrears. This is in sharp contrast to other sectors of industry, such as manufacturing, where the product normally has to produced before it is sold to the customer and cash is received by the company.

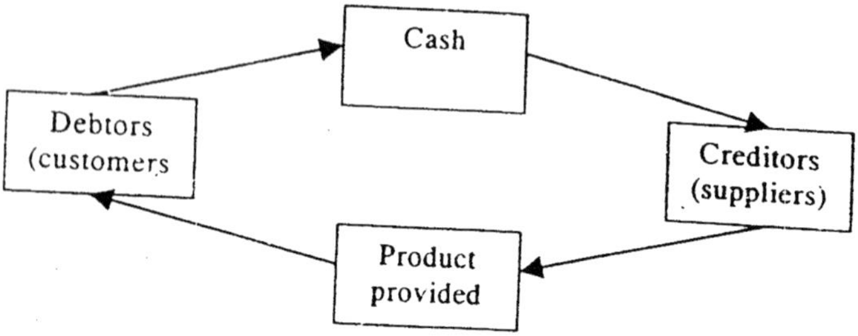

Figure 7.3 : The cash flow cycle

This feature of travel and tourism has a highly significant effect on company cash flows. Cash management is, consequently, one of the most important aspects of financial management in many travel and tourism businesses, with many companies within the sector holding large amounts of surplus cash for periods of the year. The income earned on these surplus cash balances is important. Indeed, in a business where trading margins are often low (or even negative), interest income is often a vital source of income. Taking the Airtours Group (which includes Airtours Tour Operations, Going Places travel agencies and the airline Airtours International) as an example, profit figures reveal substantial interest income even over a period of relatively low interest rates (Table 7.2).

Table 7.2 : Airtours profits (£mn), 1999 and 2000.

	2000	1999
Profit from operations	38.0	125.9
Bank Interest receivable	38.2	40.7
Operating profit and interest receivable	76.2	166.6

Source : Airtours plc Annual Report and Accounts.

Table 7.2 illustrates the significance of interest income and, hence of cash management to a company such as Airtours. In both years, interest income was highly important to overall group profitability (although interest expenses were also incurred on loans and lease agreements). In 1999 and 2000, the group had significant amounts of cash and bank deposits amounting to £554.2m and £793.3m respectively.

The pattern of earnings demonstrated by Airtours is repeated throughout the travel and tourism industry. Hence, the importance of, in effect, 'making money out of money', as well as from the operations of the business, should not be under- estimated. David Crossland, Airtours Chairman, speaking on the publication of his company's 1992 results in January 1993, gave an indication of the significance of this area of management to his company. There is, says Crossland (1993).

> *a degree of seasonality to this cash flow, but even at its lowest point in February 1992. Airtours' net cash balance did not fall below 65 million. Effective cash management is therefore a very important part of managing the business.*

Seasonality of cash flow

Travel and tourism has one of the most highly seasonal patterns of demand for any product or service, with less variation than the demand for Christmas cards or air conditioners, but more than nearly all high value individual purchases. This seasonality is largely due to climate, but is also related to factors such as school holidays, festivals and historic travel patterns.

Seasonality of demand for the product leads to a highly seasonal pattern of cash in-flows and out-flows. Consequently, at some times of the year, companies often have large surplus cash balances to invest whilst, at other time only small amounts of cash may be available to invest or it may even be necessary to borrow in order to meet cash requirements. If we take, as an example, a typically UK tour operator selling mass-market package holidays largely to Europe, the company is greatly affected by the seasonality of the product which directly affects its cash management.

Such an operator may have a number of operating characteristics:

- The bulk of holidays sold would be summer sun with the season lasting from April to September, but with the peak months being July and August during school holidays.
- Summer sun holidays are typically booked in there distinct periods:

  the early booking period starting in August or September, when a significant number of people book. This applies especially to families, and these who are tied to taking holidays between certain dates, or are trying to take advantage of particular offers such as 'free child places', or low deposits.

  the post Christmas period form January to March which is usually the large *booking* period, and during which customers may be targeted with a second edition of brochure.

  the late booking period, from April onwards, which become increasingly *significant* in recent years, and may be a time of intense competition as operators try to sell remaining capacity and vary prices in order to do so.
- Many tour operators have attempted to widen their range of activities, and reduce the effects of seasonality, by, for instance, introducing winter sun and skiing programmes. The winter sun season normally lasts from October to April, whilst the skiing season normally lasts from December to April with peaks in February and at Easter. In most cases, the combined size of these programmes is far smaller than the summer programme, representing perhaps 25 per cent of the summer programme in terms of receipts. Booking for the winter sun and skiing programmes are taken throughout the summer and autumn, but the winter ski programme in particular is subject to a great deal of late booking in late autumn and early winter as customers wait to see what snow conditions are likely for the season.
- The tour operator will have a number of seasonal costs such as airline fuel, staff working at resorts, and accommodation charges. However, the tour operator will also have a high level of costs that have to be met throughout the year, such as the costs of head office staff, aircraft, and computer facilities.

The characteristics of the tour operating business outlined above have certain implications for cash management. Cash builds up and declines in a seasonal way and, therefore, the cash position of a typical tour operator will vary greatly over the course of a normal years, as shown in Figure 7.4

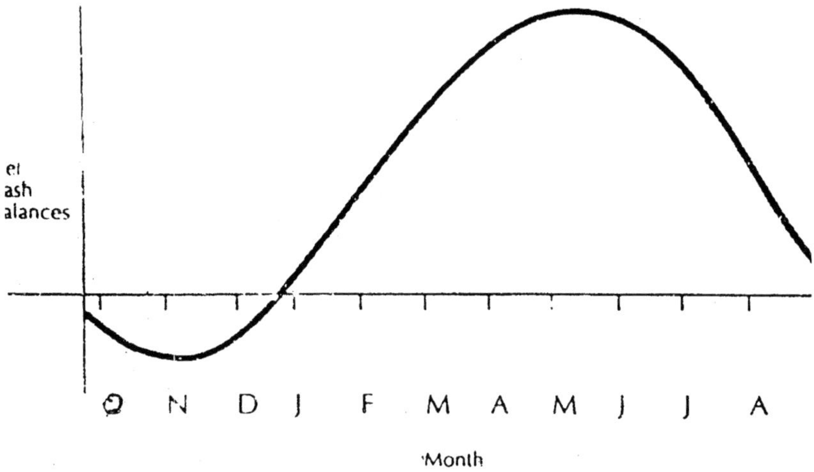

Figure 7.4 : The cash flow profile of a tour operator.

The cash flow profile shown in Figure 7.4 is, perhaps, typical of a mass tour operator in a normal year. It shows that during certain times of the year, particularly the first five months of the calendar year, large surplus cash balances are free to be invested until the cash is needed to pay bills during the summer season and for the remainder of the year. The size and timing of the cash balances and the interest to be earned from the invested balances will vary from year to year, since the profile of bookings and level of interest rates also vary from year to year.

The period of greatest risk for many travel and tourism companies, however, usually comes in the autumn and winter. Cash balances have been run down as seasonal payments have been made during the preceding summer season and the bulk of bookings for the subsequent season have yet to be made. The position is often exacerbated by companies offering favourable payments terms to customers whereby a low initial deposit is required and, as a result, companies often have to rely on bank support to help them through this period. The problem may be compounded, however, if the early summer booking period for the forthcoming season and winter ski and sun bookings are poor and post Christmas bookings are delayed.

In a case where a bank (or other party) fails to lend the necessary support, insolvency is the inevitable result. Insolvency, (the inability to pay bills as they become due), has often befallen companies in this sector when revenue from expected bookings has failed to materialise. When a company reaches an insolvent position, it normally leads to the company's failure and liquidation. A company can sometimes survive for many years without making profits or making very low levels of profit but, if they run out of cash, it is difficult for them to survive become employees and creditors must be paid. Many travel and tourism companies routinely rely on banks to provide short term finance for a part of the year, but it is when these negative case balances are larger or more prolonged than usual and banks feel unable to provide finance that problems occur.

Cash forecasting

An essential starting point for efficient cash management is to produce cash flow forecasts. Cash flow needs to be carefully planned and monitored so that the necessary action can be taken when cash surpluses of deficits are indicated. The main purposes of cash flow forecasts are :

- To plan/forecast the organisation's cash shortages or cash surpluses over the forecast period.
- To monitor how actual cash in-flows and out-flows vary from forecast cash flow.

Detailed cash flow forecasts should, ideally, be produced for all travel and tourism businesses and these forecasts should be continually updated as and when new information becomes available. The cash flow forecast involves the calculation of future cash in-flows (receipts) and cash out-flows (costs), but it is usually easier for a business to forecast its costs than its revenuers.

Costs are made up of major items such as salary costs, administrative costs, accommodation costs and transportation costs. Money of these costs can be estimated in advance with some degree of accuracy since they are subject to contracts agreed before the costs are incrurred. Further more, uncertainties with regard to costs can be minimised by management actions. For instance, the costs of foreign currency and jet fuel purchases can established in advance through purchasing forward contracts. In the case of receipts, however, the forecasting process is much more difficult and usually less accurate since, ultimately, the forecast depends upon the attitudes of customers. Customers can be fickle and their attitudes are influenced by a range of factors and events, such as wars, political instability, recession, unemployment and mortgage rates. Nevertheless, despite the inherent difficulties and inaccuracies involved in forecasting, it is an important management activity and an essential pre-requistic for successful cash management.

An example of cash flow forecast for a tour operator is shown below in figure 7.5. This cash flow forecast follows a similar pattern to the cash flow profile of a tour operator shown in figure 7.4.

The forecast shown indicates that, for nine months of the year, the company involved has a positive net cash balance. That is, it has a surplus of cash over and above the amount that is necessary in order to pay its bills. For the remaining three months, the company has a negative net cash balance. That is, it has a deficit of cash and must find other sources of cash in order to pay its bills as they become due. The questions posed by such a cash flow are :

- How are the cash surpluses to be invested?
- How are the cash deficits to be financed?

	Oct 1999	Nov 1999	Dec 1999	Jan 2000	Feb 2000	Mar 2000	Apr 2000	May 2000	June 2000	July 2000	Aug 2000	Sep 2000	Total
Inflows:													
Receipts from debtors	300	610	2,300	3,300	2,615	2,600	3,550	6,530	6,600	7,701	7,733	2,050	45,889
Interest income					13	23	33	44	47	29	17	4	210
	300	610	2,300	3,300	2,628	2,623	3,583	6,574	6,647	7,730	7,750	2,045	40,099
Outflows:													
Payments to creditors	900	905	1,000	1,000	1,083	1,078	1,648	5,539	8,062	8,545	8,565	1,869	40,194
Salaries	160	160	250	250	250	250	640	640	640	640	640	640	5,160
Admin	55	35	35	45	45	45	45	45	45	45	45	45	510
Interest payments	5	10	15	5									
	1,100	1,110	1,300	1,300	1,378	1,373	2,233	6,224	8,747	9,230	9,250	2,554	45,889
In-flows less out-flows	800	500	1,000	2,000	1,250	1,250	1,250	350	–2,100	–1,500	1,500	–500	200
Opening balance b/f	–200	–1,000	–1,500	–500	1,500	2,750	4,000	5,250	5,600	3,000	2,000	500	
Closing balance b/f	–1,000	–1,500	–50	1,500	2,750	4,000	5,250	5,600	3,500	2,000	500	0	

Figure 7.5 : The cash flow forecast for a tour operator ($000s).

Principles of Investing Surpluses and Financing Deficits

It surplus cash is available, an investment decision is required. This decision will be based on a consideration of the pertinent facts :

- The size of the amounts available.
- The period for which the cash is available.
- Whether there is a possibility that the cash will be required sooner than forecast in order to make unexpected payments.
- A knowledge of the competing institution with which funds can be placed and the terms and rates that they are prepared to pay in *bidding* for the cash.

The aim of the investment should be to secure the maximum interest possible consistent with a satisfactory level of risk and the required level of liquidity (Samuels, Wikes and Brayshaw 1990). Liquidity is the ability to access the funds invested as and when required.

Similarly, a cash deficit requires a decision as to how the deficit is to be financed. The decision will also depend on the length of time financing is required, the size and certainty of the financing requirement and knowledge of the terms and rates upon which cash will be *offered.*

Investment of cash surpluses

Cash can be invested and deficits financed in a number of ways. As with most from of investment, returns on the investment of surplus cash will be higher if the level of risk accepted is higher, if the funds are invested for long periods and if a longer period of notice to uplift the funds is accepted. That is, the consideration of investment in detail is concerned with risk, maturity dates and liquidity.

There are many ways in which short term funds can be invested that very in relation to risk, maturity dates and liquidity. Four of these methods of investing short-term cash surpluses at relatively low levels of risk are now outlined.

(i) Call accounts

Call accounts are similar to personal deposit accounts and are provided by all banks. They provide flexible accounts whereby cash can be called upon, should it be needed, at short notice, such as on the same day, with one or two days' notice or sometimes with one weeks' notice. In return for the flexibility, a fairly low interest rate is applied to such accounts and the rate of interest varies in accordance with money market rate movements.

***(ii)* Term deposits**

All major banks takes cash on term (or time) deposits in amounts from about £50,000 upwards. A term deposit is an investment of a fixed amount of cash for a fixed period of time (i.e., there is a set maturity date for the investment) and at a dixed rate of interest. Consequently, the cash is tied up for a set period of time so that this form of investment offers a low level of liquidity and requires a good knowledge of expected future cash flows. It the cash was to be required at an earlier date, the deposit could in some circumstances be *broken* (received back earlier than the maturity date), but a penalty would be applied. The rate of interest earned on term deposits is fixed at the time the deposit is made, but is like to be substantially higher than on call accounts due to the lack of flexibility with such a deposit. Term deposits can be made for periods ranging from overnight to several years.

In addition to the large British commercial banks, there are over 400 foreign banks in the City of London that quote competitively for term deposits. Therefore, the market for such cash deposits is large and extremely active (especially in the major currencies), and it pays a company to shop around for the best rates available at the time.

The term deposit represents the primary investment method used by most Travel and Tourism businesses. Airtours, for instance, 'invests surplus funds on term deposits with mainstream banks but, as the rates decline, it has indicated that it is examining other areas of investment for these funds'.

(iii) Certificates of deposit

A certificate of deposite (CD) is a certificate acknowledging a deposit issued by a bank. These are issued for periods ranging from three months to five years on amounts usualy over £50,000 and carry a fixed rate of interest which is likely to be at a rate similar to a term deposit of the same maturity. The main advantage of the CD over a term deposit is that it is a *negotiable* form of investment and is, consequently, more liquid. That is, if the investment needs to be realised, the CD can be sold to another party at a price agreed through negotiation. In London and other financial centres, there are large secondary markets for CDs so that buyers can usually be found if CDs need to be sold.

(iv) Commercial paper

Large companies with good credit raings can raise short-term finance by issuing commercial paper. Only larger companies can normally raise finance in this way, but all companies can use the market to invest during the short term. Commercial paper represents a promise to pay back the investment by the company that issues the commercial paper at a fixed maturity date (typically between 7 days and three months), in return for cash deposited.

One company can invest in another's commercial paper. For instance, Thymosin might purchase Shell Oil Company commercial paper. The *instrument* is like a certificate of deposit, negotiable, so that the investment can be sold if it is no longer required, thereby providing flexibility.

The market for commercial paper has grown considerably in recent years and interest rates (agreed at the time of purchase) tend to be slightly higher than those available on term deposits or CDs, reflecting a slightly higher level of risk.

Financing of cash deficits

At certain times of the year, many travel and tourism organisations have cash deficits which have to be financed in some way. Cash deficits can be variously financed but, before resorting to external sources for the necessary finance, there are a number of broad methods of easing temporary cash shortages that a company will probably wish to consider. Some of these measures might include the following :

(i) Postponing capital expenditure

Some capital expenditure items are more important and urgent than others. It might be imprudent to postpone expenditure on fixed assets (such as new aircraft) which are needed for the growth and development of the business. It may, however, be possible to postpone some capital expenditure without serious consequences, such as the routine replacement of company cars.

(ii) Accelerating cash in-flows which would otherwise be expected in period

The most obvious way of bringing forward cash in-flows would be to press debtors (customers) for earlier payment. This might be achieved, for instance, through early payment discounts or through providing commission incentives to agents to collect and pass on cash from customers at an earlier date. Such actions must, however, be seriously considered before they are taken, since they might result in some loss of goodwill with customers.

(iii) Decelerating cash out-flows

Longer credit might be taken from suppliers, by taking longer to pay hotels, airlines and so on. The longer credit might be the result of a negotiated agreement or a decision may be taken unilaterally to take longer to pay bills. Such a policy might run a serious risk of incurring bad feeling among suppliers and make renewing contracts difficult or expensive.

(iv) Reversing past investment decisions

Some assets are less crucial to a business than others, so that if severe cash flow problems occur, the option of selling off investments or property might have to be considered.

Although internal method of avoiding cash deficits may be implemented, most companies will need to obtain short-term finance from external sources at some time. This need for short-term external finance in either because they do not want to use the internal methods, on because there is still a cash shortfall after the internal methods have been exhausted. There are many methods of obtaining short-term finance for a business including short term loans, factoring, commercial pager, sale and lease-back of assets. By far the most popular form of short-term finance in the UK is provided by banks in the form of overdrafts. The overdraft has a number of characteristics:

- It is a very flexible form of finance with limits on borrowing set by negotiation.
- It given enterprises the scope to move freely within these limits and only be charged on the outstanding debit balance (although small commitment fees on undrawn balances are often charged).
- Overdrafts can generally be arranged quickly.
- The rate of interest charged normally fluctuates with market rates.
- Technically, the overdraft is 'repayable (to the bank) on demand', but usually some notice is given of repayment.

The overdraft is a very flexible and commonly used method of short term fainancing. However, the fact that the finance can be recalled on demand, or at least at short notice by banks, has often given cause for concern and sometimes has led to the insolvency of travel and tourism companies. For instance, the failure of Barclays Bank to agree to an annual overdraft facility to provide finance for the slack winter period for Exchange Travel (then the country's seventh largest travel agency group), was the event that pushed the company 'over the edge' into failure is September 1990.

Good cash management practice involves the building of a relationship between the bank and the company so that the bank fully understand the company's financing requirements. Requests for overdrafts do not then come as a surprise to the back but are seen as a normal part of the company's operations. Consequently, overdrafts are often renewed from one period to the next or agreed on a annual basis without problems.

Conclusion

This chapter has considered two aspects of financial management that are of vital importance to an international business such as travel and tourism, namely foreign exchange management and cash management. It has argued that these two areas (that are normally seen as being part of the treasury area of financial management) are vital to the well being of most travel and tourism companies. These two areas of management concern are important primarily because :

- In the case of foreign exchange management, the risks stemming from movements in foreign exchange currency rates are so large that if they are not managed in an appropriate fashion, profits derived from the operations of the business can be completely eliminated and the business as a whole placed at risk.
- In the case of cash management, the short term investing of cash balances is often a major source of income for travel and tourism companies, so that it is imperative that these balances are managed in an active way and invested at competitive market rates, thereby maximising profitability, whilst cash deficits need to be planned for and financed appropriately.

These two areas of travel and tourism management have received little attention in the travel and tourism literature, but their importance to the profitability and well being of many companies in the sector should not be under-estimated.

8

Travel and Tourism Economics

Introduction

The study of economic is usually defined in terms of scarcity. How can the imbalance between scarce on the one hand, and people's needs and 'wants' on the other, be reconciled? The basic economic problems is that resources are finite whereas people's needs and wants appear to be unlimited, said, consequently, exceed the resources available in order to satisfy these needs and wants.

Economics usually divide resources (sometimes referred to as 'factors of production') into those which can be considered 'free' and those which are scarce. Free resources are those resources available in such, abundance naturally (such as air and the sea) that there is no need for an allocative mechanism to allocate them to users or consumers. Scarce resources, conversely, are those which are limited in their supply relative to the demand of consumers.

These resources are often categorised as:

Land—including not only the land resources themselves but the earth's mineral resources;

Labour—the human skills used in the creation of wealth; and

Capital—the man made resources that have been created using the other two resources. Machinery and financial resources are included in this category.

Everyone needs air, food and water in order to support life and have basic wants, such as clothing and shelter, but once these basic needs and wants have been satisfied more advanced wants present themselves, such as wanting to travel or wanting to take a holiday. Business is involved with combining the factors of production in order to produce goods and services which are wanted by consumers.

The existence of this imbalance between resources on the one hand, and consumer's needs and wants on the other, means that choices have to be made in the allocation and distribution of resources to consumers. Economics, then, is largely concerned with analysing the problems of choice arising from this scarcity and, in so doing, gaining an understanding of the behaviour of households and firms in the economy.

Tourism Economics

In a tourism context, the economics of tourism has been defined by one writer as being.

> concerned with the use of scare resource, labour, capital, land, and environmental resources, to produce the product, tourism, and with the distribution of this product between different (Sincalir 1991).

It should be noted that in this definition, environmental resources are differentiated as a separate resource (rather than included as part of the 'land' resource.) In so doing, the underlying critical importance to the tourism product of the environment in terms of air and water quality and the aesthetic beauty of nature and the landscape is recognised.

Indeed, Bull (1995) argues that the basis for tourism lies in building upon these 'free' resources (or 'renewable resources' as they are sometimes termed), with a mixture of public sector and private sector resources. These free resources, together with the other scarce resources, are combined to form what most tourists perceive as the tourist 'product' they consume and which suppliers produce. As Bull (1995) points out, in today's world there are few truly free resources since any human activity makes demands on the world's resources and, as a consequence, ultimately someone will have to pay a price.

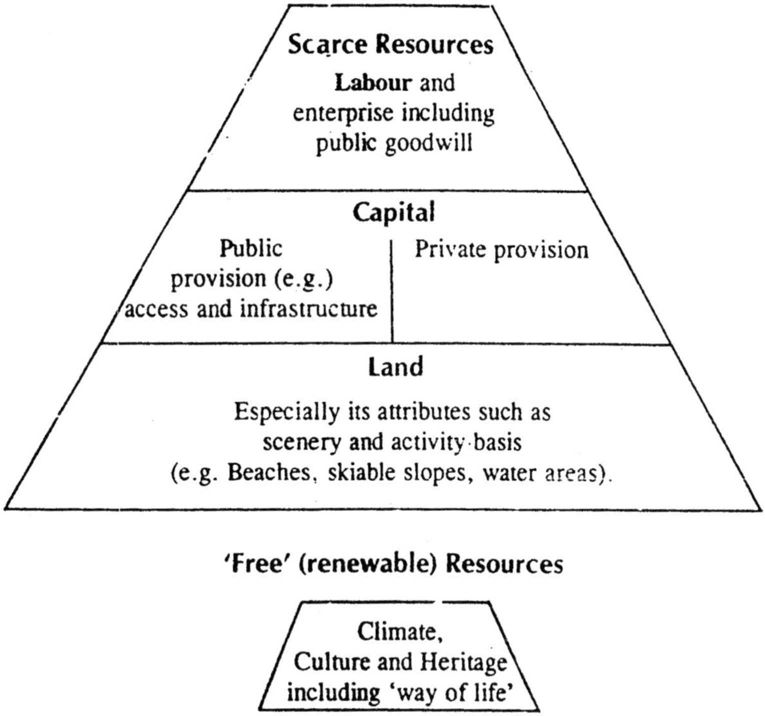

Figure 8.1 : Resources used in travel and tourism.

Figure 8.1 shows Bull's interpretation of the way in which resources are combined in travel and tourism to produce the tourism product.

All the resources have competing demands made upon them so that, if they are used for one form of development, they cannot be used in others ways. For example, a large flat land coastal area might be suitable for the development of a resort area for tourism or as a site for heavy industry. If tourism is chosen ahead of heavy industry, an opportunity to develop heavy industry on this site has been lost and the cost of this choice is known as the 'opportunity cost', which represents the potential economic returns that are being given up in favour of developing tourism.

Economics, then, can be viewed at two levels. The *micro* level considers individual business and consumers and the *macro* level considers the economy as a whole in a particular area or in relation to the national or international economy. *Microeconomics* in tourism is therefore, concerned with how economic decisions are reached at the level of the individual tourism business or the individual tourism consumer. Key questions to consider include:

- What makes consumers decide which tourism products they are going to buy, and in what quantities?
- How do specific tourism businesses, decide with tourism products are going to be sold and distributed to consumers and in what quantities?
- How are the market prices for buying and selling tourism products arrived at?

Microeconomics in tourism is concerned with the study of the total (usually termed aggregate) effects of economic phenomena affecting the local, national or international economy. Key questions include:

- What factors determine the level of aggregate tourist spending?
- What is aggregate economic effect of tourism on the economy through the so-called 'multiplier' effect?
- In this chapter we will consider some of these questions first at the micro level and thereafter at the macro level.

Economic Choices

The cornerstone of economic analysis at the micro level is the consideration of supply and demand and the interaction between them. Every individual demands goods and services (products) and, when all these demands are put together, the resulting aggregate demand is what the industry must supply if all consumers are to achieve satisfaction.

The interaction of the forces of supply and demand determine the price of a product. Products have a price because they are useful (or have *utility* to use the economists' jargon), and because they are scarce. Their usefulness is shown by the fact that consumers demand them and scarcity is revealed by the unwillingness of firms of provide unlimited amounts of a product. Neither demand nor supply are static but vary with changing condition. Furthermore, the nature of demand and supply will vary according to the nature of the product in question.

Before going on to consider the nature of demand and supply in tourism, it is necessary to consider briefly where the interaction of these forces takes places in a market.

> Markets are situations where buyers and sellers of products come together in order to exchange.

To an economist, the term 'market' does not represent the geographical place where buyers and sellers meet buy instead, refers to all those buyers and sellers who exert an influence on the price of a product. Some markets are world-wide, such as the markets for oil, gold or foreign exchange, whereas others are more localised, such as the markets for holidays or transportation.

In analysing markets, economists distinguish between *perfect* and *imperfect* competition in markets. All markets have some imperfections, but economics often study perfect markets as they provide useful insight to the theoretical behaviour of markets and demonstrate what would happen if all the imperfections were to be removed.

A perfect market exists where there are a large number of buyers and sellers and no individual buyer or seller has enough market power to influence the market price. In a perfect market:

- Individual firms must sell at the prevailing market price.
- All buyers and sellers have the same information about prices.
- The consumer will act rationally by purchasing at the lowest available price.
- The product is uniform across the market (i.e. it is homogeneous).
- There is freedom of entry into the market for new sellers.
- It is easy and cheap of transfer purchases from one seller to another.

These conditions, outlined above, ensure that price difference in the market are rapidly eliminated and that one market price is established for each product.

In the world, of course, perfect markets do not exist, although some markets such as the market for foreign exchange, come close. All markets exhibit some degree of imperfection. Reasons for this include:

- Suppliers creating the impression that their products are different or better than those of their competitors.
- The loyalty of consumers to particular products preventing rational buying decisions being made.
- Buyers and sellers not having complete access to information on prices.
- An individual buyer or seller (or a group of buyers and sellers) being powerful enough to influence the price of the products on offer.

At the opposite end of the spectrum of market types from perfect markets are monopolistic markets where there is only one seller in the market, and the seller thereby has a very large influence on the price (unless the market is regulated by outside bodies). For example, the aviation market is heavily regulated by government agencies.

Having briefly considered the nature of markets, we can now move on to consider demand and supply and how they interact in markets through the *price mechanism.*

Demand

The concept of demand

Demand represents the quantity of a product buyers are willing and able to buy at a particular price over a specified period of time.

Demand to an economist is not quite the same as wants. Everyone might want to go on a round-the-world cruise, but not everyone has the ability to pay for it. Thus, wants are unlimited, but demand is limited by the ability to pay.

Several factors influence the total market demand for a product such as:

- The price of the product.
- The price of competing products.
- The size and distribution of household incomes.
- Fashion and tastes.
- Opportunities for consumption (e.g. leisure time).

Central to a consideration of demand is the theory of demand which states that:

Other things being equal, the quantity of a good or service demanded is inversely related to its price.

In other words, as the price goes down the quantity demanded goes up and, conversely, as the price goes up the quantity demanded goes down.

The demand curve

This relationship between demand and price is usually shown graphically as a demand curve. A demand curve can be drawn:

- For an individual consume.
- A *market* demand curve which represents the aggregate quantity of a product demanded by all consumers together, at a given price.

A demand curve is constructed from a *demand schedule,* which shows the quantities of a product that are demanded at different prices. Figure 8.2 shows a typical demand curve DD which plots the relationship between price and the quanties demanded.

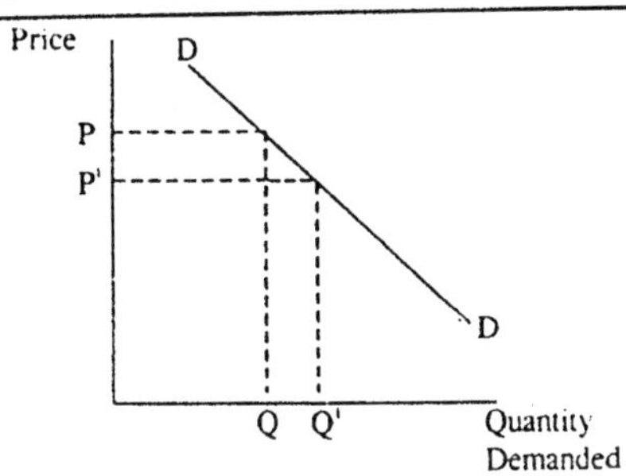

Changes in demand caused by changes in price are represented by movements along the demand curve, from one point to another. In Figure 17.2, for instance, if price is reduced from P to P^1 the Quantity Demanded increases from Q to Q^1.

Note that the demand curve is drawn as a straight line. Straight line demand curves are often drawn in economics of illustrative purpose because it is more convenient to draw them in this way. In reality a demand curve's shape is more likely to be concave indicating that there are progressively larger increases in the quantity demanded as the price falls.

Figure 8.2 : *The demand curve*

The market demand curve generally slopes downwards to the right because:

- As prices fall the product becomes cheaper relative to other products and, therefore, expenditure will shift to the product whose price has fallen. That is, a fall in the relative price of a product increases the demand for it—*the substitution effect.* (An increase in the relative price of a product decreases the demand for it).
- A fall in the product's price means that people with lower incomes will be able to afford it and the overall demand therefore increase. That is, a fall in the absolute price of a product increases in the demand for it—*the price effect.* (The converse is also true if the product's price rises).

Analysis of a given demand curve gives a great deal of information about the nature of demand for a particular product. In particular two factors are of interest:

1. The shape or slope of the demand curve.
2. The position of the demand curve.

The shape or slope of the curve is a reflection of its steepness, and tells us how sensitive demand is to changes in price; that is, the *elasticity of demand.* This is discussed in more detail in a later section. The position of the curve refers to its position in relation to each axis. As already established, changes in price result in movements along the curve.

Changing Conditions of Demand in Tourism

However, factors other man price will also affect demand. These factors will alter the position of the demand curve, causing the curve to shift its position to the left or to the right. These factors can be referred to collectively as the conditions of demand.

In Figure 8.3, demand increases for some reason, such as an increase in overall levels of income, and this is reflected in a shift to the right; from curve DD to curve D^1D^1. Every point on curve D^1D^1 is further from the Y axis, indicating that at every price level demand is stronger and a greater quantity is being demanded.

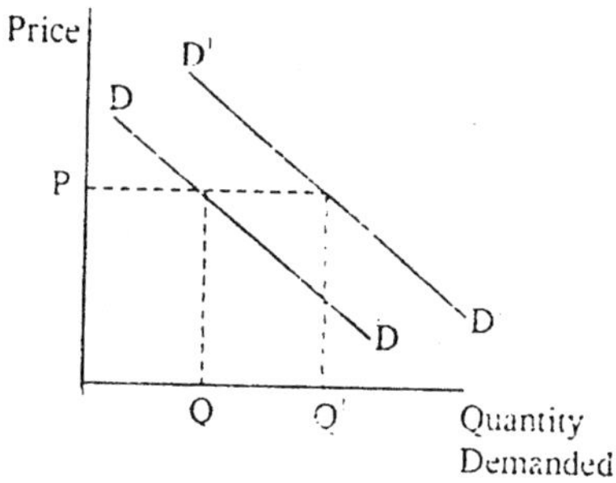

Change in demand caused by changes in the conditions of demand are represented by a shift in the demand curve to the left or the right. In Figure 8.3, for instance, at price P^1 the quantity demanded increase from Q to Q^1.

Figure 8.3 : Changing conditions of demand.

Many factors other than price are likely to influence demand for any product and, in the case of tourism, these factors are numerous and the interaction between them complex. Some of the factors are economic, whilst further factors are related to the competitive environment and other are more social or cultural in their nature. Here we will consider firstly the economic factors before going on to consider the non-economic factors affecting demand.

Tourism is, in many ways, an unusual product in that consumers must physically go to the place of production (the tourist destination) to acquire the product, and the travel element is part of the product itself. The distinguishing features of tourism as a subject for economic analysis are enlarged upon the Sinclair and Stabler in the extract in Figure 8.4.

Since economic conditions prevailing in the destination area can be quite different from those prevailing in the tourist generating area, variables in both areas and the comparison between them need to be assessed when considering their effect upon aggregate demand. Table 8.1 outlines some of the major economic factors influencing tourism demand.

> 'The application of economic concepts, theories and methods raise fundamental issues concerning both the characteristics of tourism which distinguish it from other commodities and the core elements of economics as a discipline. Tourism is distinct, even as a service activity, in that it is usually purchased without inspection, consisting of a range of goods and service which are consumed in sequence, including transportation, accommodation and natural resources. Because both natural and human-made resources are a substantial proportion of total inputs, it comprises a set of industries and markets involving significant no-priced features, such as the positives benefits which are associated with attractive and freely available environments and the negative effects of pollution (positive and negative externalities). It is, thus the unusual composite nature of tourism, frequently taking place in different countries, which requires, specific analysis.'

Figure 8.4: ***The application of economic concept to tourism.***

Table 8.1: Economic factors influencing demand.

Tourism Generating Area	• Levels of personal disposable income • Distribution of incomes • Holiday entitlements • Value of currency • Tax policy and controls of tourist spending • Company competitive endeour.
Tourism Destination Area	• General price level • Quality of tourism products • Economic regulation of tourists
'Link' Factors	• Comparative prices in generator andestination areas areas • Promotional effort by destination in generating area • Exchange rates • Time/cost of travel

In assessing the nature of demand, it is important to realise that products are sold in competition with each other in order to gain consumers scare resource—their income. For example, different tour operating companies vie with each other to fly customers to the same destination, destinations compete with each other to achieve the maximum number of tourist visits and customers can choose which airline to fly on between two points.

Consequently, a change in the demand for one product can result in a change in the demand for another product and result in a shift in the demand curve facing the companies or destinations concerned. For example, an increase in market share for Thomson tour operating products (a shift in its demand curve to the right) may result in a fall in the market share for Airtours' tour operating products (a shift in its demand curve to the left). In other cases, products that appear to be unrelated are found to have a considerable influence on each other's demand. For example, since consumers only have a finite amount of *disposable income* (their income available to spend in a discretionary manner after essentials have been paid for), an increase in the demand for cars may result in a fall in the demand for holiday products.

Products where the market demand is in some way related are referred to as either *substitutes or complements.*

Substitues: are products that are alternatives to each other, so that increase in the demand for one products is likely to cause a decrease in the demand for another product. Examples of substitutes include:

- Differing brands of the same product, such as Thomas Cook travel agencies versus Lunch Poly travel agencies.
- Differing modes of transport, such as have versus air and car journeys.
- Differing decisions of high value purchases, such as the decision to purchase household equipment rather than travel and tourism products.

Complements: are products that tend to be bought and used together, to that an increase in the demand for one likely to lead to an increase in the demand for another. Examples of complements are:

- Hotel rooms and bars, restaurants and night clubs. If demand for bed-spaces at a destination increase it is likely that demand will also increase for restaurants, bars, night-clubs and so in the vicinity.
- Flights and airport facilities. If demand increase for flights from a particular airport the demand for airport facilities such as car parking, surface transportation, shopping and catering will also increase.

Other non economic factors can also have an effect upon tourism demand resulting in a shift in the demand curve. These factors include fashions and tastes, and seasonality.

Fashion and tastes change over time. In Europe, for example, mass tourism mainly from northern Europe to southern Europe has shown enormous growth in the post war period spurred largely by the advent of jet aircraft and the development of a sophisticated travel industry. But within this overall picture of growth, changes have occurred from one season to the next, with Spain, for instance, being out of favour one year and resurgent the next Recent years have also seen the growth of long haul travel. Encouraged by the introduction of larger more fuel efficient long range aircraft? and the growth of the tourism infrastructure in many of the tourist receiving countries concerned. Consumers tastes also change as, for instance, more activity oriented holidays are demanded and consumers demand independent arrangements rather than mass packaging.

Tourism is highly seasonal in its pattern of demand. As such the product is not unique since cars, heating products and ski equipment also face seasonal fluctuations in demand, but it is certainly an important characteristic of tourism the requires consideration when assessing demand, Bar on identified several factors contributing to the seasonality of demand in tourism. The principal factors he identified in his study in terms of recereational travel were climate, festivals and special events and academic holidays. Typically, a UK, seaside resort, for instance will have a high season, an off peak season and a low season. The high season is perhaps the school period of July and August with off peak periods either side of these months and a low season for the rest of the year. Resorts attempt to extend their high season demand as much as possible into the peak periods. In Blackpoll, for instance, conferences and its famed illumi-nations extend the period of high demand into the autumn.

Changes in any one of the factors outlined in Table 8.1 above (or, indeed, a combination of these factors) will affect demand in some way. In reality, the analysis of such changes is complicated, not least by the non availability of reliable data.

Table 8.2 summarises some of the likely effects of changes to the conditions of demand.

Table 8.2 : The likely effects of changes in the conditions of demand.

Demand curve shifts to the left	*Demand curve shifts to the right*
• Fall in income (normal products)	• Rise in income (normal products)
• Rise in income (inferior products)	• Fall in income (inferior products)
• Rise in price of complementary products	• Fall in price of complementary products
• Fall in price of substitutes	• Rise in price of substitutes
• Fall in quality	• Rise in quality
• Unfashionable	• Fashionable
• Less advertising	• More advertising
• Less leisure time	• More leisure time
• Fall in population	• Rise in population

Note that in Table 8.2 reference is made to *normal* and *inferior* products. Most products are normal products where demand increases as income goes up. Some products, however, are bought as cheap substitutes for other products and are termed inferior. As income increases, consumers switch to the normal products and therefore, demand goes down as income increases.

An example is provided by the demand for airline seats by businesses in times of recession. In an economic recession (where business income decreases), businesses switch their employees from business class to economy class in order to save money. As the economy improves (and business incomes increase), businesses switch back to make fuller use of business class products. In terms of demand from business travellers, therefore, economy class can viewed as an inferior product.

Supply

The Concept of supply

Supply represents the quantity of a product existing suppliers or suppliers coming into the market would be willing to make available at a particular price over a specified period of time.

Several factors influence the total market supply for a products. These factors include :

- The price obtainable for the product.
- The price of competing products.
- The cost of providing the product.
- Changes in technology.
- The ease which providers of products can enter or leave the market-*barriers to entry or barriers to exit.*
- The extent to which the market is regulated by governments or other bodies.

Central to a consideration of supply is the theory of supply which states that:

> Other things being equal, the quantity of product supplied is directly related to its price.

In other words, as the price goes up the quantity of a product that suppliers will wish to supply goes up and, conversely, as the price goes down the quantity of a product that suppliers will wish to supply also goes down.

The Supply Curve

This relationship between supply and price is usually shown graphically as a *supply curve.* A supply curve can be drawn for:

- an individual supplier; or
- (more usually) for all firms which provide the product. This aggregate supply curve for all suppliers is the *market* supply curve.

A supply curve is constructed in a similar manner to a demand curve (from a schedule of supply quantities at different prices), but shows the quantities that suppliers are willing to provide at different price levels.

Figure 8.5 shows a typical supply curve SS which plots the relationship between price and the quantity supplied.

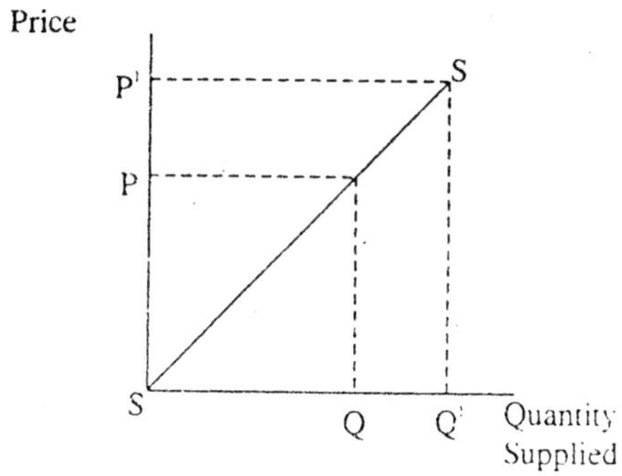

It should be noted that a supply curve shows how the quantity supplied will change in response to a change in price. Changes in supply caused by changes in price are represented by movements along the supply curve, from one point to another. In Figure 8.5, for instance, form P to P^1 the quantity supplied increases from Q to Q^1.

Figure 8.5 : The supply curve.

The market supply curve generally slopes upwards to the right because at higher prices supplying additional quantities of a product is financially more attractive to companies.

A great deal of information about the nature of supply for a particular product can be discovered by analysis of the supply curve. In particular, (as with demand) two factors are of interest:

1. The shape or slope of the supply curve; and
2. The position of the supply curve.

The shape or slope of the curve is a reflection of its steepness and tells us how sensitive demand is to changes in price i.e. the *elasticity of supply*. This is discussed in more detail in a later section. The position of the curve refers to its position in relation to each axis. Changes in price result in movements along the curve.

Changing conditions of supply in tourism

As with shifts to the demand curve, factors other than price, referred to collectively as the conditions of supply, will alter the position of the supply curve, causing the curve to shift its position to the left or to the right. In Figure 8.6, supply increases for some reason. This could result from lower operational costs, improved technology in taxation for instance.

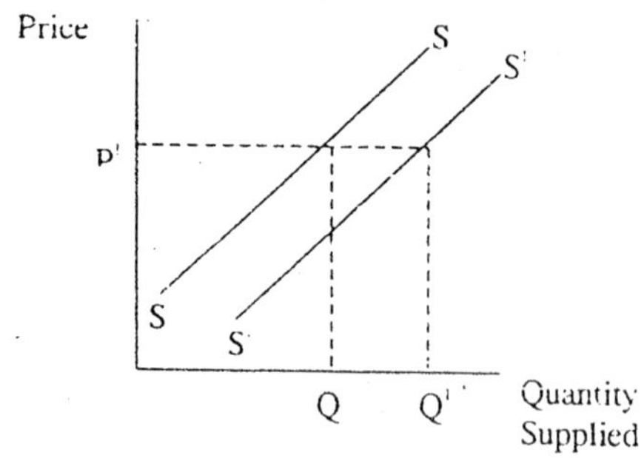

In Figure 8.6, changes in the conditions of supplier relected in the supply curve's shift to the right; from curve SS to curve S^1S^1. Every point on curve S^1S^1 is further from the Y axis, indicating that at every price level quantities supplied are increased. At price P^1 the quantity supplied increases from Q to Q^1.

Figure 8.6 : Changing conditions of supply.

Many factors other than price are likely to influence supply for any product, as outlined above. In the case of tourism in particular perhaps two aspects can be highlighted: firstly, so called barriers to entry and secondly the relative inflexibility of supply.

Barriers to entry describe the barriers preventing potential suppliers coming into the market to compete for sales. Economics talk in terms of the relative size of the barriers. In some cases, the barriers are virtually impossible to overcome, as, for example, where the government grants one company a monopoly to provide flights or rail services on certain routes. In most cases in travel and tourism. The entry barriers are not insurmountable, but large variations occur in the various sectors. In the tour operating and travel agency sectors, barriers are generally thought to be quite low. This was indicated by the conclusions drawn from the UK Monopolies and Megress Commission Report, published in 1998, which made a detailed investigation of the UK travel industry. In the transportation and accommodation sectors, however, entry barriers are often quite high, with significant capital requirements and brand loyalties in both sectors and additionally important regulatory barriers in the transporia-tion sector, Significant barriers to entry include:

- Government requirements for companies to hold bonds or licenses in order to operate. These requirements often apply to travel agencies, tour operators and airline routes. For example, UK air inclusive tour operators require a license in the form of an Air Travel Organisers' Licence (ATOL) issued by the Civil Aviation Authority, the UK regulatory body for air travel. The licence specifies the number of passengers that a particular tour operator can carry and thereby restricts the ability of new entrants to the market to trade at whatever level they choose;
- .Some tourism enterprises have requirements for significant quantities of capital in order to start up. For example, aircraft, accommodation and cruise ships require considerable initial capital investment. However, the separation of ownership of the assets from their

management can lead to the costs being borne by another company and thereby a reduction in start up costs. Various forms of management contracts, leasing and franchising operate within the accommodation and transportation sectors of the industry in particular which can lower start up costs for firms entering the industry.

The Holiday Inns hotel chain, owned by the UK brewing group Bass, for instance, has grown largely through franchising with Holiday Inns as the franchiser providing the brand identity, marketing and reservations support but with the capital for hotel construction being provided by other companies—the franchisees. It is common for property companies and pension trustees to own the physical fabric of hotel buildings but to place the management of the hotels in the hands of a well known international hotel operator such as Hilton or Marriott through management contracts. Airlines have been able to start up with comparatively low initial outlays through their aircraft requirements rather than outright purchases. In doing so, start up airlines, such as Easyjet, have been able to gain access to a modern fleet while deferring payments until cash-flow ticket sales builds up.

- Planning restrictions or competing land uses may limit the degree to which new resorts and attractions can be developed. For example, large new hotel developments are usually restricted in national parks and other protected areas.
- Established companies in a sector may act in a way that restricts competitors coming in to the market to compete by the use of price wars and other tactics. For example, the low cost airlines operating in Europe, such as Ryanair and Easyjet, have frequently accused the large full service carriers, such as British Airways and Aer Lingus, of using unfair pricing methods to limit competition on certain routes. The accusations have focused on the use of *predatory pricing* (using profits generated by other routes in order to offer fares on one route at unprofitable levels), in response to their own by cost operations.

In most areas of travel and tourism, supply is relatively inflexible, at least in the short term. Supply in the industry is usually referred to in terms of capacity. Most travel and tourism enterprises have the aim of operating at full capacity and, in the short term at least, this capacity cannot easily be varied. Thus, hoteliers measure their occupancy levels, transport providers measure load factors, tour operators measure the percentage of total capacity sold, and many tourist attractions measure their usage me.

A distinction must be made between the short run and long run reponses of supply and demand. In the case of supply, many tourism products, such as hotel rooms, airlines seats and cruise ships, require heavy investment and additional capacity cannot be brought on stream quickly. Sumilarly, tour operators can often find it difficult to alert capacity quickly. Contracting of accommodation and transport arrangements, and the printing and distribution of brochures may take place many months price to travel and, therefore, flexibility can be limited. However, it is true to say that many companies are expecting ever greater flexibility from their supplier in order to effectively match their supply with demand.

As a result of the inflexibility experienced in the supply of travel and tourism products, suppliers will do what they can in the short run to adjust demand (instead of supply) so as to equal capacity supply through altering prices or through promotional efforts. Indeed, oversupply caused by the relatively low entry barriers and continual striving among operators for increased market share led UK tour operators to repeated try to stimulate demand through lowering prices. These 'prices wars' have been a characteristic feature of the UK outbound tour industry at various times and led to an erratic accord of profitability. Since the early 1990s, however, the picture has changed as the maturing industry has targied profitability rather than market share as the key objective and has generally been able to avoid damaging price was by more closely matching supply to demand.

The Price Mechanism

Having considered supply and demand separately, we can now bring them together through a consideration of the *price mechanism.*

The price mechanism is a system where the economic decisions in the economy are reached through the workings of the market: changes in the relative scarcity of goods and services are reflected in changes in prices and these price changes produce incentives for procucers to reallocate available resources towards reducing market shortages and surpluses.

The price mechanism does not require co-ordination or intervention, the necessary adjustments occurring automatically as a result of the separate decisions taken by a large number of individuals, all seeking to pursue their own bets interests. Supply and demand are brought together by the price mehanism to create a situation of stability (*equilibrium*) where an equilibrium *price* for a product prevails.

The equilbrium price for a product is the price at which the volume demanded by consumers and the volume that firms be willing to supply the product are the same.

In a competitive market, price acts as a mechanism which signals demand and supply conditions to producers and to consumers.

In order to understand how the equilibrium situation comes about and an equilibrium price is established we can consider the action of consumers demand on the one hand and firms in the way in which they supply on the other. If demand for a product exceeds its supply, consumers must either stop demanding what is unobtainable or must be prepared to pay more in order to achieve satisfaction. At a higher price, producers will be prepared to supply more of the product thereby satisfying the demands of consumers. On the other hand if the price of a product is at such a level that producers want to supply more of the produces than consumers are willing to buy, then supply must be reduced or the price must be reduced so as to stimulate demand.

Figure 8.7 shows the interaction of demand and supply through the price mechanism and the establishing of an equilibrium price.

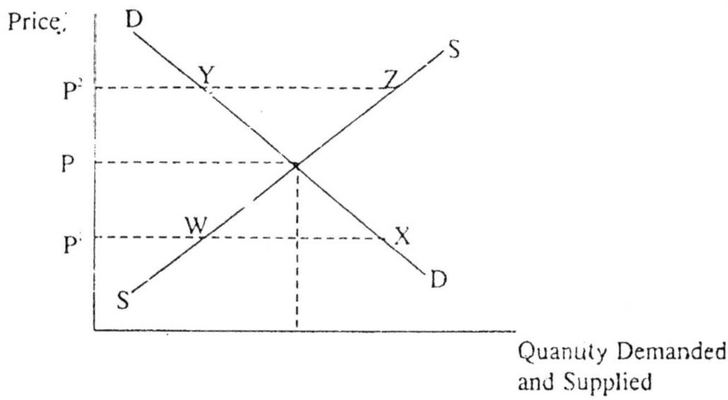

At price P^1 there is an excess in the demand of consumers over the quantity supplied at that price shown by the distance WX. The reaction of suppliers in such a case would be:

- To increase output ; and/or
- To increase prices.

The opposite will be the case at P^2 where there is an excess in the quantity that suppliers want to supply over the quantity demanded shown by the distance YZ. Output and/or prices would fall in this case.

Price P shows the equilibrium price at which the amount that sellers are willing to supply exactly matches the amount that consumers are willing to buy.

Figure 8.7 : The interaction of demand and supply through the price mechanism.

The force of supply and demand will always push a market towards its equilibrium price, as suppliers and consumers react to the signals given by the market.

Elasticity

The concept of elasticity

In previous sections, mention was made of the importance attached to the study of the steepness of the demand and supply curves. The steepness, or elasticity, indicates how responsive supply or demand is to a change in one of the variables influencing demand or supply.

> Elasticity is a measure of the responsiveness of demand or supply to a change in one of the variables influencing demand or supply.

There are a number of variables influencing demand and supply such as income levels, avaliability of competitors products and price, and consequently there are a number of different types of elasticity. Here we will consider price elasticity.

From an economic perspective price elasticities are important for the suppliers of tourism products, since they have an impact on their total revenues. Since total revenues=price×quantity sold, any change a supplier makes to the price of the product directly affects the total revenue, but by how much? Will an increase in price lead to higher or lower total revenues? The answer lies in the study of elasticity.

Price elasticity of demand

Price elasticity of demand measures the responsivence of demand to a change in price and can be expressed by the formula:

$$\frac{\text{Percentage change in quantity demanded}}{\text{Percentage change in price}}$$

Where demand is elastic it means that demand is highly responsive to changes in price whereas where demand is inelastic demand is relatively unresponsive to price changes. Figure 8.8 shows graphically a range of possibilities for price elasticity of demand.

a		Perfectly Elastic - Any increase in price causes demand to fall to zero
b	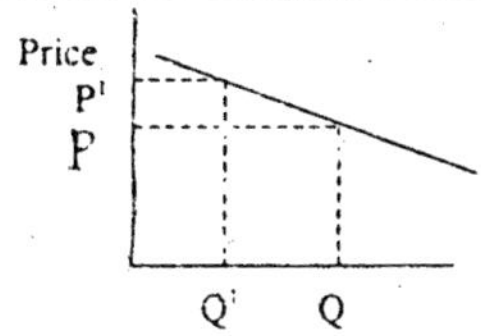	Elastic - Demand changes by a greater proportion than price
c	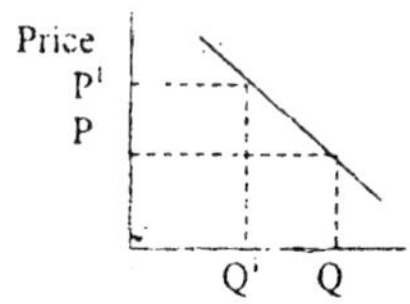	Unit elasticity - Demand changes by the same proportion as price
d	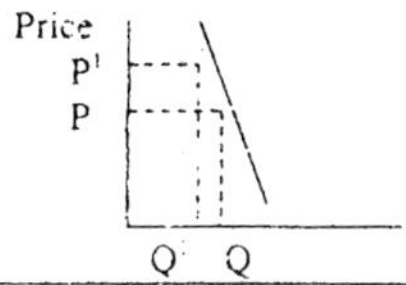	Inelastic - Demand changes by a smaller proportion than price
e	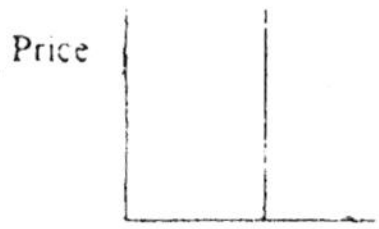	Perfectly inelastic - Demand is totally unresponsive to a change in price

Figure 8.8 : Price elasticity of demand.

The main factors affecting price elasticity of demand in tourism are:

- The availability of substitutes—the greater the degree of competition and hence the availability of substitutes the more elastic demand is likely to be.
- In the UK, for instance, out-bound recreational tourism is highly competitive, with many companies and destinations competing. Over 1, 500 companies have Air Travel Organisers License, giving them the authority to operate air inclusive tours. Hence, this sector is usually considered to be highly elastic, with consumers very

sensitive to price changes and willing to switch suppliers readily in order to save money.

- Some air routes, on the order hand, are highly regulated through intergovernmental bilateral agreements. Hence, in some cases routes are operated by a very limited number of airlines (often the national 'flag carries'). Consequently, airlines operating such routes are faced with relatively inelastic demand curves as consumers wishing to fly between the two points have a limited choice.
- The time period—over time, consumers' demand patterns are likely to change. An increase in the value of the pound relative to the Turkish lira, but not the Greek drachma (or euro) is unlikely to make an initial impact on demand. In the longer term, however, as consumers become allowance of the better value on offer in Turkey relative to Greece, their preferences will switch to Turkey rather than Greece. In other words, the elasticity of demand for Greece is likely to become more elastice over time.
- Proportion of income—the higher the proportion of a consumer's income that a particular product takes up, the greater the price elasticity of demand is likely to be.
- Thus, generally, the price elasticity for a holiday will be relatively high as it represents a high value item of expenditure and accounts for a high proportion of consumers' disposable income. Consumers will search for the best available deal as it a significant purchasing decision. On the other hand, the market for ballpoint pens is likely to be relatively inelastic, since they represent low value items accounting for a small proportion of consumers' disposable income.
- Luxury versus necessity—generally, the price elasticity of demand for luxury products is lower than that of necessities. Those that seek luxury are usually prepared to pay a premium in order to obtain it and demand is therefore relatively inelastic, whereas those who regard travel and tourism as a necessary part of their lives are likely to be relatively elastic in their demand. For instance, rooms in luxury hotels are sold to clients on the basis of the standard of facilities and service available rather than on the basis of price so that customers are relatively unpresponsive to price changes. On the other hand, a mass market tour operator selling family holidays sells to

customers who are likely to demand value for money and who are likely to be highly responsive to price changes.

- Business versus pleasure—business travellers are likely to be far more inelastic in their demand than leisure travellers, since time and reliability are highly valued as opposed to price and the employer rather than the individual is likely to be footing the bill.

Price Discrimination

An understanding of price elaticities of demand for a product can allow a company to sell basically the same product to different groups of customers (market segments) at different prices so as to increase revenues. This so-called *price discrimination* is common in travel and tourism with many airlines, transport operators and hotels, for example, operating such a pricing strategy. This serves to underline the importance of elasticity as an economic concept.

Three conditions for price discrimination to take are necessary :

- There must be market imperfections. In particular, there is likely to be a situation of monopoly power that allows companies to charge higher prices. Otherwise, companies would always compete to ensure that the lowest price was achieved.
- The product cannot be resold. If a product could be bought at the lower price in one segment of the market and then re-sold at the higher price in another segment, it would underline direct sales to the higher price segment and ultimately prices in the two segments would equalise.
- Crucially, the seller must be able to identify different market segments exhibiting different price elasticities of demand. The market may be segmented may be segmented for example by age, different times of use, and business versus leisure.

An airline, for instance may distinguish between two basic segments of the market on a particular route: business travellers. As already noted, business travellers are likely to have a more inelastic demand curve than leisure travellers, because business travellers usually have to make the trip at a particular time whereas leisure travellers are usually more flexible in their requirements. The lack of flexibility in the business travel segment (the more inelastic demand curve) allows the supplier to charge higher prices to this segment and thereby increase total revenues.

Figure : 8.9 shows the effects of price discrimination on a travel business.

Price discrimination resulting from differences in elasticities of demand explains why:

- Hotels offer lower rates at weekends.
- Airlines are able to charge more for full economy tickets which can be altered than they charge for advance purchase tickets the terms of which cannot be altered.
- Rail operators are able to charge more for early morning services.

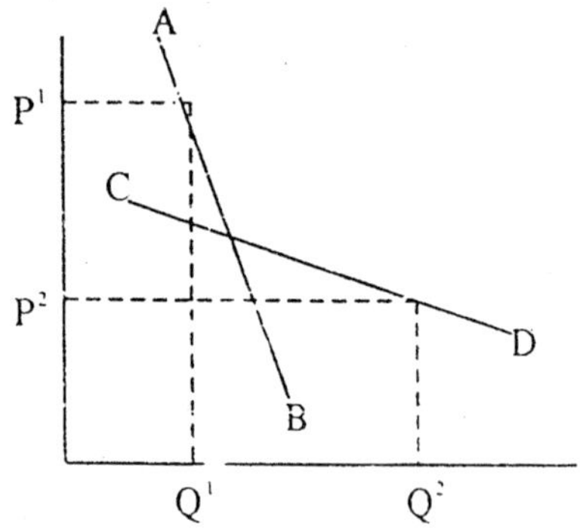

Here, the line AB represents the relatively inelastic demand of business customers whereas line CD is the relatively elastic demand curve for leisure customers. The graph shows that quantity Q^1 can be sold to business customers at the higher Price P^1 while an additional quantity shown by the distance Q^1 to Q^2 can be sold to leisure customers at the lower price of P^2. The total revenue for the travel business through being able to segment the market into business and leisure customers is $(P^1 \times Q^1) + P^2(Q^1 - Q^2)$. If the business were to have sold all its capacity at P^1 the revenue achieved would only have been $P^1 \times Q^1$ whereas if all sales had been at P^2, then total revenue achieved would have only been $P^2 \times Q^2$. Therefore price discrimination allow for total revenues to be increased.

Figure 8.9 : Prices set by a price discriminating travel business.

Yield management represents a sophisticated of price discrimination. Computer technology allows from travel companies to identify patterns of demand for a particular product and then set prices in such a way that allows revenue to be maximised. An individual or company's historic buying behaviour can be analysed and prices set accordingly. A supplier can also build up sophisticated data bases behviour patterns that allows it to make strategic pricing decisions in order to gain a competitive advantage over rivals. American Airlines, for example, using a sophisticated yield manage-ment system, gained an advantage over competitors in early 1992. Full fares were reduced and all but two basic discount fares were eliminated. Other airlines had no option but to reduce fares in a similar manner (or react in some other way), despite being unable to accurately assess the impact of such moves.

Another form of yield managements is the so-called fluid pricing adopted by major UK tour operators in recent years. Fluid pricing allows the tour operator to adjust prices in the important 'late booking' period (eight weeks or so before departure) in order to react to changing demand conditions and the actions of competitors. In so doing, tour operators are able to increase flight load factors and maximise occupancy in resorts and thereby optimise revenues.

In the past, UK customers had grown accustomed to 'late offers' advertised in travel agents' shop windows or on Teletext. Tremendous savings over brochure prices were sometimes available due to excess supply over demand and intense competition. In recent years, however, as tour operators have become more sophisticated in managing their capacity and in pricing their products, late offers are often likely to mean an increase over the brochure price (although they are still heavily promoted in the traditional ways).

Fluid Pricing—An Illustration

The staff of the late bookings section of Airtours, bear more than a passing resemblance to a group of City dealers. What they do, however, is not to trade currencies or sell shares. On the basis of up to the minute information about their competitors in the UK's they

(Contd...)

seek to adjust their own prices to maximise profitability. Travel agents, whether multiple chains or independent shops, look up destinations on screen. The prices they see are set and communicated to them by the tour operators, which arrange flights and accommodation. Airtours changes its prices several times a day.

Along with the rest of the holiday industry, Airtours much of its cost-cutting campaigns. But like all companies, it strives to charge whatever the market can bear, pushing prices up when demand is strongest. Late bookings indeed play a central role in determining a holiday company's profitability. The companies begin selling summer holidays in the August of the summer before, when they publish the first edition of their brochures. In January, they publish a second edition, with either higher or lower prices, depending on how sales are going and what competing companies are doing. It is in the last eight weeks before departure that price competition becomes most intense. A third of holidays are sold during this period.

Apart from trying to get the highest price possible, the late booking team tries to ensure that all the company's airline seats are filled. Tour operators pay for most of their accommodation in holiday resorts only if they use it, although they do guarantee to fill a certain proportion of beds. If bookings are disappointing they do not end up owing hoteliers large sums of money.

Airlines seats are another matter. The seats have to be paid for whether they are filled or not. Flights that depart with empty seats represent a loss for the tour operator. The Airtours late booking team's first task of the morning is to look at the prices competitors have set overnight. They do this by using the computer information available to travel agents. Airtours own the Going Places travel agents chain, which sells holidays organised by other operators as well. This gives Airtours access to other operators' prices.

If a competitor drops the prices on holidays to a particular destination, Airtours will not necessarily do the same. The competitor's price reduction could be temporary: the company might be attempting to fill a particular aircraft or ensure it can sell its guaranteed beds. On other occasion, the pric drop might signal an attempt to take market share from rivals like Airtours. The team says it gets to know the psychology of rival price setters, as well as customers. A further aspect of the process carried out by team is to closely monitor how soon each individual week's capacity will sell out given current sales. If for instance capacity for Majorca four weeks hence given current sales trends is likely to be completely sold out be week two, prices will be raised so as to achieve additional margin on sales and take advantage of the strong effective demand.

a

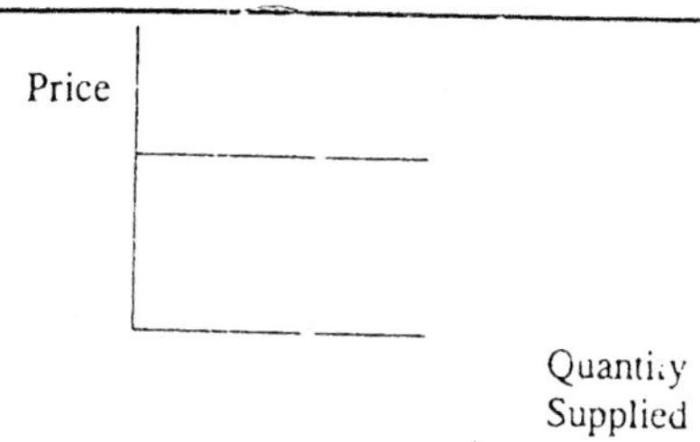

Perfectly Elastic - Any decrease in price causes supply to fall to zero

b

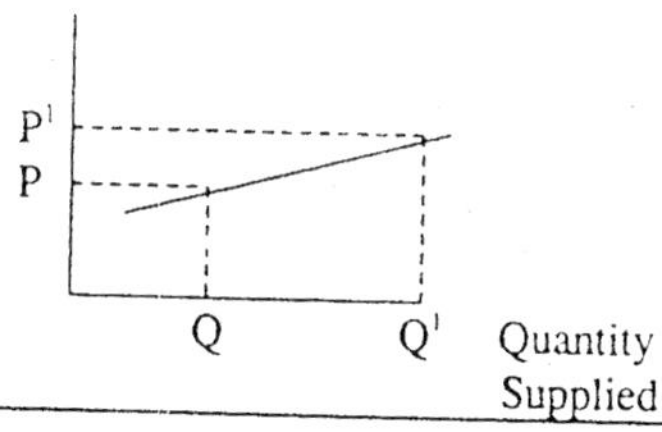

Elastic - Supply changes by a greater proportion than price

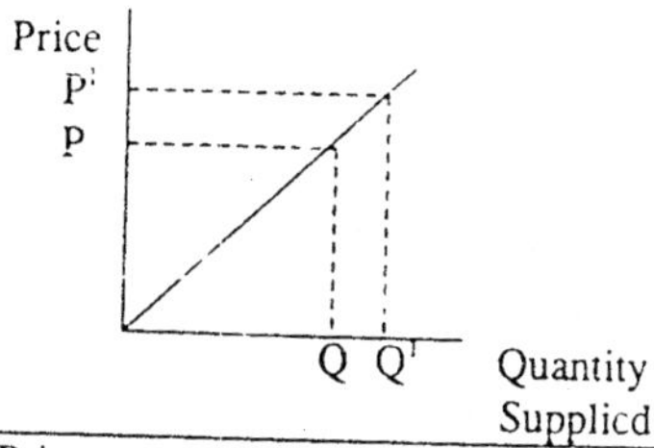

Unit elasticity - Supply changes by the same proportion as price

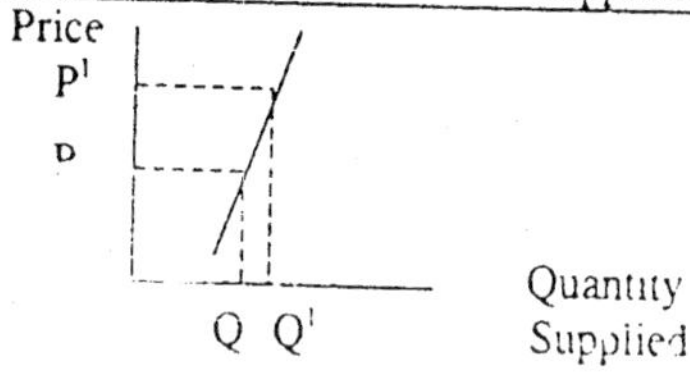

Inelastic - Supply changes by a smaller proportion than price

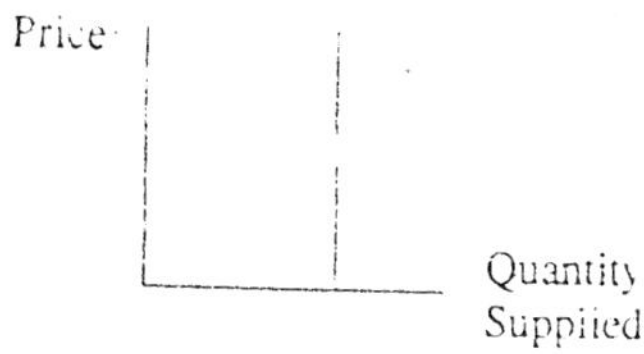

Perfectly Inelastic - Supply is totally unresponsive to a change in price

Figure 8.10: Price elasticity of supply.

Price elasticity of supply

Price elasticity of supply measure the responsiveness of supply to a change in price and can be expressed in the formula:

$$\frac{\text{Percentage change in quantity supplied}}{\text{Percentage change in price}}$$

Where supply is elastic, it means that supply is resonsive to changes in price whereas, where supply is inelastic, supply is relatively unresponsive to price changes. Figure 8.10 shows graphically a range of possibilities for price elasticity of supply.

The main factors affecting price elasticity of supply in tourism are:

- The Time Period—generally, the longer the time period allowed the easier it is for supply to be changed in response to price changes. In order words supply becomes more elastic over time.
- For example, suppose that there is an increase in the demand for hotel rooms in a city (shown by a rightward shift in the demand curve for hotel rooms). The capacity of hotels in that city is limited by the number of rooms available in the hotels. Efficiencies might be possible allowing available rooms to be used more intensively and so supply is not perfectly inelastic, but there is a limit to this process so that supply is relatively inelastic. As a result of the supply shortage, in the short-term there is likely to be a large increase in price. In the longer term, the increased price levels attainable will encourage entrepreneurs to open new hotels. In the long term, therefore, supply is more elastic as capacity is expanded to meet demand.
- In some recent year, tour operators operating from the UK have cut their summer capacity (supply) in the period leading up to Christmas in order to match supply more closely with expected demand prior to the main booking period. As the actual season approaches, it becomes progressively more difficult to trim capacity as contractual arrangements with consumers and suppliers would entail financial penalties.

- Capacity utilization—in the case of manufactured goods, stocks are held at retailers, wholesalers or factories. Modern 'just-in-time' production methods are designed to reduce stock levels and make production more reponsive to demand. A manufactured product's elastic to the extent that stocks can be released or production schedules altered to the level of demand.
- In the case of tourism, a service product, the position is different. No stocks are held and the product is 'perishable', in that the product is available at a certain date and price and if not consumed at that date disappears forever. Stocks in tourism terms are measured in terms of the amount of spare capacity that is available for certain dates. If spare capacity is easily obtainable, then supply will be relatively elastic but, if on the other hand, capacity is fully utilised, supply will be relatively inelastic.
- For example, a hotel with 100 per cent occupancy will experience perfectly inelastic supply (in the short term). Since no beds are available, supply cannot be increased, regardless of the price. However, if the hotel is say, only 30 per cent full on a particular night since there is spare available the position with regard to elasticity is somewhat different. The product, a hotel room on a particular night, is perishable and, importantly, there are many fixed costs (rent rates utility costs, salaries and so on) the hotel must pay for regardless of occupancy levels. Thus, there is a strong incentive for the hotelier to substantially reduce the price of the product in order to drive some revenue for that night to contribute towards the costs; in this case, the supply is relatively elastic.
- Flexibility of capacity—in some cases, capacity can easily be shitted from one market to another whereas, in other cases, it is much more difficult to change the focus of capacity.
- For example, a cross-channel ferry operator can adapt to changing demand patterns by moving a ship from the Dover—Calaris route to the longer western channel routes. A small family run city centre hotel cannot easily become an exclusive 'town-house' hotel as this depends upon reputation, decor and cuisine which cannot be changed quickly. Supply is relatively elastic in the case of the ferry but relatively inelastic in the hotel case.

Supply, Demand and Elasticity—Conclusion

This chapter has briefly examined the cornerstones of micro-economic analysis, namely, demand and supply, and has considered the elasticity of both concepts. It is of considerable economic importance for a tourism enterprise or a tourism destination to be able to measure and forecast the demand and supply for their products. In so doing, business can successfully match up supply with demand, plan effective use of resources for the future, and maximise their revenues.

Knowledge of price elasticity is crucial when making pricing decision since, if the price elasticity of a producer is known, a tourism product supplier can increase total revenues by making an appropriate adjustment to the price of the product. Conversely, an understanding of elasticity of demand and supply allows companies to forecast the impact changes in demand or supply will have on prices.

In practice of course, as Lunberg *et. al.,* (1995) point out, it is not so simple because price elasticities vary considerably between products and change over time. Furthermore, price elasticities are impacted by a multitude of factors that are difficult to model and, in some cases, reliable data is extremely difficult to obtain and interpret.

Having looked at some of the important micro-economic aspects of travel and tourism, this chapter now turns to briefly examine the macro-economic consequences of tourism—the economic impacts of tourism.

Economic Impacts of Tourism

The development of tourism may lead to positive impacts on a country's economy though improvements in its balance of payments, earing in foreign exchange and through the *multiplier* effects (detailed below), as well as an increase in employment opportunities. These are widely discussed in the tourism literature.

The economic impacts of tourism will also apply on a regional or local scale and can be increased through tourism related events such as local festivals and events and larger 'halmarx' events, such as the Olympic Games and football's World Cup, indeed, there is increasing recognition of the economic impact of events and festivals in particular. Even small-scale sports events and cultural festivals a are now viewed as contributing to a local community's tourism and economic prospects, as well as to its recreational and culture well being.

The magnitude of the economic impact of tourism is determined a number of factors. Fletcher (1995) identifies the most critical factors as being.

- the level of economic development of the host economy;
- the degree of diversification of economic activity; and
- the extent to which the economy is dependent upon imports of goods, services and capital.

Economic impact assessments

In assessing the economic impact of tourism, it is not sufficient to simply look at the value of tourism receipts. The direct expenditure by tourists triggers expenditure on other goods and services by tourism business, which must also be measured in order to estimate accurately the total value of tourism. Economic impact assessments usually include a multiplier calculation of demonstrate that expenditure has both direct and secondary benefits to the economy.

This 'multiplier effect' measures the impact of extra expenditure introduced into the economy and which filters through it thus stimulating other sectors of the economy. The multiplier principles of assessing the economic impact of tourism is derived from several major studies that have been carried out in the UK and around the world that seek to assess the economic benefits derived from tourism.

> A Tourist Income Multiplier is a coefficient which expresses the amount of income generated in an area by an additional unit of tourist spending.

In other words, if the total known tourist spending in an areas is, say £ 1 million and this generates, say £ 800,000 of additional income for other (non tourism business) in that area, the value of the multiplier is 0.8.

The multiplier effect is based on the premise that firms in the local economy are dependent upon other firms for their supplies and that, consequently, any changes in the level of expenditure, as with tourists entering the area, will bring about a change in the local economy's overall level of income. These changes may be greater than, equal to, or less than the value of the change in expenditure that brought them about. That is, the multiplier may be greater than, less than or equal to 1.

Money will flow initially to 'front-line' establishments linked with tourism, such as hotels, attractions, restaurants and gift shops, which provide services directly for the tourist. This expenditure will be used by the recipients in various ways:

- A proportion will leak directly out of the local economy in that goods and services are bought from outside the area.
- A proportion will be used to purchase local goods and services.
- A proportion will be used to pay wages and salaries and become part of household income.
- A proportion will be used to pay taxes, licences and fees.

These are all direct effects

The leakages will be lost to the local economy and in the same way that imports at the national level represent income for foreign nationals. However the business, individual households and government which receive money in payment for their goods and services will also make purchase which will be spent in the same way as the direct effects shown above.

These are all secondary effects

This multiplier effect, whereby the initial direct expenditure filters down through the economy and thereby generates additional secondary effects in subsequent tertiary rounds of expenditure, is shown in Figure 8.11

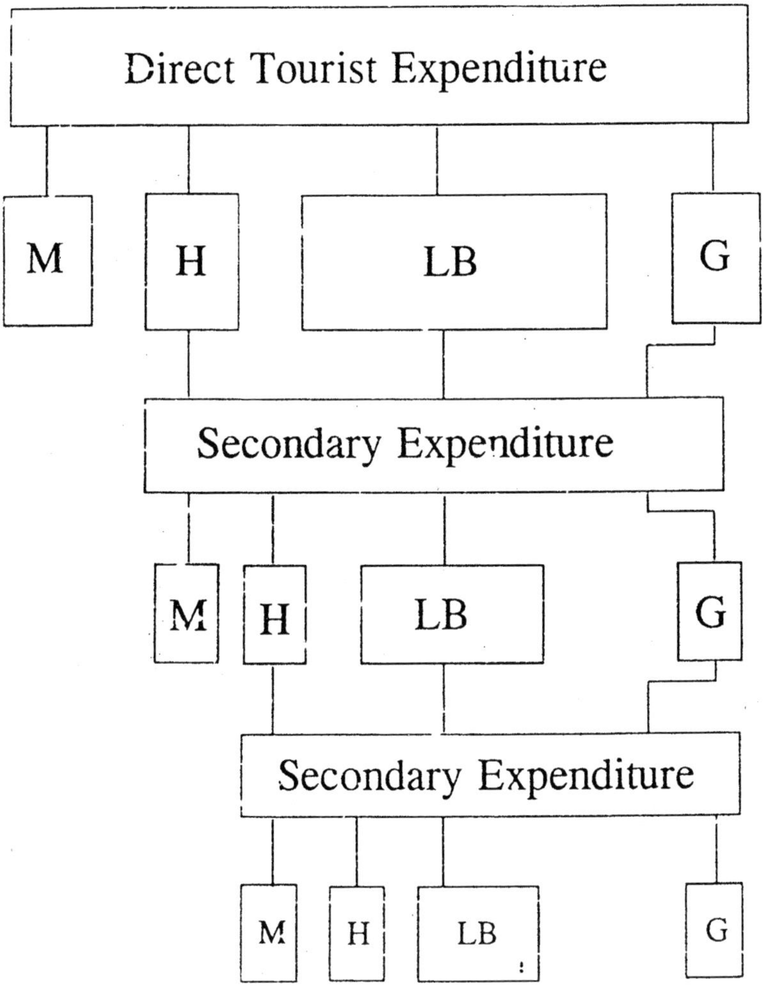

Key:

M = Imports of Leakages from the regional economy
H = Household income
LB = Local Businesses
G = Government

Figure 8.11 : The income multiplier process.

It is conceptually possible (but in practice difficult), to measure various types of multiplier. For example, additional expenditure of £ 1m may generate:

- Output of £ 2.5 million within an economy (*output multiplier*).
- Direct and secondary income of £ 0.5 million to nationals in the area (*income multiplier*).
- Extra jobs totalling 380 of which 180 are created as a result of secondary effects (*employment multiplier*).

In the example above, the output multiplier therefore is 2.5, the income multiplier is 0.5 and the employment multiplier is 1.9 (380/200).

Most studies carried out in the UK, North America and elsewhere have concentrated on studying in the income multiplier. A selection of tourism income multipliers from a multitude of individual studies are shown in Table 8.3.

Table 8.3 : Selected tourism income multipliers.

Country / Region / City	*Tourism income multiplier*
United Kingdom	1.73
Republic of Ireland	1.72
Dominican Republic	1.20
Bermuda	1.09
Fiji	1.07
Missouri, USA	0.88
Hong Kong	0.87
Walworth Country, Wisconsin, USA	0.78
Iceland	0.64
British Virgin Islands	0.58
Victoria, Candada	0.50
Carliste, UK	0.40
Edinburgh, UK	0.35
East Anglia, UK	0.34

The results shown in Table 8.3 need to be interpreted with some care since they were determined using detailed variations in methodology. However, the results clearly show a distinction between the economic impact at the national level and the economic impact at the regional or city level, and the results also show higher coefficients for North America than are to be found in the UK.

The higher figures at the national level and particularly for island economics, reflect the extent to which the sectors of the economy are linked together. For an island economy, for instance, it is likely that most of the goods and services would have to be serviced from within the island itself to be cost effective. Similarly, in the case of US states and counties, higher coefficients are to observed than in the UK, reflecting the extent to which these regions and counties trade with the rest of the country. Given the relative distances between centres in the US compared with the UK, it is not surprising that regions and counties in the US are more self-sufficient, sourcing goods and services from within the region or county resulting in a higher income multiplier.

In the UK, the impact of tourism expenditure is diminished by the high level of leakages of business payments to firms located outside the region. For example, a hotel is likely to have employees who live outside the local area and some of their supplies will be provided by suppliers from outside the local area. Higher coefficients are likely to be observed in island economics or where a population centre is comparatively remote from other centres of population. In both these cases, the area has to be fairly self contained due to the access difficulties thereby leading to higher coefficients.

Tourism Satellite Accounts

As mentioned previously, measuring multipliers is conceptually possible but in practice very difficult due to the very nature of tourism. Difficulties include:

- The definition of tourism. There is no universally accepted definition of tourism, despite efforts by the world Tourism Organisation to encourage adoption of their definitions and statistical methods.
- Tourism is not industry in the traditional sense. However it is defined, tourists make purchases in many traditional

industries, while non-tourists purchase tourism products or commodities.

- Measurement is laborious. To collect reliable data for multiplier analysis requires extensive, expensive and time-consuming fieldwork.

As a result of these difficulties, 'the tourism industry has defiled easy analysis. However, in response to the complicated nature of tourism and the difficulty in obtaining reliable data, approach that has been tried (in Canada, for instance), is the Tourism Satellite Account (TSA). The TSA represents a new accounting framework for tourism based upon Canada's system of national accounts.

A full description and analysis of TSAS is beyond, since they are highly complex, Briefly, however, the TSA is envisaged as 'an information system that collects, orders, and interrelates statistics describing all significant and measurable aspects of tourism within a framework that organists tourism data according to the 'real world' relationship from which a they originate' (Canadian National Task Force 1987). As such, the TSA, concept can be viewed as having the potential for providing data on national tourism industries that are, for the first time, consistent, and coheret with statistics available for tradi-tional industries (Smith 1995).

Conclusion

Tourism will generate a variety of economic problems, which can be studied at the micro or at the macro level. The nature of tourism is, however, complex as it comprised of a range of inter-connected components. Consequently, the assessment of the interaction of supply and demand at the micro level and of the economic impact of tourism at the macro level is a complex task. Conceptually measuring and forecasting tourism demand and supply and its the economic impact may be relatively simple but, in practice, collecting and interpreting such information is extremely difficult.

9

eBusiness and Travel and Tourism

Introduction

Information technology has always an important part in much of the travel and tourism industry. However, perhaps the most significant and exciting development in the sector in the last few years has been the emergence and development of the Interned. The Internet has grown from a small network of computers, set up in the USA the late 1960s for defence purposes, into today's global network linking millions of computer users around the world. Private users and small companies can connect to the Internet via the phone line using a mode and by opening an account with an Internet Service Provider (ISP), whist larger companies or organisations will have dedicated connections provided by telecommunications companies.

Digitised business or managerial information can be disseminated throughout the network and specially designed computer applications can analyse this information and respond accordingly, thereby interacting with customers, other businesses and organisations. This activity is now known as eBusiness of eCommerce.

The purpose of this chapter is to preview of the role of eBusiness in the tourism sector and, in particular, to consider how it is affecting both industry players and customers. It also on to look at some future developments in eBusiness technologies and the implications that these may have for those involved in tourism. It does not, however, delvin to Internet engineering and communication technologies but, nevertheless, assumes that the reader understands basis Interment concepts, terminology and, indeed, jargon. Examples of interesting or useful web sites are given in parentheses throughout.

Definitions

eBusiness is business or management activity conducted by electronic means over computer networks. It is more commonly referred to as eCommerce; however, eCommerce tends to focus on the transactions between customers and suppliers, whereas the term eBusiness can encapsulate the total business process, both within and without the firm, including the relationship between customer and supplier. eBusiness, then affects a variety of business activities, such as marketing, human resource management, procurement and distribution, as well as having implications for the state in terms of the law, taxation and government regulation. Most notably, however, it is changing consumer behaviour whilst, at the same time, providing the consumer with increased power and choice.

Therefore, the scope of eBusiness extends well beyond the popular view of web pages being used to advertise and sell things. The components of eBusiness will include email, internative websites, mobile phones, television and, possibly, other household appliances!

Characteristics of eBusiness

Global reach

The Internet is a global network which means that eBusiness has, theoretically, a global reach. However, although this characteristic is true as far as communication is concerned, the picture is more complicated when the distribution of tourism products in considered. It is not practical, for example, for a Brities travel agent to sell a Spanish holiday to a customer in Australia because the customer would, of course, have to come to the UK to take the holiday.

Global reach is also constrained by consumer protection law and other kinds of regulation both of the tourism sector in particular and, increasingly, of eBusiness generally. This will affect the ability of tourism firms to market their products on global basis and may mean that companies engaged in eBusiness will have to adapt their activities and procedures in order to comply with such regulations in different parts of the world. At the same time, consumers are ways of buying from sites overseas because consumer law has not yet caught up with the new legal situation being created by the Internet. For example, if a consumer in Brazil arranged to rent a country cottage from a web site in Sweden and a dispute over the transaction arose, to which country's consumer protection law could that customer appeal? In other words, in the age of the Internet, an important yet unresolved question is which counuy's laws protect the consumer when they are making purchases across national boundaries?

This is one reason why some companies have localised domain names as well as the more common international dot.com (.com) suffix. An example of this is *eBookers,* the online travel agency that has a main site at www.ebookers.com as well as various international sites, including www.ebookers.com/fr for France, and www.ebookers.no/ for Norway. Indeed, some sites' computers advise surfers that they should go to their 'national' site. *Expedia,* (http://www.expedia.com/) does this, reminding customers that they cannot buy American air tickets if they are browsing form outside the USA.

Of course, different rules and regulations may not be the only reason for a firm to have a variety of localised domain names- there are good marketing reasons for them as well. Potential customers may feel more confident interacting with a web site presented in their own language and with one that appears to be based in their own country.

In some cases, government regulation may lead to companies leaving particular geographic locations precisely because they can set up and conduct business anywhere by using the Internet. For example, in 1999, the large bookmakers *coral* and *William Hill* threatened to move their operations overseas to reduce the tax burden imposed on those who bet. A private bookmaker, *Victor Chandler International,* had set up an offshore operation on Gibraltar and was able to reduce the tax on betting.; The big bookmaking companies were beig squeezed by the rival operation's success. In late 2001 the taxation rules on betting were changed and taxes that were imposed on the customer are now levied on the bookmakers' profits. The change was largely as a result of the increase in betting on the Internet (BBC 2001).

Disintermediation/reintermediation

It was believed that one of the consequences of the growth of the Internet and the development of eBusiness would be the elimination of intermediaries between supplier and customer, a process that has been termed 'disintermediation'. This potentially occurs because the Internet allows customers to communicate directly with the supplier or producer of a product. Thus, a potential package holiday customer can buy place tickets from an airline, accommodaton from a hotel, car-hire from a hire company, and so on (in effect, creating their own package) and this can all be carried out if the suppliers have a 'web presence'. This means that, in theory, the need to have travel agents based in the high street is unnecessary. However, this process of disintermedication has not yet happened, for several reasons:

- It is very difficult for individuals to buy components of their holiday by surfing the Internet-it is time consuming and, in the long run, usually more expensive because individual consumers cannot benefit from the economies of scale that are available to travel agencies and tour operators.
- New intermediaries have emerged that specialise in marketing travel products on the Internet. Companies such as *Travelocity,* (www.travelocity.com), *Expedia* (www.expedia.com) and *Lastminute* (www.last-

minute.com) new allow customers to search, select and buy tourism products in one place.

- Sometimes the new intermediaries get it wrong and do not provide the customer with the best deal.
- The development of the new intermediates, referred to as 'reintermediation', has meant that many of the traditional travel agencies now also have web sites to market their products. Originally, these sites were advertisements for their high street shops and had no interactive facilities at all. Many, indeed, directed surfers to their branches by providing phone numbers. However, they have now developed into sophisticated sites from which to market their products (www.lunnpoly.com and www.firstchoice.co.uk).

It does seem likely that there may be a slight fall in the number high street travel agencies over the coming years, in much the same way that the UK banking sector closed unprofitable branches during the late nineties. However, the traditional agencies that are now trading on the Internet appear to be seeing this as complimentary to their marketing strategy in respect of their 'bricks and mortar' presence, rather than as a replacement. This begs the question, though, of whether the Internet is allowing these particular companies to reduce costs. Indeed, the setting up Internet operations as well as having shops may, in fact, have the opposite effect and actually increase costs.

Virtualisation

The Internet allows companies to contract out business activities to other firms more easily. An airline, for example, could outsource its aircraft, catering, in-flight and ground services, and so on, to specialist firms. Whilst this has always been possible in the past, the Internet makes this much less difficult and it can be much more efficiently organised. This is because all the suppliers could be locked into the airline's computer network where communications and operations between all the parties can be managed electronically. In some cases, the contracted company could even be based in another country.

Automation

eBusiness is ideal for automating business processes. Costly manual processes involving paper, telephones and the staff to carry them out can be, to a large extent, eliminated or redeuced. Storage efficiencies can also be achieved because most information can be held on electronic databases for easy retrieval, comparison and manipulation. This, in turn, allows companies to obtain information at a very detailed level both in terms of its internal processes and its customers. This all leads to cost reductions and to other benefits both for the supplier and the customer.

Cost reduction

As already mentioned above, eBusiness technologies allow companies to reduce costs, primarily because the physical requirements of information collection, manipulation, analysis and storage can be radically reduced. Furthermore, because customers interact with web sites in order to collect much of this information, human intermediaries, such as telephone sales staff, can also be reduced in number. Thus, 'cost reduction in service is largely achieved by moving towards customer self-service, with the help of technology. Part of the cost reduction can be passed on to the customer'. Indeed, some corporate customers are already switching from using traditional travel agencies to book business travel arrangements, to booking online (Rice 2001).

Collaboration

The Internet allows companies and their suppliers to be electronically linked via 'subnetworks' called *intranets* or *extranets*. An intranet is a closed network which a particular company or organistion. An extranet is a network that may link a company with its suppliers or other stakeholders. In other words, suppliers have access to a particular company's network to exchange information-the general public would not, however, have access to this network. Three major areas where the internet is making an impact in collaboration are in product development, rocurement and joint marketing.

(i) Product development

Companies can involve their suppliers in the development of new products through network technology. Being, the aircraft manufacturer, has, for example, engaged a specialist company, Aeronet, to build it a wide-ranging intranet that allows suppliers and subcontractors to obtain technical information about its planes. Boeings's suppliers and subcontractors to obtain tecchnical information about its planes. Boeing's suppliers and customers can now directly download information, such as maintenance manuals and customers can now directly download information, such as maintenance manuals and engineering drawings, that used to be distributed in 'hard' form. Keeping and supplying information in this way means that, when updates are necessary, the company does not have to order another print run of documentation- it just updates the digital information on its server. Again, this information would be available only to authorised individuals or organisations like the maintenance staff of airlines that fly Boeing aircraft and would not be accessible to casual net 'surfer'.

(ii) e-Procurement

e-Procurement is the procurement and tendering of goods and services using electronic means. Many airlines now do business with their suppliers electronically. For example, a company in the USA, *Free Markets,* has recently signed a contract with the *One world* airline alliance of 31 airlines. The company, which has been working with airlines and other aviation related industries since 1998, believes that it has saved an estimated $2.7 billion for its customers (www.ebizchronicle.com).

(iii) Joint marketing

The Internet allows tourism principals, such as airlines, to jointly market their products, thereby avoiding other travel intermediaries. The Orbitz site, which was established by five US airlines, (www.orbitz.com), promotes itself as offering 'access to the most low airfareson the Internet, plus great values on rental cars, hotel rooms and more. In addition, Orbitz brings you the latest in fare-finding technology, so you can be sure that you're getting the most complete list of available airfares.' The is just one example of how airlines are moving into areas that were once the preserve of the travel agent. Furthermore, some of the new start-up companies are now collaborating with older, more traditional companies in their marketing strategy. For example, in 2001, *Lastminute* and *Thomas Cook* established an arrangement whereby Thomas Cook would be the preferred supplier of airline tickets.

Marketing and eBusiness

The most immediate effect of the growth of the Internet in the tourism sector has been its using marketing. Many early web sites acted as promotional tools for tourism enterprises, whether they were large tour operations companies or small rural hotels. To use the Internet for marketing is relatively simple, inexpensive and extremely cost effective. A bed and breakfast business can, for example, design its own web page, arrange with an Internet Service Provider to put it online and, after registering it with a few search engines, wait for the customers to make enquiries. Many of these sites still exist but, as Internet technologies and software applications have developed, larger tourism businesses have been looking for more than just a means to promote their products and interactivity, multimedia presentations and page customisation have become commonplace (www.thomas-cook.co.uk).

Interactivity–getting the customer close to you

Before the advent of the Internet, consumers were largely passive recipients of promotional information provided to them by the tourism industry. The Internet, in contrast, allows customers to interact with the medium, actively seeking out the information they desire. This also means that the companies providing this information can react to this activity by identifying what the consumers' interests and needs are. More tailored information can then be sent back to the surfer and the cycle of information exchange is repeated. A simple example of how a web server can interact with a surfer is at '*Ask Jeeves*', a search engine (www.ask.co.uk). If an enquiry is made about a specific country or destination, the results page will include advertisements for that country. It is likely that regular surfers will revisit the same sites, thereby allowing the companies to further refine their knowledge of the customer. This has several implications has far as interactivity is concerned:

- Sites must be available constantly as, nowadays, customers may want to buy products at any time of the day or, indeed, night. This has implication for staffing and servicing-especially if a site is complemented by the human touch through help lines and so on.
- Sites must be easily 'navigable' so that interactivity can be made as straightforward as possible. This means that web site design and site 'stickiness' becomes critical.
- Companies need to try to enter into closer relationships with customers once they can identify who they are. This entail, for example, encouraging customers to give more information about themselves through the completion of forms or the 'Personalisation' of their own version of the company's web site.
- Customers can now seach for tourism services much more quickly and efficiently on the Internet. This means that comparisons can easily be made between companies and the competition between them in intensified.

Market Research—getting closer to the customer

Interactivity is one way in which tourism companies can obtain information about their customers but other eBusiness technologies can also provide sophisticated tools for carrying out market research. When surfers browse web sites, information can be obtained regarding their interests and activities either overtly or surreptitiously. This information can then be stored, retrieved and analysed, although any eBusiness operation that does this is still subject to the Data Protection Act, 1998.

Some techniques that are commonly used to gather information on customers are given below:

- Electronic order forms.
- Electronic registration.
- 'Cookies'.

(i) Order forms

An obvious and open way of acquiring information is for companies to ask surfers to provide them with information. If a customer is looking to book a holiday they will have to provide information about himself or herself to the operator in question. This is normally done by completing a form online. The form itself can ask questions that are not directly related to the ordering of the holiday and the customer can, if he so wishes, provide this additional infor-mation. The details on the form can then be processed to complete any order that has been made by the customer. However, the information, because it is provided electro-nically, can be analysed and stored for further market research.

(ii) Registration

Sometimes, web sites encourage surfers to register themselves with the web site and this, again, helps firms obtain useful information regarding their wants and needs. Once registered, users will be offered additional benefits over and above those offered to casual surfers. For example, page customisation might be available where customers can adjust the 'look'n 'feel' of the page to suit their own testes, or regular emails will be sent to those registered regarding special offers.

(iii) Cookies

A less transparent way of obtaining information on surfers is to send a 'cookie' to the surfer's computer after they have loaded a web page. A cookie in a small file that is stored on the users computer by the company's web site. It will contain information regarding the consumer's activity on the web. This may be information about what the customer has ordered on the Internet in the past, or about which advertisements have attracted his attention. When the customer revisits the web site in question, the cookie is accessed so that the customer and his web activity, can be identified. The web page can then be 'personalised' for that customer.

In some cases, the management of cookies can be highly sophisticated. For example, information can be contained in the cookie regarding the frequency or likelihood that a customer may place an order. This means that, when a regular customer returns he, or rather his surfing activity, is directed to much faster computer servers so his order can be processed more quickly. Causal browsers, identified by their cokies, are directed to slower servers.

Cookies and similar software are giving rise to some concern about privacy on the Internet and many surgers object to the idea of outsiders placing files, however small, on their computers. Some browsers now allow surfers to choose whether to accept cookies before they are downloaded (www.opera.com); however, if cookies are refused in this way, it may mean that the customer is unable to access the site.

The new capability to gather large quantities of information about customers using customer interaction, and the processing of it using electronic databases, means that companies can develop both the ability and the flexibility to be able to offer customised products to individual customers-one-to-one marketing.

Promotion-getting the message to the customer

Early web sites concentrated almost entirely on promotion. They were effectively little electronic posters or brochures-'brochureware'. One major advantage over physical promotional tools like brochures, is that tourism suppliers are able to rapidly update their information regarding prices, timetables and product attributes etc. online. Some consequences of how promotion has been affected and developed by the Internet are given below.

Web page design

As with all promotional devices, design is critical. Too many pages look cluttered and confusing and this detracts from the promotional effect. Clean dsign with a logical navigation system is critical if a page is to be effective as a promotional tool.

Corporate identity and branding can also be reinforced using the web page. As noted above, existing travel and tourism companies are already presect in cyberspace. Their web sites will have been designed so that their corporate identities are highly visible and integrated into their overall real world brand image.

Advertising

Soon after the emergence of the Internet as a marketing tool, 'banner' advertising developed whereby tourism companies could buy space on more generic Internet portals. Banner advertising consists of a small advertisement or *banner,* usually placed at the top of a web page, where a firm can promote its products. If a customer clicks on the banner, he gets taken to the site advertised. It is thought, however, that the 'click through rate' for banner advertisements is only about 0.5 per cent. Another form of advertising is 'interstitial advertising, where a small additional window opens when a web page is accessed. However, a reading of the popular computer press indicates that these forms of advertising are extremely irritating and software now exists to prevent them loading on to a web page, thereby defeating the purpose of the practice. Any company thinking of using this form of advertising needs to think carefully about whether more people may be put off the product than be attracted to it.

The Internet also encourages 'affiliate' advertising. This is where a firm with a complimentary product places small advertisements on another company's web sites. A car hire company might buy some space on a tour operator's site, for example, or an airline might use a hotel site to promote itself. (http://berlin.hyatt.com/bergh/).

Finally, technology is now becoming so sophisticated that 'geo-location software' has been developed that enables companies to identify where a particular surfer lives. This means that advertisements and other promotions can be targeted at people's browsers based on their location, and of course, location can be an indicator of age, lifestyle and class. This targeting can be further refined depending on the time of day or day of the week. For example, an airline could promote discounted tickets for weekend travel to potential customers within a defined radius of a particular airport. The advertisement would only appear on those customers screens—it would not appear on screens outside the designated zone even if those surfers were looking at the same web page.

Email

Email can also be used to promote goods and services on the Internet. Unsolicited emails, however, are viewed with suspicion surfers. Therefore, companies that want to use email as a promotional tool will ask site visitors to register their interest with a particular site, thereby inviting emails about special offers, late availability, on new products (www.klm.com and www.britishairways.com). Email can also be customised to reflect a particular company's corporate identity: however, this does not seem to have caught on and most emails still appear to surfers as plain text. This may be because some email programmes have difficulty hanging such content.

Text Messaging

Text Messaging (SMS) is now increasingly being used as a promotional technique. It is especially useful when used tactically, In the summer of 2000, a company called *Worldpop* (www.worldpop.com) began promoting clubs, and other products, in Ibiza using text messaging, Clubbers needed to register to receive the SMS service and about 800 did so. The SMS system was also used to control capacity at certain clubs, advising clubbers where the longest queues were. This kind of promotional strategy is likely to grow in the future as it offers firms the ability to target carefully selected audiences with specific information while at the same allowing them to measure the response. '*Mobiles offer marketers the aluminate direct, personalised, time-and location-sensitive method of advertising*' (Day 2001).

Market Development—getting more customers

As the Internet makes international markets more accessible it allow organisations in the tourism sector to attract customers and visitors from far and wide. A country house hotel or a National Park can use the Internet in this way; for example, both the Langley Castele Hotel in Northumberland (www. Langleycastle.com) and the Dartmoor Natonal Park (www.dartmoor-npa.gov.uk) have web sites that can now be used to market both organisations around the world.

The Internet has enabled companies reach parts of the market that might once have been difficult and expensive to attract. For example, a specialist firm that offered walking holidays would, in the past, have probably concerntrated on reaching its target market through specialists magazines and the weekend leisures supplements in newspapers. By going online the company has the ability to reach a much wide market-especially if it makes sure it has registered with several search engines. (www.nzwal-kingcompany.com). 'If you run a small travel agency or tour operation, it is very important to realise that it pays to specialise on the Web. Specialist operators and agents will not only be sought out by travellers for their specific expertise, but there is actually less competition' (Travel Trade Gazette 2001a).

The Internet has also allowed new business models to develop. One of these is the online auction. Instead of an auctioneer gathering together a lot of potential customers in one physical space, an online auctioneer gathers them together in cyberspace. Surfers can long on to dedicated web sites and make offers for the products that are for sale. The web based travel site *Priceline* (www.priceline.com) offers customers the chance to bid for air tickets online. Other generic sites like *eBay* (www.eBay.com) also offer this facility for all kinds of tourism products.

Product characteristics and distribution

The characteristics of a particular product are crucial when considering whether that product can be sold and distributed over the Internet. 'Digitsed' products, like software, or 'digitisable' products, such as music, can easily be delivered through computer networks to customers' computers. Small products, such as books or CDs, can be transported via conventional delivery system like the post or courier services. In both these sases, distance is not a particular issue. However, with some services it might be. For example, if a plumber used the Internet to advertise and promote his services he could still only operate whitin the geographical area in which he did before. A plumber in London, however stylish and sophisticated his web page, could not relay offer to carry out repairs in Los Angeles. So how does this affect tourism products?

Tourism products are intangible yet they do have certain tangible aspects—an air ticket is tangible, the flight itself is intangible. This means that an air ticket can be ordered over the Internet and can be delivered to the customer by post, courier or at the departure airport itself. Interestingly, the function that the air ticket performs, that is, to show a check-in clerk that a customer has paid for a trip to a particular destination, can be now be digited. If the customer is sent a code by a computer instead of a paper ticket, that code can perform the same function of an ordinary ticket. The budget airline EasyJet used this system (http://easyjet.com/en/info/howToBook.html). This model extends to other to other tourism products like hotel accommodation or theatre bookings.

Digitising the tangible aspects of the tourism product, like a ticket or a hotel reservation, means that tourism companies will need build in added reassurance for customers who may not feel that they have bought anything because they do not have any physical evidence to prove that they have done so. Therefore, email, containing a unique reference number, is usually used to confirm that a purchase has been made.

Furthermore, the more complicated a product, the more difficult it might be to sell over the Internet. A air ticket, virtual or otherwise, is far simpler to sell through the Internet than a package holiday. A package holiday contains far more variables than a simple ticket—variables such as full-boards or half-board, bength of stay, type of hotel, transport from the airport, day trips, insurance, child prices, food, etc. Therefore, the customer may want the reassurance of a human salesperson with whom to discuss such things, as well as tangible objects like glossy brochures, complicated from and baggage tags.

Market segmentation

The fact that the product can be digitised and distributed electronically may have implications for segementation in tourism marketing. Tourism consumers, as in all markets, can be segmented along certain lines based on behavour, culture and needs. Those who currently use the Internet tend to be from the more affluent and better-educated groups and they may have less fear about making eBusiness transactions. This means that companies that traditionally target this kind of customer and able to make more of the Internet than others Youth market segments are also prime targets for tourism eBusiness whereas the grey market might be less so (www.gite.com).

eBusiness and Staffing

Touism businesses wanting to become ebusinesses will need to think about having to recruit new people to handle this new way of doing things. Most of these staff are likely to come from the information technology sector but some may need to bring with them new skills in relation to marketing and operations. Firms can, of course opt to retrain existing staff but, given the technological nature of eBusiness, this may sometimes be difficult. An alternative, especially for a large operation, is to engage the services of specialist companies who can set up the appropriate web structures to do business online. In 1995, Japan Airlines contracted IBM to explore 'the opportunity to launch e-commerce services via the Web' (www-3.ibm.com).

eBusiness technologies also allow for more home working and distance working as working with the Internet means that workers do not have to occupy one building in a particular location. Furthermore, eBusiness is not constrai-ned by the traditional working day and the workforce will need to be managed so that 24-hour cover is given. This also means that opportunities for part-times may increase—maybe at the expense of full-time workers.

Restructuring and redundancy

The development of an eBusiness may have the effect of 'flattening' the management structure. For example, if a travel agency company wanted to move out of the high street and sell its products on the Internet, it would want to close its high street shops down. This would lead to redundancies, unless those staff could be easily relocated and retrained. It would also be likely that the network of shops would be replaced by a single operation in a large office with smaller number of workers. There would be less need for these workers to interact with customers as most of the business, formally carried out face to face in the travel agencies, would take place electronically. These workers too would be managed by fewer managers. All the hierarchies that previously existed in the agencies would have disappeared, being replaced by a flatter, broader structures located in one place. Finally, it might even be more cost effective to have this new operation based abroad. So, in this scenario, the dynamics of eBusiness have removed a travel agency's presence in the high street, reduced its workforce, flattened its management structure and moved its operations over-seas.

Public Sector Tourism

So far this chapter has dealt with eBusiness as applied to the private sector. However, the public sector can also benefit from eBusiness. Public Sector tourism is involved in the promotion of tourism in geographic areas usually to promote economic development. For example, in former industrial areas, many local authorities are keen to promote tourism to replace jobs and economic activity lost with the decline of older industries (www.durham.gov.uk), whilst others may be concerned with managing tourists within certain geogrphic boundaries (www.cumbria.gov.uk).

As with the private sector, public sector tourism can use the Internet to market tourism. Destinations and attractions can be marketed on the Internet and local authorities and tourist boards draw together many of the tourism operators and attactions in a particular area, and promote them on a single web site under one local or regional umbrella (www.zurichtourism.ch). This allows small operators, like bed and breakfast operators and museums, organisations and firms that are never awash with money, to benefit from the power of eBusiness without having to invest in the technology themselves (www.wooler.org.uk).

The public sector, however, can do more with Internet technologies than just promoting a particular area. The large number of small businesses that make up tourism can be brought together by public sector bodies via the Internet. Local authorities can easily communicate with these businesses using the Internet. Tourism policy, marketing plans and other issues involving tourism can also be disseminated through the Internet to all those involved in tourism in a particular locality.

Other public sector bodies can also use the Internet to enhance their services. National parks, for example, can use the Internet to communicate with potential visitors about weather conditions or special events. They can augment their education and interpretation services (www.nnpa.org.uk) and they can manage the park more effectively in terms of communication with remote field offices, inventory management and so on by using the Internet.

Finally, public sector bodies can also use the Internet to disseminate information regarding tourism to those who have a professional interest like companies, researchers and academics (www.tourism trade.org.uk).

Future Developments

The eBusiness revolution started with access to the Internet via personal computes. While the personal computer will remain a key device for many tourists and tourism companies when engaging in eBusiness, new hardware is also being seen as crucial to the development of eTourism. Perhaps the most important of these will be the mobile phone but PDAs (Personal Digital Assistants) and other electronic devices, such as televisions, will also begin to play a role in eBusiness.

The personal computer allows surfers to browse at leisure looking for tourism products but the advantage with the mobile phone is that most of the time they are switched on. This means that those that can interact with the Internet are online all the time and when they are on the move. This 'nomadicity' offers many opportunities for eBusiness, especially when it comes to engaging in short tactical communications with owners. 'Current uses of mobile devices take into account the limitations and focus on providing targeted information that frequently requires only short responses. Once the current limitations are overcome, increased sophistication of mobile applications is anticipated. Further application enhancements are expected in the areas of localisation, personalization and instant connectivity.' (www.dmreview.com). Telephones also have a familiarity that computers do not, thereby avoiding the fear some people might have when using 'new technology'.

The two areas where mobile phones will prove critical are text messaging (SMS) and third generation mobile telephony services (3G).

(i) SMS

SMS is proving to be a very attractive way for suppliers to maintain contact with customers. This comparatively simple technology has achieved the same level of market penetration in three years that took email twenty years. Already, many airlines offer a mobile call service regarding flight schedules and other information that connects directly to subscribers' phones (www.china-airlines.com/us/index/htm). Furthermore, there are now companies that provide a price comparison service on the Internet for consumer goods (www.pricerunner.com). These sites can be assessed via mobile phones to carry out instant price comparisons based on product search criteria. It seems inevitable that this kind of facility will soon exist for travel products. SMS is also now being developed to handle more sophisticated information like simple graphics and sound.

(ii) 3G

In the late 1990s, I-mode and WAP (Wireless Application Protocol) phones were introduced: These were the first attempts at providing internet access from a mobile phone. I-mode is however, confined to Japan and WAP to Europe. Although I-mode has proved popular, WAP has failed to take off in Europe, mainly because the technology is still an ineffective way of communicating with the Internet-it is slow and expensive and unable to handle much more than textual information. The real advance in Internet connectivity will come with 3G phones, which will be able to handle far more sophisticated information, including multi-media applications, at a much higher speed-expected to be 40 times faster than WAP.

In 2000, Swissair introduced a service for selected mobile phone users where the checking-in process could be done from a moblie phone using WAP technology. This kind of service is likely to increase with the advent of 3G services where, for example, travellers will be able to make and adjust booking arrangements for air trips and accommodation from their mobile phones. Payment for theses services will be charged on the basis of the service provided, or the quantity of bytes downloaded, rather than the time spent on the phone. Furthermore, with the development of 'agents' or 'bots' (http://botspot.com), tourists will one day be able to ask these software entities, via their computers or phones, to search for specific travel products online and report back with the results.

Related to these developments are biometric technologies, which might remove the need for passwords, boarding cards and even, one day, passports (http://webusers.anetstl.com/~wrogers/biometrics/). The technology is based around certain unique physical attributes of the human body, such as the iris or the face, some airlines have already begun to experiment with this when screening passengers boarding planes.

Conclusion

eBusiness in tourism has grown significantly in the past few years and looks to grow even faster in the years to come. This growth originated with simple web applications and has now developed to include mobile phone techonologies. Research carried out by Energies indicates that travel and tourism in believed by industry experts to the leading sector in eBusiness development in the future (Travel Trade Gazette 2001b). Moreover, Forrester Research (www.forres-ter.com), estimate that between '2001 and 2004 more than $212 billion of business and leisure travel services will be bought online in the US, Canada, and Europe,'

The Gartner Group www.gartner.com) sees eBusiness as going through four phases (Leemakdej 2001). These are :

(i) The 'cyberspace placeholder' phase, where businesses used the Internet to advertise their products;

(ii) The Common Gateway Interface (CGI) phase, which saw the beginnings of interaction between surfer (customer) and server (supplier);

(iii) the transaction phase, by which time firms were creating 'virtual stores' and began to integrate their online presence with existing information systems; and

(*iv*) The transformation phase, whereby companies' web resources will connect with their suppliers information systems to improve supply chain management, while at the same time integrating the management of human resources, processes and production.

The nature and characteristics of each of the myrlad of organisations that make up the tourism sector will determine how fast each one goes through these four 'phases'- some, like major airlines, are nearing phase for. It seems inevitable, however, that those companies that fail to understand the potential offered by eBusiness will struggle to survive today eBusiness is business.

Bibliography

Adams, I. (2000), *Leisure and Government, 3rd Edition,* Sunderland, Business Education Publishers.

Andrews, M. (1989), *The Search for the Pictuesque: Landscape, Aesthetics and Tourism in Britain 1760-1800,* Aldershot: Scolar Press.

Armstrong M. (1999). *A Handbook of Human Resource Management* Practice, London: Kogan Page.

Atkinson. J. (1984). *Manpower strategies for flexible organisa-tions.* Personnel Management. August: 28-31.

Ball A. R. and Peters, B.G. (2000), *Modern Politics and Government, 6th Edition,* Basingstoke: Macmillan.

Barke, M., Towner, J. and Newton M.T. (1996), *Tourism in Spain: Critical Issues.* Oxford: CAB International.

Baum, T. and Mudambi, R. (1999), *Economic and Management for Tourism and Hospitality Research,* Chichestar: John Wiley & Sons.

BBC (2001), *Radio 4 News Report,* 6th October 2001.

Beardshaw, J., Brewster, D., Cormack P. and Ross. A. (2001). *Economic: A student's Guide, 5th Edition,* Harlow UK: Prentice Hall.

Beardwell, I. and Holden, L. (1997) *Human Resource Manage-ment:* A Contemporary Perspective.

Beardwell, I. and Holden, L.(1997). *Human Resource Manage-ment:* A Contemporary Perspective. London: Pitman.

Bratton, J and Gold, J. (1999), *Human Resource Management:* Theory and Practice, London: Macmillan.

Budowski, G. (1976), Tourism and environmental conservation: conflict, coexistence or symbiosis? *Environmental Conservation* 3(1): 27-31.

Buckey, A. (2000), *Multinational Finance, 6th Edition,* London: Financial Times Prentice Hall.

Bull, A (1995), *The economic of Travel and Tourism, 2nd Edition,* Harlow: Longman.

Burns, P.M. and Holden. A. (1995), *Tourism: a new perspective,* Hemel Hempstead: Prentice Hall International.

Butler, R. (1980), The concept of a tourism area cycle of evolution, *Canadian Geographer* 24: 5-12.

Burkart, A.J. and Medlik, S. (1992), *Tourism: Past, Present and Future, 2nd Edition,* London: Butterworth Heinemann.

Chen, S. (2001), *The Strategic Management of e-Business,* Chichester: John Wiley & Sons.

Cole, D.N. (2000) Biophysical impacts of wildland recreation use, in W.C. Gartner and D.W. Lime (2000), *Trends in Outdoor Recreation, Leisure and Tourism,* Wallingford: CAB Inter-national: 257-264.

Cooper, C., Fletcher, J., Gilbert, D., Wanhill, S. and Shepherd, R. (1998), *Tourism: Principles and Practices, 2nd Edition,* Harlow: Longman.

Cooper, C., Fletcher, J., Gilbert, D. and Wanhill, S. (1993), *Tourism: Principles and Practice* London: Pitmans.

Cooper, C., Fletcher, J., Gilbert, D., Shepherd, R. and Wanhill, S. (1998), *Tourism: Principles and Practice, 2nd Edition,* Harlow, Longman.

Cooper. C., Fletcher J., Gilbert D. and Wanhill S. (1998), *Tourism: Principles and Practice, 2nd Edition,* Harlow: Longman.

Crick, B. (1995), What is politics?, *New Statesman and Society, Political Studies Guide:* 3-5.

Cullen P. (1997), *Economics for Hospitality Management,* London: Thomson Business Press.

Day. J. (2001), Hard sell in your hand, *The Guardian,* March 19th 2001.

DCMS (1999), *Tomorrow's Tourism: A growth industry for the new Millennium,* London, Department of Culture, Media and Sport.

Department for Education and Employment (1997). Employment News. June.

Department of Employment (1974). Company Manpower Planning, HMSO.

DMReview, *Mobile eBusiness* Magic White Page, http://www.dmreview.com/portal.cfm? NavID = 95 & Topic = 65 & PortalID = 196, 2001.

Drummon, S, and Yeoman, I. (eds.) (2001), *Quality Issues in Heritage Visitor Attractions,* Oxford: Butterworth-Heine-mann.

Dunleavy, P. (1995), Policy disasters: explaining the UK's record, *Public Policy and Administration* 10(2): 52-69.

Elliott, J. (1997), *Tourism: politics and public sector management,* London: Routledge.

ETC (2000), *Sightseeing in the UK 1999,* London: English Tourism Council.

ebiz chronicle (2001), http://www.ebizchronicle.com/news01/apr/apr12.htm, April 2001.

Financial Times (2001), *Lastiminute signs deal with Thomas Cook as losses mount,* ft.com staff, February 12th 2001.

Fietcher, J. (1995), Economics impact, in S. Witt and L. Moutinho (eds). *Tourism Maketing and Management Handbook, 2nd Edition,* London: Prentice Hall.

Fombrun. C.J..Tichy, N.M. and Devanna, M.A.(1984), *Strategic Human Resource Management.* New york: John Wiley & Sons.

Getz., D. (1997), *Even Management and Event Tourism,* New York: Cognizant Communications.

Goudie, A. and Viles, H. (1997), *The Earth Transformed: an Introduction to Human Impacts on the Environment,* Oxford: Blackwell.

Gilliatt, S. (1987), Being political: a quarrelsome view, *International Political Science Review,* 8(4): 367-384:

Hall, C.M. (1994), *Tourism and Politics: Policy, Power and Place,* Chichester: John Wiley & Sons.

Hall, C.M. (1994), *Tourism and Politics: Policy, Power and Place,* Chichester: John Wiley & Sons.

Hall, C.M. and McArthur, S. (1998), *Integrated Heritage Management: Principles and Practice,* London: The Stationary Office.

Hall, C.M. and Lew, A.A.(1998), *Sustainable Tourism: a Geographical Perspective,* New York:

Harrop, K. (1999), The political context of public services management, in A. Rose and A Lawton (eds.) *Public Services Management,* Harlow: Pearson Education: 3-25.

Harrop, K. and Long, P. (1994), Government and tourism, in P. Callaghan, P. Long and M. Robinson (eds.) *Travel and Tourism, 2nd Edition,* Sunderland: Business Education Publishers: 161-193.

Hague, R. and Harrop, M. (2001), *Comparative Politics and Government, 5th Edition,* Hampshire, Palgrave.

Harrison. R.(1999). *Employee Development,* London: CIPD.

Halpern, L. (2001), You've got email: are you using it?, *The Gaurdiun,* November 30th 2000.

Henry, I, and Bramham, P. (1993), Leisure policy in Britain, in P. Bramham, I, Henry, H. Mommaas and H. Van der Poel (eds.) *Leisure Policies in Europe, Wallingford:* CAB Interna-tional: 101-128.

Holloway, J.C. (1998), *The Business of Tourism, 5th Edition,* Harlow: Longman.

Holloway, J.C. (1998). *The Business of Tourism, 5th Edition,* Harlow: Longman, Chapter.

Holden, A. (2000), *Environment and Tourism,* London: Routledge.

Holden, A. (2000), *Environment and Tourism,* London: Routiedge.

Humphreys, A. (1992), The arts in eighteenth century British, in B. Ford (ed.) *Eighteenth Century Britain: The Cambridge Cultural History,* Cambridge: Cambridge University Press: 3-46.

Hunt, J. (2001), We know where you live, *The guardian,* October 22nd 2001.

IBM (2001), *Japan Airlines Building an e-business on IBM technology,* http://www-3.ibm.com/e-business/casestudy/44720.html, November 2001.

Institute of Personnel and Development (1995), *Codes of Practice.* IPD.

ICOMOS. (1993), *Tourism at World Heritage Cultural Sites (rev. ed.).* Washington: ICOMOS/WTO.

Jones, B. *et. al.* (2001), *Politics UK, 4th Edition,* Harlow, Longman.

Lea, J.P. (1993), Tourism development ethics in the Third World. *Annuals of Tourism Research,* 20(4): 701-715.

Lee, L. (1992), *Red Sky at Sunrise,* London: Viking.

Leemakedej, A (2001), The four e-phases: All elements of business being linked online, *Bangkok Post, August* 2001.

Liddle, M.J. (1975), A selective review of the ecological effects of human trampling on natural ecosystems, *Biological Conservation,* 7: 17-34.

Lockwood, R. D. (1989), Foreign exchange management, in S Witt and L. Mountinho (eds.) *Tourism Marketing and Management Handook,* Hemel Hampstead UK: Prentice Hall: 175-178

Lundberg. D., Stavenga, M. (1995), *Tourism Economics.* New York. John Willey & Sons.

Mathieson, A. and Wall, G. (1982), *Tourism: Economic, Physical and Social Impacts,* New York: Longman.

Miller, D. (ed) (1987), *The Blackwell Encyclopaedia of Political Thought,* Oxford, Blackwell.

Nairn, G. (1998), Business benefits come first, *Financial times,* March 4th 1998.

Nepal, S.K. (2000), Tourism in protected areas: the Nepalese Himalaya, *Annuals of Tourism Research,* 27(3): 661-681

Pearce, D. (1989), *Tourist Development, 2nd Edition, Harlow:* Longmans.

Prentice, R. (1993), *Tourism and Heritage Attractions.* London: Routledge.

Pearce, D. (1992), *Tourist Organisations,* Harlow: Longman.

Priestly, G.K. (1995), Sports tourism: the case of golf, in G. Ashworth and A. Dietvorst (eds.) *Tourism and Spatial Transformations: Implications for Policy and Planning,* Wallingford: CAB International : 205-224.

Prebble, J. (1969). *The Highland Clearances,* Harmondsworth, Penguin.

Rhodes, R.A.W. (1997a), *Understanding Governance,* Milton Keynes: Open University Press.

Rhodes, R.A.W. (1997b), From marketisation to diplomacy: It's the mix that matters, *Astralian Journal of Publci Administration* 56: 40-53.

Richards, G. (ed.) (2001), *Cultural Attractions and European Tourism,* Wallingford: CABI Publishing.

Ross. D. (1996). *International Treasury Management, 3rd Edition,* London: Euromoney Publications.

Rural Development Commission (1996), *Green Audit Kit: the DIY guide to greening your tourism business,* Bristol, Rural Development Commission.

Ryan, C. (1991), *Recreational Tourism,* London: Routledge.

Salem, N. (1995), 'Water Rights', *Tourism in Focus,* 17, 4-5.

Samuels, J., Wilkes, F. and Brayshaw, E. (1995). *Management of Company Finace, 5th Edition.* London: Chapman and Hall.

Shakley, M. (1996), *Wildlife Tourism,* London: International Thomson Business Press.

Simmons. P. (1998), 'Apres ski le deluge', *New Scientist,* 1, 469.

Sinclair, M.T. and Stabler, M. (1997), *The Economics of Tourism* London: Routledge.

Stoker, G. (2001), Pop heavies, *The Guardian,* June 13.

Towner, J. (1997), *An Historical Geography of Recreation and Tourism in the Western world 1540-1940,* Chichester: John Wiley & Sons.

Torrington, D. and Hall, L.(1998). *Human Resource Management,* London: Prentice Hall.

Tribe, J. (2000), *The Economics of Leisure and Tourism, 2nd Edition,* London: Butterworth Heineman.

Vogel, H.L. (2001), *Travel Industry Economics—A Guide for Financial Analysis,* Cambrdge: Cambridge University Press.

Vogel, H.L. (2001), *Travel Industry Economics-A guide for financial analysis,* Cambriage: Cambridge University Press.

Williams, s. (1998), *Tourism Geography,* London: Routledge. *Chapter 5.*

Williams, S. (1998), *Tourism Geography,* London: Routledge.

World Tourism Organisation (1997), *International Tourism: A* Global Perspective, Madrid: WTO.

□□□